# Learning While Black and Queer

# Learning While Black and Queer

## Understanding the Educational Experiences of Black LGBTQ+ Youth

ED BROCKENBROUGH

HARVARD EDUCATION PRESS
CAMBRIDGE, MASSACHUSETTS

Copyright © 2024 by the President and Fellows of Harvard College

All rights reserved. No part of this publication may be reproduced or transmitted in any form or by any means, electronic or mechanical, including photocopy, recording, or any information storage and retrieval systems, without permission in writing from the publisher.

Paperback ISBN 9781682539071

Library of Congress Cataloging-in-Publication Data

Names: Brockenbrough, Edward, author.
Title: Learning while Black and queer : understanding the educational
   experiences of Black LGBTQ+ youth / Ed Brockenbrough.
Description: Cambridge, Massachusetts : Harvard Education Press, [2024] |
   Includes bibliographical references and index.
Identifiers: LCCN 2024020025 | ISBN 9781682539071 (paperback)
Subjects: LCSH: Youth, Black—Education—United States. | Sexual
   minorities—Education—United States. | Students, Black—United States. |
   Teaching—Social aspects—United States. | Safe spaces—United States. |
   Curriculum change—United States. | Health education (Secondary)—
   United States. | Social justice and education—United States.
Classification: LCC HQ73.4.A37 B76 2024
LC record available at https://lccn.loc.gov/2024020025

Published by Harvard Education Press,
an imprint of the Harvard Education Publishing Group

Harvard Education Press
8 Story Street
Cambridge, MA 02138

Cover Design: Endpaper Studio
Cover Photo: smartboy10/DigitalVision Vectors via Getty Images

The typefaces used in this book are Adobe Garamond Pro and Myriad Pro.

*This book is dedicated to two beautiful Black gay men and my dear friends, Jeffery C. Mingo (1974–2017) and Jasan M. Ward (1972–2021). You were here. You are loved.*

# Contents

| | | |
|---|---|---|
| CHAPTER 1 | Lesbian Safer Sex 101: An Introduction to Learning While Black and Queer | 1 |
| CHAPTER 2 | Queerly Responsive Pedagogy: Insights and Implications for Supporting Queer Youth of Color | 19 |
| CHAPTER 3 | Black Queer Resistant Capital | 45 |
| CHAPTER 4 | Trans Fugitivity in a Black Queer Youth Space: Thinking Beyond Safety | 65 |
| CHAPTER 5 | Queerly Responsive Sex Education for Young Black Queer Males | 91 |
| CHAPTER 6 | A Pedagogy of the Closet | 119 |
| | Notes | 137 |
| | Acknowledgments | 169 |
| | About the Author | 171 |
| | Index | 173 |

# Learning While Black and Queer

CHAPTER 1

# Lesbian Safer Sex 101

*An Introduction to Learning While Black and Queer*

"If a girl does it with another girl, she can't catch nothing, right?" So began my journey toward this book during what was supposed to be an uneventful visit to a gay-straight alliance, or GSA, in a predominantly Black public high school in Midtown, a pseudonym for a city in the northeastern United States.[1] The GSA's faculty advisor had invited me to speak to the group's members after leadership turnover begat organizational inertia. With my background in LGBTQ+ educational advocacy and my status as a Black and openly queer tenure-track university professor, I was tasked with finding a way to inspire the group. That inspiration took an unexpected turn when a soft-spoken Black cisgender-presenting girl self-consciously stammered, "I have a question. It might sound silly, and I probably shouldn't ask it. But I am kind of curious. But it's silly, I probably shouldn't . . ."

In my head, I thought, "Sweetheart, just ask the question." Aloud, I used more compassionate language. She replied, "If a girl does it with another girl, she can't catch nothing, right?"

Up to that point, my conversation with the GSA had been decidedly desexualized. For queer educators like me, being cast as sexual deviants who prey upon innocent children places us in a precarious position when it comes to in-school discussions of queer sex.[2] I could already see the headline: "Gay Professor Teaches Lesbian Sex to Midtown High Schoolers," which would rile parents and derail my career path. Yet, somehow I steeled myself, replied to the girl's question with "no, that's actually not true," and launched into a brief, impromptu Lesbian Safer Sex 101 talk. By posing her question, this soft-spoken student exercised queer pedagogical agency as her visible anxiety was conquered by her courage to acquire queer sexual knowledge. As a Black queer educator, my fears around job security were outweighed by my pedagogical and political commitment to prepare Black students to strategically navigate their out-of-school lives. Learning—and in this case, teaching—while Black and queer required the audacity to speak queer sex into existence, and the fortitude to bear the prospect of anti-queer repercussions.

As I left the school that morning, I found myself wondering if and how students who were not in the GSA meeting would learn about queer sexual health. Through subsequent work I initiated with Black queer youth (BQY) at an HIV/AIDS community-based organization in Midtown, I learned that the local school district's thin sexuality education curriculum promoted abstinence while covering safer sex practices for presumably heterosexual penile-vaginal intercourse. Thus, the students I met that morning in the GSA meeting had no direct and sanctioned access within Midtown's schools to sex-positive, queer-inclusive information on sexuality. They also lived in a city where, at the time of my visit, new HIV infections among young Black men who have sex with men (MSM) had risen a staggering 91 percent, exceeding the nationwide rate increase of 48 percent.[3] These sexual health disparities were *in addition to* the high poverty rates, food and housing insecurities, gun violence, lack of access to culturally competent health care, and limited employment and postsecondary educational opportunities facing many of the city's racially minoritized youth.[4] For students who identified as Black and LGBTQ+, intersecting inequities pervaded their lives in and out of schools. My brief visit to the GSA, though well-intentioned, suddenly felt woefully inadequate.

The urgency I felt in the days and weeks following my GSA visit sparked a scholarly trajectory that is represented in this book. For over a decade, my teaching, research, and advocacy efforts have foregrounded the educational perspectives and experiences of BQY. With its title playing on "driving while Black" and similar phrases that acknowledge the dangers associated with Black people's participation in everyday activities in American public spaces, *Learn-*

*ing While Black and Queer: Understanding the Educational Experiences of Black LGBTQ+ Youth* shares my investigations of the precarities and promise of BQY's educational lives.[5] The stories and analyses that appear in subsequent chapters pose a series of responses to the following questions: How do BQY navigate a range of pedagogical contexts in their quests for knowledge and belonging, and what are the implications of these experiences for educational and community-based practitioners committed to queerly responsive pedagogical work with BQY? As I explain in detail in chapter 2, queerly responsive pedagogy counters anti-queerness and other forms of domination that marginalize LGBTQ+ youth with critically caring approaches to affirming these young people's identities, agency, desires, community-building, and knowledge production. With that pedagogical framework in the backdrop, this book (1) identifies several key barriers that undermine BQY's learning experiences; (2) underscores the significance of those barriers by locating them within larger social and pedagogical contexts; (3) draws upon the voices of BQY to unpack how these young people perceive and respond to those barriers; and (4) invokes my conceptualization of *queerly responsive pedagogy* to pose potential strategies for enhancing the learning and well-being of BQY. By centering these young people's voices, this book seeks to help readers comprehend social and pedagogical injustices through the eyes of BQY, as doing so is crucial to creating queerly responsive spaces that effectively and compassionately serve these young people's educational needs.

Along with centering their voices, this book situates BQY's experiences at the intersections of multiple, systemic forms of subjugation. As other scholars and advocates have noted, anti-queer hostilities in Black families and communities and anti-blackness in predominantly White queer settings—spaces that BQY might otherwise call home—can pose intimate and enduring threats to their safety, belonging, and self-worth.[6] Their precarious membership in Black and queer communities leaves BQY all the more vulnerable to the structural inequities that produce their marginality, thus resulting in their disproportionately high rates of depression, homelessness, HIV infection, and participation in survival sex.[7] Sadly, though not surprisingly, their marginality in American society at large is reproduced in the nation's schools, where BQY face harassment from peers and adults, and where they and other queer youth of color (QYC) are disproportionately targeted by disciplinary policies and procedures.[8] These predicaments are in addition to the challenges they already face as students who identify and/or are identified as Black and queer, among other historically minoritized identities.[9] The cumulative impact of these burdens does not foreclose the possibility of BQY success, but it can certainly make these young people's journeys arduous, violent, and unjust. Hence, this book underscores the relevance of its analyses and recommendations by recognizing the intersecting oppressions it seeks to disrupt.

Lastly, this book treats learning while Black and queer as a phenomenon that unfolds over multiple social, institutional, and technological contexts. Analyses throughout reference BQY's experiences across several sites, including public middle and high schools, public health-funded community-based organizations, and digital media and social networking platforms. Some of these sites had more intentionally pedagogical designs than others, yet all of them emerged across data sources as spaces that significantly influenced the wellness, awareness, and knowledge acquisition of BQY. Hence, my descriptions of learning experiences extend beyond schooling to also include interactions in out-of-school settings that shape BQY's sense of self and knowledge of the world around them. Ideally, this book will drive queerly responsive supports that are informed by BQY's myriad domains of living and learning.

**NOTES ON TERMINOLOGY**

In my efforts to document how BQY learn about themselves and the worlds that surround them, I quickly noticed that *Black, youth,* and *queer* were not static terms. For starters, although the two empirical research projects featured in this book were conducted within the United States, the data that were generated included perspectives from young people born within and outside of the country who claimed a range of ethnic and national identities associated with members of the African diaspora. Consequently, I use *Black* throughout this book to signify race, with exceptions for when youth study participants described themselves with more specific identity markers associated with members of the African diaspora like *African American, Haitian,* or *Jamaican.* I also use *youth of color* and *racially minoritized youth* when discussing issues that affect Black as well as Latinx, Asian American, Pacific Islander, and Indigenous youth.[10]

All of the young people who participated in my research on BQY were recruited through and interviewed at community-based organizations that were funded partially or significantly to engage *disconnected youth* or *opportunity youth,* the latter being an assets-oriented alternative to the former. Both terms refer to young people between the ages of sixteen and twenty-four whose disconnections from family, schools, employment, and/or other potentially affirming institutions and networks place them at increased risk for negative life outcomes.[11] While my ultimate intent was to improve urban secondary schooling for BQY by offering examples of their empowering educational experiences elsewhere, some of my research findings spoke to out-of-school endeavors as well. Consequently, I use *youth* and *young people* interchangeably to describe life points spanning from the beginning of high school (around fourteen) to the upper end of opportunity youth status (twenty-four). Doing so allows me to honor the breadth of experiences associated with *youth* by community-based organizations and the young people they serve while also paying particular attention to the relevance of my study findings for two audiences: urban secondary educators—my primary audience—and practitioners in urban community-based organizations who serve a similarly aged population. Readers who train and support those two groups may also find this book a useful resource. Although six participants in my second research project were twenty-five, they were enrolled in that study after being identified by community-based organization staffers as individuals who had participated in youth programming.

Regarding *queer,* I use that term to denote same-sex desires, identities, and intimacies, as well as transgender, gender nonbinary, and other gender identities and expressions, that fall outside the bounds of cisheteronormativity, the structural and ideological privileging of cisgender (or *cis,* the identification with the gender assigned to one at birth) and heterosexual identities as norms. While sexuality and gender are not identical, my use of queer rests on two factors: the similar manner in which cisheteronormativity disparages and polices the sexualities and genders it deems deviant; and the coalitions and community forged under the queer moniker among those who are targeted by cisheteronormative power.[12] I also use *LGBTQ+*—Lesbian, Gay, Bisexual, Transgender, Queer, and other related identities—interchangeably with *queer* since the acronym offers another way to render the ever-evolving and ever-expanding range of identities, desires, and behaviors that are surveilled by cisheteronormativity. I should note that my use of *queer* to represent noncisheteronormative individuals runs counter to the growing trends of pairing *queer* and *trans* in educational scholarship and utilizing *LGBTQIA2S+* (an acronym that includes intersex, asexual, and two-spirited) in social services and advocacy efforts.[13] I decided to stick with *queer* for the sake of a book title and prose that (hopefully) are legible to a wide audience of readers. However, I do use *trans* when referring specifically to those who do not identify with the gender identity assigned to them at birth. I also use *cis* when describing individuals who have confirmed their identification with the gender assigned to them at birth.

## QUEER OF COLOR CRITIQUE

My inquiries into the educational perspectives and trajectories of BQY are grounded in a field of study known as *queer of color critique.* Inheriting its name from Roderick Ferguson's seminal sociological and historical treatise on Black queerness in the United States, queer of color critique has coalesced over the past two decades into an interdisciplinary body of scholarship that probes the interplay of domination and resistance in the lives of queer people of color.[14] Centering the often disregarded ways of knowing and being located within queer of color communities, queer of color critique spotlights the social and historical forces that have marginalized those communities, and it surfaces forms of agency rooted in queer of color lived experiences. Its dual attention to subjugation and agency is indebted to its theoretical anchor, US women of color feminisms from the 1970s and 1980s, which combined examinations of the multiple and intersecting oppressions shaping the lives of women of color with considerations of their shifting strategies of resistance.[15] Additionally, queer of color critique incorporates queer theory's yearning to disrupt cisheteropatriarchal surveillances of transgressive gender and sexual identities.[16] The result is an analytic lens with two key affordances: the discipline to name and contextualize the marginalization of queer of color difference, and the commitment to differentiate strategies of resistance to address the evolving exigencies of the lives of queer people of color.

The analytical affordances of queer of color critique drive two of this book's critical, and admittedly provocative, interventions. First, the field's intersectional lens on identity and power has enabled educational scholars to disrupt white-centered depictions of queer youth that often struggle to attend to forms of domination beyond anti-queerness.[17] In doing so, queer of color critique in educational research has insisted on acknowledging the presence of QYC and the complexities of their lives. This book is similarly invested in centering BQY and tracing the social and educational inequities that confront them. In some cases, this intervention surfaces issues that typically are avoided or prohibited in urban secondary schools and in some community-based spaces as well. Chapter 5, for example, explains how exorbitant HIV infection rates, hypermasculine and violent internet pornography, and the absence of comprehensive sexuality education in schools undermine the sexual health, autonomy, and safety of young Black queer males. Responding to these factors by embedding sex positivity, porn literacy, and queer affirmation in school-based sexuality education is a hard sell in the most permissive of times, let alone in our current milieu of "don't say gay" bills, attacks on trans youth rights, and firings of queer-supportive and sex-positive K–12 educators. And yet BQY, as cited earlier in this chapter, remain disproportionately vulnerable to HIV infection, survival sex, and other risks that are exacerbated by the lack of access to queer-inclusive sexuality education. Doing nothing to contend with these factors is an unconscionable option. Grounding my work in queer of color critique means raising dilemmas in this book that, to some, may seem too taboo to even mention in their youth work, let alone attempt to address. In such cases, I encourage readers to consider how they might support efforts led by practitioners and organizations that are better equipped to ameliorate the impact of social and educational inequities on BQY's lives, if doing so in their own domain of influence proves too impractical or perilous.

The second intervention by queer of color critique that drives this book is the focus on agency. While not dismissing the complicated and compounded dilemmas that QYC face, queer of color educational scholarship, as discussed in detail in chapter 2, has foregrounded young people's agency. This stands in stark contrast to the victimization narratives that have dominated attempts to address LGBTQ+ issues in American K–12 schools.[18] Guided by queer of color critique, I cast agency throughout this book as the degree to which BQY can determine their actions and shape their sense of self at the intersections of white supremacy, cisheteronormativity, adultism, and other hierarchies that produce their alterity. This builds on Boni Wozolek's work with BQY, in which agency is defined as a contingent phenomenon negotiated with other actors amidst the power dynamics of a given time and place, ultimately producing shifting degrees of determination over one's actions and being.[19] Given the complicated decision-making required across the multiple domains of their lives, BQY's agency can resist and reproduce the oppressive sensibilities that surround and inevitably shape it. Such is the case in chapter 3, where I describe how some BQY agentively resist anti-queer violence in schools through their own physical retaliations, subverting perceptions of queer vulnerability while concurrently reproducing cultures of violence. Because of the authenticity and nuance afforded by queer of color critique, what emerges in chapter 3 and elsewhere in this book is a portrait of agency that, while neither romantic nor unproblematic, realistically reflects the decisions BQY have to make at times to protect and advocate for themselves. By highlighting the agency behind such moments, my hope is that readers will bring two qualities to their encounters with BQY: a sensitivity to the complicated decision-making these young people sometimes face; and a willingness to help them make decisions strategically and on their terms. These qualities underscore the spirit behind my engagement with queer of color critique.

## DATA SOURCES

The data presented in this book come from two empirical research projects. The first project, the Midtown AIDS Center (MAC) study, was an ethnographic examination of how MAC, an urban, community-based, HIV/AIDS services agency, operated as a pedagogical space for BQY. Located in Midtown, a mid-sized city in the northeastern United States, MAC was the only local organization with an explicit mission to improve the health and wellness of queer communities of color. As BQY became disproportionately affected by the HIV/AIDS epidemic during the 2000s, MAC's programming became increasingly youth-focused. Volunteering for a year at MAC allowed me to witness its dynamism as a queerly responsive pedagogical space for BQY. Subsequently, sharing MAC's pedagogical insights with secondary schools became the aim of my study. In all, seven adult staffers and volunteers and ten youth agreed to participate. Table 1.1 summarizes the demographic characteristics of the MAC study participants.

Since the purpose of the study was to understand how MAC operated as a space that engaged BQY, an ethnographic methodological approach was employed to grasp the myriad factors that shaped MAC's institutional culture and secured its significance in the lives of youth attendees. As cis male scholars who identified as queers of color, my graduate research assistant at the time and I volunteered at MAC in various capacities from November 2009 through December 2010 in order to gain the trust of staff and youth, and to develop pre-study insights into the life of the organization. Data collection began in January 2011 and ended in July 2011 when staffing turnover prompted some internal reorganizing at MAC. An in-depth, one-on-one interview lasting ninety minutes to two hours was conducted with each study participant and transcribed for analysis. Adult staffers and volunteers were asked about their personal and professional histories and their involvement at MAC, and youth study participants were asked about their personal histories, K–12 schooling experiences, and MAC experiences. Observations were conducted and field notes were taken on a range of youth-oriented MAC programs and events, and agency reports, PowerPoint presentations, fliers, events calendars, and other artifacts were also collected for insights on the organization.

Data analysis consisted of two phases. In the first phase, my graduate research assistant and I reviewed each data source together to develop an initial sense of the range of themes across data sources, generating a tentative list of codes. In the second phase, I revisited each data source multiple times with particular attention to four overarching themes that emerged during phase one: organizational dynamics and community social contexts that shaped life at MAC; details and insights on programs and services; adult staffers and volunteers' identities, biographical and professional backgrounds, and involvement at MAC; and youths' identities, biographical and educational narratives, and participation at MAC. Analytical profiles on major coding categories were

TABLE 1.1  MAC study participants

| Pseudonym | MAC role | Age | Race | Sexual orientation | Gender[a] |
|---|---|---|---|---|---|
| 2 | Youth | 20 | Black | Gay | Nonbinary |
| Aaron | Youth | 21 | Black | Gay | Male |
| Binky | Youth | 19 | Black & Latinx | Open | Trans female |
| Concerned Activist | Youth | 20 | Black | Bisexual | Male |
| GoGo | Youth | 22 | Black | Bisexual | Male |
| Levi | Youth | 21 | Black | Gay | Male |
| M | Youth | 18 | Black | Gay | Male |
| Mystery Man | Youth | 16 | Black & Latinx | Bisexual | Male |
| Nicole | Youth | 17 | Black | Straight | Trans female |
| Twizzler | Youth | 22 | Black | Gay | Male |
| Armando | Adult staff / Volunteer | 41 | African American & Puerto Rican | Gay | Male |
| Collette | Adult staff / Volunteer | 45 | Biracial, Jewish, & white | Bisexual | Female & androgynous |
| Kal-El | Adult staff / Volunteer | Between 27 & 35 (direct quote) | African American | Gay, lesbian, & bisexual | Male |
| Peggy Lee | Adult staff / Volunteer | 32 | White & Jewish | Pansexual | Genderqueer & female |
| Roman | Adult staff / Volunteer | 33 | Black Caribbean | Gay | Male |
| TJ | Adult staff / Volunteer | 34 | Black / African American | Gay | Male |
| Travis | Adult staff / Volunteer | 34 | Black / African American | Homosexual | Male |

[a] Those who identified as male were cis-presenting, but since they were not asked at the time to confirm their identification with the cisgender label, their gender is listed here as male. When analyzing their gender identity politics in chapter 4, male MAC study participants are described as cis-presenting.

constructed to refine data analysis and were followed by the drafting of detailed outlines of major findings. These outlines were shared with my graduate research assistant for his insights, and they were used to solicit feedback during member reflection sessions with a subset of four youth and two adult study participants. Preliminary presentations of findings to multiple audiences outside of the study generated additional feedback that further refined data analysis.

To date, MAC study findings have been featured in four of my prior publications: two solo-authored articles in peer-reviewed journals, one solo-authored chapter in an edited book, and one co-authored chapter in another edited collection.[20] Throughout this book, I put MAC study findings in conversation with more recent research—including previously unpublished data from my follow-up project, the Sexual Engagements with Networked Technologies (SENT) study (described below)—and with several media artifacts. I also situate the findings within new, robust theoretical frameworks. Together, these moves allow me to demonstrate the ongoing relevance of MAC study findings as I use them to make new contributions to the scholarship on BQY.

The second empirical research project that I draw upon in this book is the SENT study, which I conducted with Dr. Mitchell Wharton, a faculty member at the University of Rochester's School of Nursing, with funding from the University of Rochester's Center for AIDS Research. Despite a growing awareness among HIV/AIDS researchers and service providers that young Black queer males (YBQM) were using online dating and hookup sites to meet sexual partners, Mitchell and I noticed that research on the topic routinely undersampled these young men and/or accorded minimal attention to them in analyses.[21] Responding to the gaps in the extant research literature, the goal of the SENT study was to explore how YBQM used networked technologies like internet sites, geolocation hookup apps, and texting for four purposes: to learn about sex and explore their sexual identities and desires; to consume, produce, and/or exchange sexually explicit content; to connect with and participate in YBQM and other sexual and community networks; and to comprehend and negotiate the risks of HIV infection.

The SENT study was grounded conceptually in danah boyd's work on networked publics.[22] Building upon sociological perspectives on a public as a sociohistorically situated collection of people with shared identities and worldviews, boyd explains how membership and activity in publics have been radically reorganized by networked technologies. Digital platform features like user profiles, algorithm-generated content thumbnails, and the persistence and replicability of content create new and ever-evolving conditions for constructing one's identity and participating in social collectives. Drawing upon boyd's work, the SENT study explored how the key features of networked technologies shaped YBQM's sexually oriented engagements of these platforms. Focusing on participants' meaning-making as they maneuvered through pornographic video sites, geolocation hookup apps, and associated sociosexual networks afforded new insights into how these experiences affected their learning and well-being.

SENT study participants were recruited through community-based health and advocacy organizations that served queer communities of color and sponsored youth-focused programming. All participants lived in one of four cities in the northeastern United States where the community-based organizations were located. In total, twenty-two participants enrolled in the study. Table 1.2 summarizes the demographic characteristics of those who participated in the two studies that are featured in this book.

Data collection, which occurred from July 2015 to July 2016, began with each participant taking a twenty-minute computer-based survey that collected descriptive data on demographic characteristics and sexual history and included a HIV knowledge questionnaire specifically tailored for YBQM.[23] This was followed by the administration of the Internet Usage Scale for Sexual Purposes—Modified, a validated, twenty-five-item measure that assessed respondents' viewing of sexually explicit materials, their seeking of sexual partners, and their seeking of sex-related information on the internet.[24] After completing both surveys, each subject participated in a one-on-one interview that lasted between one hour and ninety minutes and covered the following topics: their general technological knowledge and patterns of engaging networked technologies; their sexual identity and behavior; their sexually oriented engagements with networked technologies; and the pedagogical implications of those technological engagements. During the interview's third section, each participant was provided with a computer tablet and asked to visit the

TABLE 1.2  SENT study participants

| Pseudonym | Age | Race | Sexual orientation | Gender |
|---|---|---|---|---|
| Adonis | 25 | West Indian / Black | Gay | Cis male |
| Alec Jerrodd | 25 | Black | 70% guys, 30% girls | Cis male |
| Batman | 22 | African American | Bisexual | Cis male |
| Black Mamba | 23 | Puerto Rican & Trinidadian | Gay | Cis male |
| Blue | 23 | African American | Homosexual | Cis male |
| Bob | 25 | African American & Guyanese American | Bisexual | Cis male |
| Bobby | 25 | Black / Jamaican | Same gender loving | Cis male |
| Chris | 25 | African American | Gay | Cis male |
| Eros | 21 | Black | Gay | Cis male |
| Janita | 22 | Black | Bisexual | Cis male |
| Josh | 19 | African American | Gay | Cis male |
| Kai | 22 | African American | Bisexual | Cis male |
| Kris | 24 | Haitian American & African American | Gay | Cis male |
| Lionel | 21 | African American | Bisexual | Cis male |
| Michael | 24 | Black | Gay | Cis male |
| Sean | 23 | Black | Gay | Cis male |
| Sora | 20 | Mixed (Latino, Black, & Irish) | Queer | Cis male |
| Stitch | 22 | Black | Gay / Same gender loving | Cis male |
| T | 21 | Black | Gay | Cis male |
| Tommy | 25 | Caribbean | Gay | Cis male |
| Tyrone | 22 | African American / Black | Gay | Cis male |
| Will | 20 | Black | Bisexual | Cis male |

websites or apps that he identified as influential on his sexual identity, sexual practices, and HIV awareness. While navigating websites or apps, each subject was prompted to explain and demonstrate how the platforms enabled him to pursue the four goals identified above in the study aims. Screenshots of key website and app features were collected as digital artifacts. The study findings presented in this book come from the analyses of the one-on-one interviews and digital artifacts, as these data sources proved especially effective in generating more nuanced and participant-driven insights into how YBQM engage multiple networked technologies for sexually related purposes.

Data analysis of the interviews and digital artifacts consisted of three phases. In phase one, my co-researcher and I reviewed interview transcriptions and digital artifacts to develop an initial list of tentative codes. In phase two, I reviewed the data a second time to fine-tune the initial coding schemes with assistance from my research assistant at the time, a queer graduate student of color with an extensive professional background in sexuality education. With a well-defined coding scheme in place, I worked with another queer graduate student of color during phase three to formally code interview transcriptions and digital artifacts using Dedoose coding software. Both research assistants' background experiences as queer people of color who were familiar with the sexual politics and cultural contexts shaping the data proved to be major assets during data analysis. Additionally, presentations at two conferences for researchers and service providers who work with YBQM provided valuable feedback on initial data analyses. This book is the first publication to include my analyses of SENT study findings.

Despite my professional focus on urban secondary education in the United States as a teacher educator, I conducted the MAC and SENT studies outside of formal schooling institutions. The potential for my research to spark resistance and backlash in those institutions, especially in response to my attention as an openly queer scholar to queer-inclusive sex education, was admittedly a deterrent. Additionally, most of the queer-affirming classroom teachers I knew of kept an intentionally low profile, engaging in what I describe in chapter 6 as a pedagogy of the closet. But perhaps most notably, readily identifiable, queerly responsive educational experiences with and for BQY were just hard to come by in the urban secondary schools to which I had access. Locating my research projects outside of schools afforded undeniably greater freedom to explore how queerly responsive pedagogical contexts could support BQY's learning and well-being. In the end, the findings that emerged from the MAC and SENT studies included eye-opening accounts of participants' formal schooling as well as illustrations of effective approaches to their education in out-of-school spaces. As I share those findings throughout this book, I consider the implications for practices within and beyond schools. I also invite readers to consider how an awareness of, and perhaps a cooperation with, efforts across these contexts might improve the lives of BQY.

## A NOTE ON BLACK QUEER DIVERSITY

The MAC and SENT studies, while generative in many respects, still had their limitations. Both studies were confined to participants who lived in urban centers in the northeastern United States. Additionally, of the thirty-two youth represented across the two studies, twenty-nine identified and/or presented as cis and male, two identified as trans and female, and one identified as nonbinary. The skewed gender profiles of my research samples were due in no small part to the funding landscape at the time of both studies. The shifting locus of the HIV/AIDS epidemic to YBQM's sociosexual networks in the 2000s spurred funding streams for HIV/AIDS-related research and services targeting that specific population. Consequently, community-based public health agencies like MAC found themselves increasingly reliant on funding for YBQM-centered initiatives, and research like the SENT study became more fundable if it, too, targeted that demographic.

I take a few steps throughout this book to compensate for the lack of gender diversity among my study participants. Most notably, I devote chapter 4 to analyzing trans female youth's navigation of MAC amid YBQM-centered programming and transmisogynist identity politics. In chapters 2 and 3, I foreground other data sources that contain more gender-diverse perspectives. Similarly, I highlight scholars in chapter 6 whose works on BQY extend beyond YBQM, and I also include curriculum and instruction examples in that chapter that center Black queer womanhood. These strategies do not alter the disproportionate representation of the lives and concerns of YBQM in my empirical research, and I want to be clear about owning that. My hope, however, is that placing my study findings in conversation with sources that include a broader array of genders moves this book closer to representing the exigencies of BQY's lives, learning, and well-being.

**OVERVIEW OF THE BOOK**

The purpose of this opening chapter has been to introduce learning while Black and queer as a fraught endeavor worthy of scholarly attention, and to provide context for how I have studied it. In chapter 2, "Queerly Responsive Pedagogy: Insights and Implications for Supporting Queer Youth of Color," I propose *queerly responsive pedagogy* as a framework for shaping the learning experiences of LGBTQ+ youth. Grounded in a review of the existing literature on school- and community-based pedagogical contexts that serve QYC, queerly responsive pedagogy, I contend, speaks to the specificities and nuances of these youths' learning experiences in ways that prior assets-based lenses like culturally responsive and sustaining pedagogies have not. At the crux of this chapter is a set of four commitments, or underlying principles, that I offer as guideposts for queerly responsive pedagogical work with LGBTQ+ youth. I accompany the explanations of the four commitments with potential examples of and strategies toward enactment targeted specifically to Black and other racially minoritized queer youth, and I conclude the chapter with suggestions for the further development of queerly responsive pedagogy as a tool for transformative work with Black queer youth and their non-Black LGBTQ+ peers.

Chapter 3, titled "Black Queer Resistant Capital," complicates queer youth victimization narratives and anti-queer harassment policies in schools by introducing an underexamined phenomenon: Black queer students who fight back. Drawing upon Tara Yosso's conceptualization of resistant capital in her work on the cultural wealth of communities of color, I argue that when BQY stand up to anti-queer violence, they are marshalling *Black queer resistant capital,* a culturally derived set of resistance strategies that enable their survival and, at times, aim to disrupt the material and ideological conditions of domination.[25] I develop this argument first by situating resistance within Black queer cultural contexts, and then by examining two categories of Black queer resistant capital in BQY narratives on school-based bullying and harassment: reading and physical self-defense. With queerly responsive pedagogy as a framework, I conclude the chapter with recommendations for making urban secondary schools more affirming for BQY, especially in cases when these young people fight back in the absence of any meaningful protections from adults.

The folly of safe space discourses that dominate efforts to support LGBTQ+ youth is the focus of chapter 4, "Trans Fugitivity in a Black Queer Youth Space: Thinking Beyond Safety." Although the convergence of structural, ideological, and interpersonal forms of violence on queer and trans youth makes their safety a rational concern, the promise of safe spaces for them belies the power dynamics that can marginalize, and in some cases harm, LGBTQ+ young people in the very spaces deemed as safe. In this chapter, I pose *fugitivity*—a framework from the field of Black studies that explores how the precarity and liminality of Black life in the United States informs the ways in which Black people produce knowledge, read the world, and develop strategies for survival and resistance—as a more nuanced paradigm for examining Black queer youth's spaces. By revisiting a previously co-authored account of Black trans female youth's experiences at MAC, I consider how to make sense of these young women's fugitive navigations of a setting that proved hostile to their presence, despite its intention to serve all Black LGBTQ+ youth.[26] While not wholly abandoning the hope of supportive spaces for Black queer youth, this chapter searches for queerly responsive strategies to negotiate the anti-trans stigma that can undermine the capacity of those spaces to serve Black trans female youth.

Sex education takes center stage in chapter 5. Titled "Queerly Responsive Sex Education for Young Black Queer Males," this chapter examines YBQM's engagements with two sources of queerly responsive sex education: MAC's sex education programming, and internet sites with sexually explicit material. Like so many of their LGBTQ+ peers nationwide, the YBQM who participated in my research projects relied heavily on out-of-school resources to learn about queer sexual practices and explore their own queer sexual identities and desires. Drawing upon the National Sex Education Standards (NSES), I illuminate how MAC and sexually explicit online material facilitated YBQM's exploration of two NSES topics: *sexual identity and orientation,* with an attention to how study participants determined their queerness and learned about the mechanics of queer sex; and *functional knowledge and skills*—that is, the information and strategies that enable safe, thoughtful, and autonomous sexual decision-making.[27] This chapter highlights affordances and challenges associated with study participants' experiences that can inform efforts to provide them with queerly responsive sex education.

All of the chapters in this book account in some way for the increasingly hostile climate for queerly responsive pedagogical initiatives in the United States, especially in K–12 schools. The sixth and final chapter, "A Pedagogy of the Closet," proposes a strategic response to that milieu. Drawing on a conceptualization of the closet as shifting degrees of queer visibility and invisibility, I pose *a pedagogy of the closet* as a possible set of maneuvers for discreetly and strategically delivering queer-inclusive curricula in secondary schools to Black queer youth and other LGBTQ+ students. Beyond symbolizing the site of queer secrecy and despair, the closet, I contend, may afford varying levels of student exposure to queer content while providing some cover for teachers from political and professional backlash. After providing examples of how a pedagogy of the closet can shape teachers' approaches to curriculum and instruction, I conclude the book with future directions for research and advocacy efforts to improve the lives of LGBTQ+ youth, Black and otherwise.

CHAPTER 2

# Queerly Responsive Pedagogy

*Insights and Implications for Supporting
Queer Youth of Color*

In chapter 1, I described an ethnographic study that I conducted at the Midtown AIDS Center (MAC), my pseudonym for a community-based HIV/AIDS services agency in a northeastern US city that offered programming and resources for Black queer youth (BQY). Findings from that study were featured in a peer-reviewed academic journal article titled "Becoming Queerly Responsive: Culturally Responsive Pedagogy for Black and Latino Urban Queer Youth."[1] As reflected in the article's title, my aim was to present culturally responsive pedagogy as a lens for educational work with queer youth of color (QYC), specifically Black and Latinx queer youth, a population that was absent at the time from scholarship in the field. Whether an oversight or exclusion (or both), the silence around the relationship between queerness and culturally responsive pedagogy has reinforced the invisibility and neglect of Black, Latinx, and other racially minoritized LGBTQ+ youth in K–12 schools. Asserting that QYC deserve culturally responsive educational experiences was, on its own, a substantial intervention.

Since 2016, scholarly investigations into culturally centered pedagogical frameworks for QYC have remained scarce. Out of the vast corpus of literature on culturally responsive and sustaining pedagogies, only a handful of publications by authors like Latrise Johnson and Jon Wargo has complemented my article by rigorously foregrounding the experiences of QYC.[2] Coincidentally, the paucity of queer analyses in this field has persisted as the visibility of QYC in schools and other educational settings has increased, accompanied at times by newsworthy failures to support and protect these youth.[3] While insightful, the current smattering of queerly framed scholarship on culturally responsive and sustaining pedagogies leaves ample room for deeper dives into pedagogical frameworks that attend directly and smartly to the nuances of QYC's learning experiences.

In this chapter, I make a case for *queerly responsive pedagogy* (QRP), a framework for teaching and learning that counters anti-queerness and other forms of domination that marginalize LGBTQ+ youth with critically caring attention to these young people's identities, agency, desires, community-building, and knowledge production. Given this book's overarching concern for BQY, I develop QRP in this chapter by drawing upon a body of scholarship that explores the educational experiences of Black and other racially minoritized LGBTQ+ youth, or QYC. By using the *queer of color* category to grapple with the intersections of race, queerness, and education in QYC's lives, this work has elevated the narratives of specific QYC subgroups while underscoring their shared struggles against white supremacy, anti-queerness, and scholarly erasure.[4] Citing research on QYC throughout this chapter allows me to envision queerly responsive pedagogical work with BQY while laying the groundwork for more culturally specific applications of QRP to other racially minoritized queer youth as well.

Although I do not review scholarly sources in this chapter that center white queer youth and/or accord little to no attention to QYC, I do contend that white queer youth can benefit from my conceptualization of QRP. As this chapter will reveal, the literature upon which I build QRP is defined by its attention to both the intersecting forms of domination that act upon QYC and the agentive responses to those forms of domination by QYC and/or the school- and community-based practitioners who support them. It is these intersectional analyses of power and agency in the lives of LGBTQ+ youth that have traditionally been underdeveloped in or missing altogether from educational scholarship that centers white queer youth and their encounters with anti-queerness.[5] White queer youth are obviously positioned differently from their nonwhite LGBTQ+ peers. However, the four commitments of QRP that I identify present language and underlying logics that can apply to white queer youth's negotiations of power, agency, and learning from their particular racialized location. While I prioritize QRP's implications for QYC throughout the bulk of this chapter, I do offer some thoughts at the chapter's end about how future work might explore QRP in white queer youth's learning experiences.

Following a brief overview of culturally responsive and sustaining pedagogies, I use most of this chapter to outline four commitments that should comprise QRP. The explanations of these queerly responsive pedagogical commitments are accompanied by recommendations for building practitioners' capacities to enact them. My aim is not to prescribe fixed practices to be applied with fidelity by all who engage them. Rather, the four commitments that make up QRP are intended as guides for practitioner strategies that adapt to the conditions they enter and the learners they serve. Finally, I conclude the chapter with several implications for growing QRP as a tool for transformative work with BQY and their non-Black LGBTQ+ peers.

## CULTURALLY RESPONSIVE AND SUSTAINING PEDAGOGIES

Sweeping bodies of academic literature spanning multiple disciplinary perspectives have charted the relationship between one's cultural identity and background and one's learning experiences.[6] Within those vast literatures, Sonia Nieto's writing on culture exemplifies the thinking that informs my analyses in this chapter.[7] Nieto has defined culture as "the ever-changing values, traditions, social and political relationships, and worldview created, shared, and transformed by a group of people bound together by a combination of factors that can include a common history, geographic location, language, social class, and religion."[8] Challenging the reduction of minoritized cultures in many K–12 settings to celebrations of food and holidays, Nieto stresses the social, economic, and political forces that shape culture and thus warrant consideration through critical perspectives on power. Her analyses also surface the intersectional nature of culture by noting how white supremacy, capitalism, cisheteropatriarchy, and other inequities position members of a cultural group to experience that very culture differently. As sociohistorical circumstances evolve, so too do people's responses to those circumstances—responses that consequently shift, expand, and reconstitute the experiences that comprise any given culture. Echoing Nieto's characterizations of culture, I view LGBTQ+ youth of color as cultural groups whose ways of seeing, learning, and being in the world unfold at and respond to similar intersections of multiple oppressions, and whose cultural identities and practices diverge in particular and, at times, significant ways from those of other queer youth and other youth of color. The aspects of QYC's lives that distinguish them from other youth populations provide the warrant for pedagogical logics that acknowledge and appeal to their cultural sensibilities.

Over my two decades of work in urban teacher preparation, culturally responsive pedagogy has been my go-to for addressing the culturally mediated learning experiences of minoritized groups like QYC. A wide collection of scholarly literature, professional development materials, and resources for practice uses cultural responsiveness (as well as cultural relevance) to describe a pedagogical orientation to culture that shapes effective and empowering educational experiences for racially, ethnically, and linguistically minoritized youth.[9] Building on the foundational scholarship of Gloria Ladson-Billings and Geneva Gay, a rich corpus of literature has established how culturally responsive educators recognize the role of cultural background and identity in mediating students' construction of knowledge and participation in learning environments, thus leading these educators to seek curricular, instructional, and engagement strategies that incorporate students' cultures into their learning experiences.[10] Culturally responsive educators treat minoritized students' cultural ways of knowing and being as assets for learning, enact culturally familiar modes of care with minoritized students, and prepare these students to negotiate and resist the sociopolitical conditions that produce their minoritization.[11] By disrupting long-standing deficit-based perspectives that presume the academic inability of nonwhite students, culturally responsive pedagogy allows practitioners to operationalize a culturally and politically rooted mission to support racially and ethnically minoritized youth in K–12 schools and beyond.

The legacy of culturally responsive pedagogy, while undeniably transformative, is also fraught. In their thoughtful presentation of culturally *sustaining* pedagogy as both a complement and corrective to prior work on approaches like culturally responsive pedagogy, H. Samy Alim and Django Paris offer three "loving critiques" of the limitations of asset-based pedagogies.[12] First, after noting how some applications of these pedagogies have sought to help youth of color adapt to white middle-class norms, Alim and Paris call for educators to commit instead to "sustaining the cultural ways of being of communities of color," thus decentering the acclimation to whiteness as a guiding principle.[13] Second, the authors raise concerns about pedagogies that recirculate portraits of minoritized cultures from decades past, urging instead for engagements with the current and ever-evolving cultural realities and practices shaping the lives of communities and youth of color. Lastly, after troubling the idealized picture of minoritized youth cultures that pervades some of the work on asset-based pedagogies, Alim and Paris stress the need to involve young people in critical analyses of misogyny, homophobia, and other forms of discrimination that can exist within communities of color. To be clear, Alim and Paris do not dismiss the critical interventions made by culturally responsive pedagogy and similar frameworks in the education of youth of color. They do, however, use their loving critiques of asset-based pedagogies to identify dilemmas that deserve further consideration.

Though Alim and Paris do not make a specific call for queer adaptations of culturally responsive pedagogy, their appeal for an inward-facing criticality (their third loving critique) gestures toward the possibility. The most decisive steps in that direction to date can be found in Wargo's proposition of *[q]ulturally sustaining pedagogy*.[14] Informed by Alim and Paris's interest in sustaining cultural practices within minoritized cultures, Wargo uses the bracketed "q" to signal the centering of queer genders, sexualities, and desires, all of which, he argues, have been sidelined in the asset-based pedagogical tradition. He also embeds intersectionality within [q]ulturally sustaining pedagogy as an analytic filter that attends to race, class, and other categories of identity and difference informing queer youth's lived experiences and pedagogical perspectives. Thus far, Wargo has recounted two applications of [q]ulturally sustaining pedagogy: one in his study of QYC's writing practices in an afterschool gay-straight alliance (GSA), and the other in his practice with predominantly white students in an undergraduate elementary teacher education class.[15] While room exists for more considerations of queer-centered pedagogies, Wargo's theorization and enactments of [q]ulturally sustaining pedagogy mark an important step toward an asset-based, culturally mediated pedagogical approach that deliberately foregrounds and values queerness as a resource for learning.

To build the case for a queer-centered, culturally mediated pedagogy even further, I turn in the following section to a growing collection of scholarship on the learning experiences of QYC. While this literature spans secondary, postsecondary, and out-of-school settings, I exclude the work on QYC's postsecondary learning experiences, staying instead within my wheelhouse as a teacher educator and researcher who supports practitioners in urban secondary education and urban, youth-serving community-based organizations. Though stretching across multiple states, these scholarly analyses are situated predominantly in urban areas.[16] They also include QYC who claim a variety of identities, and they feature a range of approaches—both within and outside of schools—to aiding the learning and well-being of racially minoritized LGBTQ+ youth. Drawing upon this body of work in its entirety presents the opportunity to construct a pedagogical framework—what I am calling *queerly responsive pedagogy*—that extends beyond the recommendations from any single analysis, building instead on our collected knowledge on QYC's educational encounters. By *explicitly* naming queerness in its title, and by developing guiding principles based on a synthesis of relevant scholarship, I offer a pedagogical framework with the potential to increase the volume, visibility, and sensitivity of efforts to support the educational aspirations of QYC.

## THE FOUR COMMITMENTS OF QUEERLY RESPONSIVE PEDAGOGY

In graduate courses with urban pre-service teachers, as well as in professional development sessions with more experienced educators, I repeatedly echo other scholars who stress that culturally responsive pedagogy cannot be reduced to a short list of discrete, decontextualized instructional techniques.[17] I also present teachers with guiding principles for culturally responsive pedagogy that have been identified by experts in the field, and I help teachers to align their curricular and instructional practices to those principles. For example, Tyrone Howard has described five key principles that repeatedly emerge in the scholarship on culturally responsive pedagogy: the eradication of deficit perspectives; the disruption of Eurocentric or middle-class ways of being and knowing as normative; a critical, sociopolitical consciousness; culturally authentic notions of care; and the use of culture as a tool for achieving academic excellence.[18] With these five guideposts, I help teachers to incorporate critical analyses of white supremacy in their lesson plans, develop a "warm demander" approach to classroom engagement, and align other aspects of their practice to culturally responsive pedagogy.[19] Underlying principles offered by Howard and other scholars capture culturally responsive pedagogy's core concerns while trusting educators to determine how to meet those concerns in their own practice.[20]

The remainder of this chapter is devoted to outlining four commitments of queerly responsive pedagogical work with QYC. Just as scholars like Howard and like Brittany Aronson and Judson Laughter have singled out the core principles of culturally responsive pedagogy based on extensive reviews of academic literature, I build the four commitments of QRP by pinpointing the major recurrent themes in the scholarship on QYC's learning experiences within and outside of secondary schools.[21] Although these commitments are intended to guide—not prescribe—practitioners' adaptations of QRP, I do draw upon my own experiences as both a teacher educator and a researcher who has worked with BQY to offer suggestions for realizing each commitment. These suggestions are intended not as roadmaps but rather as launchpads to queerly responsive engagements with QYC.

### Commitment 1: Provide a critical ethic of care to queer youth of color through queer of color peer and community networks, as well as through connections with critically caring adults.

For QYC, being situated at the intersections of anti-queerness, white supremacy, and other injustices can produce a unique set of challenges that schools and other educational contexts often struggle to resolve. The cumulative impact of harms like social isolation, familial neglect, ostracism from white-dominant queer communities and cisheteronormative communities of color, and physical and verbal harassment necessitates a *critical ethic of care,* or *critical caring,* for QYC. As discussed in the scholarship on Black and Latinx teachers' caring practices, as well as in the literature on authentic care for students of color, a critical ethic of care is informed by a recognition of the deleterious impact of white supremacy, capitalist exploitation, and other systemic subjugations on the minds, bodies, and spirits of youth of color.[22] Critical caring supplies the compassion, protection, reassurance, and sociopolitical consciousness necessary for minoritized youth to heal, persevere, and ultimately thrive. When supporting QYC, a critical ethic of care openly decries the racist and anti-queer disregard for QYC's lives, and it counters that disregard with affirmation, advocacy, and belonging. A critical ethic of care must be an essential commitment of QRP.

Despite the endemic anti-queerness and racism in American secondary schools, examples of critically caring spaces established within schools by QYC and their allies do exist. These include QYC-led GSAs, afterschool writing clubs targeted toward QYC, school-sponsored retreats for queer girls of color, and more informal gathering spaces created by QYC in schools.[23] Some QYC have found a critical ethic of care in alternative high schools committed to serving LGBTQ+ students when anti-queerness and other forms of discrimination have pushed them out of prior high school placements.[24] Highlighting the importance of critically caring school-based spaces, Andrea del Carmen Vázquez poignantly captures the mutual support among QYC who created an unofficial "gay club" at a high school in a predominantly Mexican agricultural community in central California. The following is del Carmen Vázquez's description of club meetings held in a bungalow adjacent to the main school building:

> Here the youth were free to laugh, break bread, develop as teachers and activists, and engage in life affirming politics in an intimate space away from the core infrastructure of their school. These life affirming practices were simple: sharing chips when a student did not have money for lunch, making fun of a homophobic teacher, and enjoying the pleasures of sharing a kiss. These practices were activities that could not be situated within the gaze of the broader Villa High community without the fear of repercussions. They had to take place away from the surveillance of heteronormativity, homophobia, and transphobia.[25]

In addition to the activities chronicled above, del Carmen Vázquez recounts the group's deliberation over what should happen to the school's only gender-neutral bathroom. From sharing food to debating a stance on the institutional allocation of queer space, the gay club's actions underscore critical caring's importance to QRP, and they illustrate QYC's capacity to supply that care to each other.

Locations outside of schools can serve as queerly responsive sources of critical caring for QYC as well, especially when few or no comparable sources are available within schools. Several of my publications, along with works by colleagues like Tomás Boatwright and Mollie Blackburn, examine the affirmation, security, and connectedness fostered in community-based agencies serving QYC.[26] Both Shamari Reid and I, along with scholars situated outside of educational studies like Marlon Bailey and Ricky Tucker, detail the intergenerational kinship networks, the celebration of queer Black and Latinx creativity and resilience, and the personal and political advocacy around HIV/AIDS that some QYC access through the House Ball community.[27] As discussed later in this chapter and again in chapter 4, both school-based and community-based spaces serving QYC can struggle at times to realize their caring potential. Nonetheless, the scholarship cited in this section thus far corroborates the importance of QYC's peer connections and larger queer of color communal networks as sources of a queerly responsive, critical ethic of care.

Along with QYC themselves, adults emerge in several accounts as key agents of critical caring. These adults do not necessarily have to be members of queer of color communities. For instance, in addition to my prior work, publications by Blackburn, Michael Bartone, and Therese Quinn spotlight non–queer of color adults who comforted and advocated for QYC, often in the absence of queer of color counterparts.[28] However, several examples in the existing literature reveal how caring queer adults of color can supply cultural-insider knowledge on surviving and thriving to QYC while bolstering the youth's personal confidence, social connectedness, and sociopolitical awareness.[29] In my analysis with Boatwright of MAC study data on trans youth of color, a youth participant named Binky recalled the pivotal role that Symone, a slightly older trans woman of color and a former MAC peer leader, had played in her own development as a young trans woman of color:

> Symone was a member of the Lead Team, and she's my gay mom. Symone, nonstop helping me, encouraging me never to settle for less, never to get punked, always go for the real surge. And she definitely encouraged me to

get my name changed. She was the first one to tell me, "Hey, your makeup using, stop it" [i.e., you're not applying it correctly]. So, like, she helped me with a lot. She helped me, like, "Hey, this is how you can make your chest look like yours even though it's not there," and "This is the clinic you can go to for hormones," and "This is how you get your health care."[30]

Binky's reference to Symone as her "gay mom" echoes a repeated theme in the literature on QYC: the significance of queer of color kinship formations. Finding themselves in anti-queer and transphobic biological families, some QYC turn to queer adults of color in their local communities as surrogate parental figures. As evidenced by Binky's relationship with Symone, queer and trans adults of color can guide the socialization of racially minoritized LGBTQ+ youth from adolescence into young adulthood. The familial connectedness that these young people feel with queer adults of color, as well as with each other, constitutes their *chosen family*—the kinship bonds that queer people of color nurture with one another—often as biological family connections falter under the weight of anti-queerness. As Boatwright, del Carmen Vázquez, Reid, Boni Wozolek, and others highlight in their work, chosen families can function as vital and culturally authentic sites of critical caring in the lives of QYC.[31]

Together, the sources cited above showcase examples of a critical ethic of care, ideally reinforced by caring adults, through which QYC share compassion, resources, and insider knowledge with each other. This mode of care is a pillar of the QRP for which I advocate. The four recommendations outlined below may help queerly responsive practitioners to take up and support a commitment to providing critical caring for QYC.

1. *Recruit adult staff with expertise in critical caring for QYC:* The literature reviewed above compellingly illustrates the significance of adults as agents of critical caring for QYC. While queer adults of color may have a unique capacity to fulfill this role, any adults recruited with this aim in mind need to demonstrate expertise in providing a critical ethic of care. As I note in publications on my MAC study findings, MAC staff members, in addition to being queer-identified, had educational credentials and prior work experiences that not only informed their insights into the strengths and needs of BQY, but also distinguished them from

other adult community members who resented the strong youth presence at MAC.[32] Schools and other organizations that are serious about QRP for LGBTQ+ youth of color need to do their due diligence in identifying adults, queer of color and otherwise, who have a demonstrated commitment to critical caring for QYC. Broadly yet thoughtfully worded probes into candidates' prior educational studies and professional experiences that address intersections of race, gender, and sexuality may help in this regard, particularly if political climates or legal constraints prohibit using more direct language about supporting QYC.

2. *Build relationships with local organizations that can facilitate paid professional development on a QYC-oriented critical ethic of care and/or provide critical caring spaces for QYC:* As with any area for professional growth, schools and community-based organizations that need to improve their capacity to critically care for QYC should learn from those with expertise. Local agencies with a track record for queerly responsive work specifically with QYC (e.g., agencies like MAC) are a logical starting point, especially since they may also double as critically caring spaces for those youth. In the absence of this option, the following alternatives may be worth exploring: local community-based, youth-serving agencies that engage in queer- or race-related forms of social justice work; hospitals and other local health institutions with community education departments; professional staff at college or university LGBTQ+ resource centers as well as faculty with expertise in supporting QYC; and national organizations like GLSEN, the National Black Justice Coalition, the Human Rights Campaign, the National LGBTQ Task Force, and others that can be contracted for local professional development sessions. With any of these options, direct conversations about providers' capacity to address critical caring for QYC are a must. Additionally, depending on their comfort level, QYC within a school or organization might have recommendations for local stakeholders and agencies that can facilitate professional development on critical caring and/or provide critically caring environments for QYC.

3. *Engage QYC's chosen families:* As Wozolek observes, QYC's chosen families are an undertapped resource for schools that are struggling to

support these youth.[33] Acknowledging and welcoming chosen families can afford opportunities for schools and other spaces to partner with familial networks that share a critical ethic of care for QYC. Doing so may be easier for a community-based agency like MAC, where QYC claimed several staffers and fellow youth attendees as members of their chosen families. Schools and other organizations with more conservative cultures around family engagement might benefit from the professional development sessions suggested above, as they could contextualize the significance of chosen families for QYC.

4. *Engage QYC in creating spaces for critical caring:* Across the scholarship reviewed in this section, several examples emerged of critical caring spaces within and beyond schools that were created by QYC for QYC. Ultimately, these youth are the only ones who can validate authentic attempts to supply them with a critical ethic of care. Their expertise in what constitutes that care should drive any effort—whether school-based or community-based, youth-led or adult-led—to provide it.

**Commitment 2: Pair intersectional analyses of oppression with opportunities for queer youth of color to affirm and explore their identities, desires, and agency.**

While ongoing anti-queer political attacks are certainly cause for alarm, the movement to create empowering learning opportunities for LGBTQ+ youth has made, and hopefully will continue to make, impressive strides across the United States. There are, however, two recurrent shortcomings to these efforts that warrant mention in light of this book's intentions. First, as noted by scholars and advocates who focus on the experiences of QYC, queer educational research and practice has frequently overlooked homophobia's intersections with other systemic oppressions, particularly white supremacy.[34] Second, repeated depictions of queer youth in crisis have reproduced tragic outlooks for these young people's lives.[35] The result is a white-centered, victimization-focused body of work and resources that too often minimizes the presence and agency of QYC. Against this backdrop, it is crucial for QRP to pair intersectional analyses of oppression with opportunities for QYC to affirm and explore their identities, desires, and agency.

As a whole, the scholarly works on the social and educational contexts of QYC's lives reach beyond homophobia to scrutinize white supremacy as a systemic and consequential injustice.[36] The consequences of hegemonic constructions of masculinity and femininity are also recurrent topics in QYC scholarship, and the increased visibility of trans youth has generated well-deserved attention to transphobia.[37] Several authors elucidate the exigencies of immigration status and cultural assimilation that merge with other barriers facing immigrant QYC.[38] Also of concern are QYC's negotiations of poverty and financial insecurity, along with housing insecurity and homelessness, especially in racially segregated and gentrifying urban centers.[39] The economic precarity engendered by these convergent circumstances forces some QYC to rely on survival sex, escalating their already disproportionately high risk of HIV exposure.[40] Being planted at the intersections of these and other forms of deprivation and subjugation requires QYC to develop nuanced, multifaceted strategies for surviving and thriving. A QRP that centers intersectional analyses of identity and power can throw those strategies into sharp relief.

Those analyses, though powerful on their own, cannot be where the work of QRP ends. Critical examinations of the structural and ideological forces that devalue racially minoritized LGBTQ+ youth must be paired in QRP with ongoing opportunities for these youth to affirm and explore their identities, desires, and agency. To date, this kind of self-exploration has been featured most frequently in studies of QYC's literacy practices. For example, both Johnson and Wargo describe QYC's self-reflections on their racial and queer identities, future hopes, and roles as change agents through their writing, with writing journals providing a particularly generative reflection space in Johnson's work.[41] Quinn recounts how members of a GSA at a predominantly Black, all-girls charter school used playwriting and poetry to voice their frustrations with the school's anti-queerness and celebrate their gender nonconformity and sexual desires.[42] Cindy Cruz recalls the transformative power of QYC's poetry writing and filmmaking in an alternative high school for LGBTQ+ youth, and both Blackburn and Boatwright describe working with BQY to create literacy artifacts that celebrated Black queer culture and amplified BQY's sociopolitical commentary.[43] The weight that these literacy practices carry is illustrated in this excerpt of "Pride," a poem written by Justine, a

BQY in Blackburn's study, who recounts being called a "dyke" by a male stranger while holding her girlfriend during a gay pride celebration: "Empowered by my sisters of no / mercy, convinced that my girl / is my ball and chain. I can / walk down the street kissing / and fondling her . . . And [I] couldn't / give a shit who was watching. / That's the dyke I know. / I want to be a dyke."[44] Like Justine, the QYC featured in the sources referenced above used writing, along with filmmaking in Cruz's work and collage in Boatwright's, to talk back to discrimination, proclaim their loves and desires, and avow their humanity. These outcomes speak to the queerly responsive power of literacy practices to facilitate QYC's affirming and agentive self-explorations.

In addition to rendering QYC's literacy practices, a few scholars have cited examples of QYC-affirming curriculum. Johnson and Wargo, for instance, recall assigning texts from Black queer writers and queer Black feminists, respectively, in their afterschool writing spaces.[45] Savannah Shange describes a freshman humanities class in a small, alternative high school in which students read Huey Newton's speech about solidarity with gay liberation and Carla Trujillo's *What Night Brings,* a lesbian coming-of-age novel.[46] Outside of schools, Reid has analyzed the curriculum practices in the House Ball community's initiatives to educate youth members about the community's history and values.[47] This thread within the extant academic literature has noticeable room for growth, but it still indicates some possibilities for QYC-affirming curricular approaches to adopt and expand in QRP.

Whether concerned with literacy practices, curriculum, or other nodes of learning, the queer of color educational scholarship reviewed in this chapter lauds efforts to fortify the agency of LGBTQ+ youth of color.[48] Cultivating that agency can be understood as both a warrant for and desired outcome of QRP. In several reported cases, QYC's agency has led to coordinated institutional and political action. For instance, dating back to 1972, a predominantly queer of color cohort of students formed the first school-based LGBTQ+ organization on record in George Washington High School in the Bronx, New York.[49] Historical accounts reveal this group's agenda as firmly rooted in a defiant gay liberationist politics.[50] More recent cases presented by del Carmen Vázquez and Quinn similarly show QYC founding their own school-based groups and leading them as cultural and political counterspaces.[51] The students in Quinn's account went as far as openly resisting the school administration's anti-queer maneuvers to silence and disband them.[52] In his work with Black gay and gender nonconforming boys, Lance McCready identifies a student who carved out a space within his high school's LGBTQ+ student group to address racism.[53] In addition, both McCready and Blackburn describe how QYC advocated for school reform by designing and delivering anti-homophobia workshops to educators.[54] Stepping outside of schools, some analyses follow QYC as they learn how to mobilize against local and national politico-economic injustices that disempower them as racially minoritized LGBTQ+ youth.[55] All of these accounts exemplify the cultivation of individual and collective agency that should be central to queerly responsive pedagogical work with QYC.

To be sure, QRP is not the only asset-based pedagogical framework committed to fostering minoritized youth's sociopolitical consciousness and sense of agency. However, through its second commitment—the focus of this section—QRP can account for QYC's negotiations of power and identity with a frequency and nuance that seem to elude other asset-based pedagogical traditions. Despite the growing popularity of intersectionality in educational studies, the reach of intersectional analyses has not extended to QYC in multiple fields of scholarship, including the research on culturally responsive pedagogy, as noted earlier in this chapter. The literature reviewed here underscores why intersectionality is a necessary prism on the lives of LGBTQ+ youth of color. It also illustrates how learning environments within and beyond schools can cultivate QYC's educational and political agency—an outcome made all the more urgent given these youths' victimized portrayal in and erasure from educational and popular media discourses. Though other frameworks may have the potential to pair intersectional analyses of oppression with opportunities for QYC to affirm and explore their identities, desires, and agency, the QRP that I am proposing explicitly prioritizes this commitment.

Below are four recommendations that may catalyze practitioners' engagement of QRP's second commitment.

1. *Provide professional development on intersectionality:* Since intersectionality is a theoretical framework that can shape how we understand *all* young people's positionalities and advance their sociopolitical awareness,

professional development on intersectional praxis should frankly be required for anyone tasked with educating and supporting young people. Emphasizing intersectionality's applicability to the experiences of all youth is one way to strategically create space for examining the specificities of QYC's lived experiences.

2. *Provide leadership training for QYC:* The literature reviewed in this section features multiple accounts of QYC establishing and leading their own organizations. These young people deserve youth leadership training that affirms them as QYC and prepares them to address the intersecting dilemmas they face. For those at the helm of school-based efforts, GSA networks and conferences at the district, state, regional, and even national levels are worth considering.[56] Out-of-school organizations that are not QYC-specific but successfully train youth leaders are another option, especially if they have a track record of including and affirming QYC.

3. *Encourage journal writing:* As cited earlier in this section, journal writing provided a generative space for BQY's self-explorations in an afterschool writing club led by Johnson.[57] Luckily, journal writing is a familiar and accessible practice in classrooms, writing clubs, and other educational settings. As I always impress upon pre-service teachers, establishing journals as a space for private conversations between a teacher and each student can encourage students to share ideas that might get withheld during class discussions. The flexibility for shared and private reflection makes journal writing a compelling approach to QRP's second commitment.

4. *Provide professional development on queerly responsive curriculum:* While curriculum construction is an obvious site for queerly responsive pedagogical interventions, the scholarship in this area is relatively sparse at this moment. Drawing upon my curriculum work with pre-service teachers as an urban teacher educator, I want to offer a short list of *queerly responsive curriculum guiding questions* as a possible starting point. This list consists of five questions that may help practitioners assess the queerly responsive potential of prospective curricular resources.

a. *Authorship:* Is the resource from someone, queer of color–identified or otherwise, with track records of sharing authentic insights into queer of color communities and demonstrating a commitment to queer of color justice?
b. *Corroboration:* Do other resources from credible authors or creators corroborate the claims within this resource?
c. *Intersectionality:* How (if at all) does this resource afford intersectional analyses of power that may speak to the lives of QYC?
d. *Curricular standards:* In what ways does this resource align with the curriculum standards that guide classroom content?
e. *Adjustments:* What aspects of the resource should be foregrounded, de-emphasized, excluded, or replaced to make it manageable for and relevant to particular groups of students?

In my more extensive discussion of curriculum in chapter 6, I offer an example of how these curriculum guiding questions can be applied.

**Commitment 3: Address any tensions that challenge a respect for and inclusion of variously identified queer youth of color.**

Educational scholarship on racially minoritized LGBTQ+ youth has expanded under *queer of color,* a moniker that indexes a shared sense of self amidst common struggles against white supremacy, anti-queerness, and other systems of domination. Those common struggles, however, do not preclude conflict. As with any identity category, the myriad histories, identities, and politics indexed by *queer of color* can be synergistic as well as antagonistic. It is thus incumbent upon all participants in queerly responsive pedagogical contexts to address any tensions that may challenge a respect for and inclusion of a diverse array of QYC.

One set of tensions to anticipate are those emerging among QYC themselves, often along subgroup identities. These divides generally are not the principal topic in the educational scholarship on LGBTQ+ youth of color, but the accounts that do exist expose the detriments of divisive dynamics in queerly responsive settings. Blackburn, for instance, along with Boatwright and I, traces the transphobic participatory politics in community-based agencies serving primarily BQY.[58] Blackburn spotlights interracial divides between Black and other racially minoritized queer youth in one agency as well.[59] Femiphobia, hegemonic masculinity politics, and contention over gender presentation stir additional unrest between QYC in scenarios captured by Wargo and Shange.[60] In the latter instance, Shange recounts a hallway brawl between two Black queer female students, punctuated by the following epithets: "'Dyke bitch! You wanna be a man, come out here and whoop my ass then! Always tryna look like a dude—you ain't no fuckin' dude!'"[61] Hurled by a femme-presenting student at her masculine-identified partner/foe, "bitch" and "you ain't no fuckin' dude" mark the politics of gender presentation as the site of power struggles between the two. Collectively, all of the cases cited in this paragraph offer depictions of QYC's antagonisms toward each other, and these antagonisms warrant further investigation.

The above descriptions of peer tensions are complemented by a few scholarly accounts of adult and institutional biases that challenge a respect for and inclusion of diverse QYC. Cruz offers one such account from her work at an alternative high school for LGBTQ+ youth: "'Josie'—a big girl, strong, butch, Latina—publicly challenged another male student today, she shook her fists at him, she pushed chairs over to get to him, it was an awesome display of power. The lead teacher quickly suspended her from school. I've noticed that other male students who exhibit the same damn behaviors are given two or three chances and are rarely expelled from school. Double standard for the lesbians."[62] Along with observing the unfair treatment of lesbian youth at an alternative high school, Cruz describes a trans youth being sidelined in a QYC-serving community-based agency by an adult staffer's trans-insensitivity.[63] In addition, Joan Ariki Varney, along with Boatwright and I, links the marginalization of trans youth and queer cis female youth to HIV/AIDS-related funding that institutionally privileges the participation of queer cis males in QYC spaces.[64] Fortunately, analyses by Blackburn, del Carmen Vázquez, and Shange chronicle LGBTQ+ youth of color, with some adult assistance, working through disagreements and discord.[65] While not insurmountable, tensions and conflicts that threaten the inclusion of all QYC in spaces meant to serve them must be anticipated in queerly responsive pedagogical endeavors.

To ready queerly responsive practitioners to embrace QYC's diversity and navigate potential challenges to their inclusion, I offer two recommendations.

1. *Create alternatives to safe spaces:* For over three decades, the provision of "safe spaces" has driven both school- and community-based efforts to support LGBTQ+ youth.[66] With ground rules in place to guide interactions, participants are encouraged to delve vulnerably and honestly into risky conversations with the assurance that their safety—from physical and emotional harm, peer judgment, etc.—will be protected. The references above to transphobia, femiphobia, sexism, and other discriminations within spaces designated for QYC uncover challenges to that safety. Replacing safe spaces with more accurate frameworks is one way to acknowledge the potential for conflicts—and even harm in some cases—and to establish ground rules for managing those difficult moments when they arise. In chapter 4, I make the case for "fugitive spaces" as an alternative. "Safer spaces," "brave spaces," and "truth spaces" are other possible alternatives.[67]
2. *Conduct intersectional analyses of peer interactions among, and of the spaces that serve, QYC:* Commitment 2 of QRP emphasized the necessity of centering intersectional analyses of power in QYC's learning experiences. QRP's third commitment illustrates the need for those analyses to be directed not only at systemic forms of domination, but at the spaces where QYC engage in their own world-making with each other. Queerly responsive pedagogical spaces should consider crafting intentional opportunities for QYC and the adults who support them to examine how gender, race, and other categories of identity and difference can bedevil their community-building with each other. Social media clips that identify points of contention within LGBTQ+ communities, as well as similarly oriented (and often free) online resources from queer youth–serving organizations, can prove generative dialogue starters.[68] As always, any potential learning resources should be reviewed beforehand to gauge their responsiveness to the needs of particular groups of QYC.

**Commitment 4: Advocate for educational and social justice with and for queer youth of color.**

As repeated throughout this chapter, QYC are stationed at the intersections of white supremacy, cisheteronormativity, and other systems of domination that deny their humanity. Pedagogical contexts that empower QYC are obviously important, but they can still fall short of their potential by failing to challenge the social policies and institutional practices that systemically dehumanize racially minoritized queer youth. A queerly responsive pedagogical commitment to serving QYC requires strategic, intentional engagements in educational and social justice advocacy. The efforts I am calling for should extend beyond one-on-one emotional supports for QYC to tackle the educational inequities, health-care disparities, disproportionate policing, housing insecurities, and other oppressive circumstances that can ultimately undermine queerly responsive pedagogical initiatives and thwart QYC's thriving. Ideally, these advocacy efforts should center the participation and leadership of QYC, with the caveat that a number of factors—discomfort with public disclosures of their identities, family-imposed constraints, and other possible vulnerabilities—may limit some youths' involvement. Nevertheless, it is imperative that any advocacy on behalf of QYC be informed by those youths' input. With a critical ethic of care, intersectional analyses of power, and the affirmation of youth agency making up other core commitments, QRP must incorporate deliberate mobilizations, driven by the voices and concerns of QYC, against the structural barriers to QYC's life opportunities.

The scholarly literature cited below features a few examples of queerly responsive educational and social advocacy. These include previously mentioned accounts from Blackburn and McCready of QYC who advocated for school reforms by leading anti-homophobia workshops for educators, as well as Quinn's portrait of queer girls of color who protested school administrators' attempts to silence them.[69] Looking beyond school-based efforts, both Bailey and I outline initiatives in community-based agencies and the House Ball community to fight the HIV/AIDS epidemic and other health disparities affecting BQY.[70] Other examples depict the involvement of QYC in local and national collective political organizing. These include Veronica Terriquez's analysis of QYC standing up against anti-immigrant discrimination and queer erasure in the immigrant rights movement, and Susan Driver's portrait of QYC's resistance against the police harassment, incarceration, and displacement spurred by gentrification in the West Village neighborhood of Manhattan.[71]

Together, these examples illustrate the types of advocacy efforts that can amplify the mission of QRP.

While advocating for educational and social justice with and on behalf of QYC makes sense from a queerly responsive perspective, it also presents some challenges. Whether the aim is supporting a GSA's protest against anti-queer school policies or disrupting police harassment in local neighborhoods, standing up for the rights and dignity of QYC can yield professional, political, and legal repercussions for practitioners who get involved. In addition, no single practitioner or youth-serving organization has the capacity to mobilize against all of the indignities that QYC face, and some are not as knowledgeable or well-positioned as others to address certain issues. The three recommendations that follow honor the urgency of advocacy efforts with and for QYC while accounting for the risks and constraints that come with taking a stand against social and educational injustices.

1. *Create advocacy incubators:* Earlier, I recommended youth leadership training as one response to the focus on QYC agency in Commitment 2. Extending those trainings to cover political organizing is one way to equip QYC with the requisite skills and knowledge for educational and social advocacy campaigns. Additionally, spaces that attend to the learning needs and well-being of QYC can collectively engage those youth in identifying the educational and sociopolitical concerns that matter to them. Treating these spaces as *advocacy incubators*—where QYC co-construct their reform agendas and learn how to pursue them in schools, community settings, and broader political arenas—can galvanize these youth as change agents and ensure that their voices and desires remain centered in any advocacy on their behalf.
2. *Promote collective teacher organizing:* Over the past decade, educators in cities like Chicago and Los Angeles have coupled calls for pay raises and better working conditions with demands for more nurses and social workers in schools and an end to racist "random searches" of students.[72] Dubbed "bargaining for the common good," this strategy has allowed educators to center their advocacy on behalf of students' schooling needs

within their own collective bargaining as workers.[73] Beyond the more visible actions like protests and strikes, teachers across the nation have also created their own spaces for studying social injustices, developing a common language of protest, and formulating collective advocacy agendas.[74] From a queerly responsive standpoint, these efforts can provide opportunities for school-based practitioners to embed supports for QYC—for example, QRP trainings for nurses and social workers, queerly responsive curriculum workshops in teachers' collective study spaces—into teachers' collective mobilizations for school reforms. This strategy not only underscores how all students benefit from educational justice advocacy, but it might also reduce anti-queer backlash by lowering the visibility of queer-specific reform demands.

3. *Support advocacy groups and networks:* In QYC-serving schools and community-based spaces where professional risks and other constraints associated with collective organizing are prohibitive, practitioners can consider supporting agencies elsewhere that are advocating for social and educational reforms to improve the lives of racially minoritized LGBTQ+ youth. Organizations with national profiles like GLSEN, the Human Rights Campaign, the National LGBTQ Task Force, and the National Black Justice Coalition have track records of mobilizing around issues that affect QYC, even during times of elevated social and political repression. Supporting these national organizations and more local agencies, too, with donations and/or volunteer labor can allow practitioners to push for reforms to improve the lives of QYC and, if necessary, do so away from the public eye.

## GROWING QUEERLY RESPONSIVE PEDAGOGY

Because of the glacial turnaround time of the peer review process for scholarly articles, on top of the backlog of manuscripts that many peer-reviewed journals already have in their publication queues, it can easily take a year or more for an article, if accepted, to appear in an academic journal. Case in point, my previously mentioned "Becoming Queerly Responsive" article, published in 2016, was written and submitted for peer review in 2014. That piece proclaimed the necessity of a culturally responsive pedagogy for Black and Latino queer youth based on a compelling yet relatively small amount of existing educational research on QYC and an exciting yet context-bound set of findings from my MAC study. Fortunately, the scholarship on QYC's learning experiences has proliferated since 2014, unearthing invaluable insights on how LGBTQ+ youth of color navigate an array of secondary, postsecondary, and out-of-school educational environments. Thanks to a community of scholars who have insisted on pushing queer of color scholarship to the fore, a more substantial body of work reveals the possibilities of queer-centered, asset-based approaches to teaching and learning. Proposing QRP as a model for supporting racially minoritized LGBTQ+ youth would have been premature in 2014. By contrast, this chapter can now marshal the insights from a nuanced, expanded collection of scholarly literature to imagine the contours and content of queerly responsive pedagogical work with QYC.

As the scholarship on QYC's learning experiences continues to flourish, so too will the opportunities to grow QRP into a more robust and encompassing framework. Much of the current literature, as noted earlier in this chapter, is set in urban locales, thus offering comparatively fewer insights on QYC in other settings. Studies specifically focusing on populations like Asian American, Pacific Islander, Indigenous, and bisexual youth are lacking, too. And though secondary schools are represented in the existing scholarship, they appear primarily in the form of alternative high schools and extracurricular spaces like GSAs. Further inquiries into the current gaps in queer of color educational scholarship will allow QRP to become even more responsive to varied populations of LGBTQ+ youth. Additionally, since I excluded literature on QYC's learning experiences in postsecondary settings, reviews of that work could explore the implications of QRP in higher education. In the meantime, this chapter offers a solid foundation for QRP based on the work to date on the learning experiences of QYC.

Proposals for pedagogical frameworks are invariably met with questions, debates, confirmations, and pushback. The absence of queer pedagogy from this chapter is one factor that may spark such reactions. Situated at the intersections of queer theory and critical pedagogy, queer pedagogy is a conceptually rich and dynamic attempt to disrupt the cisheteronormative strictures on knowledge production and transmission, both within and beyond schools.[75] While unquestionably innovative, the scholarship on queer pedagogy was left out of this chapter for two reasons. The first is that queer pedagogy does not recur as a major theme in the queer of color educational scholarship reviewed for this analysis. To begin laying the grounds for QRP's legitimacy, it was important to base this initial formulation of it on a coherent body of work that consistently and authentically speaks to the learning experiences of QYC. Moving forward, the potential reasons for queer pedagogy's absent foothold in the scholarship represented in this chapter deserve deliberation.

The second reason for queer pedagogy's absence from this chapter is connected to QRP's title and targeted audience. Replacing "culturally" with "queerly" is an intentional move to liken QRP to—and, thus, capitalize on urban secondary educators' familiarity with—culturally responsive pedagogy. I have even delineated four core commitments to mirror the types of guiding principles that shape practitioners' culturally responsive uptake in schools. Across my two decades of experience as an urban teacher educator, I have yet to see a comparable recognition or engagement of queer pedagogy in the K–12 sector. That said, neither reason for excluding the scholarship on queer pedagogy from this chapter should preclude future considerations of its possible contributions to QRP. Notably, the framework's queering of pedagogy itself poses opportunities for more expansive takes on queerly responsive pedagogical enactments.[76] Still, it does seem important for scholars who center QYC's learning experiences in our work to first discern and contend with potential aversions to queer pedagogy in our efforts to empower Black and other racially minoritized LGBTQ+ youth.

As with the absence of queer pedagogy, some readers may question my decision to hold off on QRP's applications to the experiences of white queer youth. Given my scholarly grounding in queer of color critique and my goal of advancing supports in this book specifically for BQY, I felt both qualified and called to emphasize QRP's implications for Black and other racially minoritized youth within the limited space at my disposal. That said, I still contend that my framing of QRP has the potential to shape the learning experiences of LGBTQ+ youth more broadly, including those who identify as white. Consider these rephrased versions of the four commitments I proposed for QRP:

- Commitment 1: Provide a critical ethic of care to queer youth through queer peer and community networks, as well as through connections with critically caring adults.
- Commitment 2: Pair intersectional analyses of oppression with opportunities for queer youth to affirm and explore their identities, desires, and agency.
- Commitment 3: Address any tensions that challenge a respect for and inclusion of variously identified queer youth.
- Commitment 4: Advocate for educational and social justice with and for queer youth.

Given their intersectional sensibilities, these commitments acknowledge the injustices that queer youth face, call for efforts to unpack and challenge those injustices, underscore the importance of affirming queer youth in the process, and stress the need to address tensions among queer youth that might undermine queerly responsive supports. At first glance, they seem capable of guiding efforts to support white and nonwhite LGBTQ+ youth alike as these young people navigate the power dynamics, identity politics, and learning conditions encountered across a range of pedagogical contexts. However, since I identified these four commitments after reviewing scholarly literature on QYC's educational experiences, similar efforts that include empirical research on white queer youth are logical next steps toward building a stronger case for QRP's potential benefits for all LGBTQ+ youth.

Finally, as with every chapter in this book, the haze of anti-queerness blanketing the United States casts its shadow over this chapter's contents. Even if QRP's resemblance to culturally responsive pedagogy makes it more palatable to practitioners, particularly those in the urban secondary schools and community-based spaces where many QYC reside, the political fallout of anti-queer surveillance will likely remain a powerful deterrent. Bottom line: All of the ideas presented in this book require concerted, sustained political organizing for more ideal pedagogical conditions to truly flourish. Additionally, researchers must do our part by building a wider and deeper empirical basis for queerly responsive pedagogical work. If we believe BQY and other LGBTQ+ young people have a right to queerly responsive learning experiences, then we must fight to prove it.

CHAPTER 3

# Black Queer Resistant Capital

In the fall of 2010, a horrific rash of suicides in response to anti-queer harassment in US schools ignited unprecedented mass media attention to the plights of queer students.[1] The launch of the "It Gets Better" campaign followed, promising brighter queer futures to those resilient enough to reach them.[2] Concurrently, K–12 schools nationwide started or renewed anti-bullying initiatives to save LGBTQ+ students from further peer torment.[3] To gain traction and buy-in from school personnel and the American public at large, all of these efforts have consistently relied on an understandable yet troubling trope: queer victimhood. As a host of queer educational studies scholars assert, the victimized queer kid dominates representations of LGBTQ+ students in both academic and popular discourses, reproducing constrained portraits of queer youth's potential.[4] To be sure, preventing physical, mental, and emotional harm against queer youth must be a priority for K–12 schools and other educational settings. But those prevention efforts can have a limited impact when they fail to extend beyond queer victim narratives.

This chapter focuses on one particular quandary stemming from the pervasiveness of the queer victimhood trope: what to do about the queer kids who fight back. In educational contexts where the recognition of and sympathy for queer students presumes the figure of the battered queer martyr—and, importantly, where resurgent concerns over school violence have reinvigorated zero tolerance disciplinary policies—what happens when some queer students mobilize their own violent responses to the anti-queer violence enacted upon them?[5] Also, what sympathy (if any) remains specifically for Black queer youth (BQY) who, like so many Black youth in US schools, may already face vilification for their blackness?[6] Situated at the intersection of Black criminality, queer helplessness, and anxieties over school safety, BQY who retaliate against anti-queer bullying must navigate an educational path riddled by conflicting notions of fairness, agency, caring, and justice. These students deserve institutional policies and practices that account for those complexities.

In this chapter, I argue that BQY who stand up to anti-LGBTQ+ violence in urban secondary schools are marshaling *Black queer resistant capital,* a culturally derived set of resistance strategies that enable their survival and, at times, aim to disrupt the material and ideological conditions of domination. Building upon Tara Yosso's conceptualization of resistant capital in her work on the cultural wealth of communities of color, I identify two categories of Black queer resistant capital, both borne out of Black queer survival, that appear in BQY's narratives on school-based bullying and harassment.[7] Based on my analyses of these narratives, I cast a shift in focus among urban secondary educators from BQY's victimization to BQY's resistance as an example of the first commitment of queerly responsive pedagogy presented in chapter 2: *Provide a critical ethic of care to queer youth of color through queer of color peer and community networks, as well as through connections with critically caring adults.* Finally, I close the chapter with implications for disrupting anti-queer violence against BQY in urban secondary schools. By conceptualizing and depicting Black queer resistant capital, my hope is to reframe educators' perspectives on BQY who defend themselves, especially in the absence of any meaningful protections from the adults entrusted with their care.

A quick note: although multiple, intersecting forms of domination are acting upon BQY at any given moment, this chapter focuses on anti-queerness since it emerged repeatedly in young people's narratives as the source of violence and harm in their urban secondary schooling experiences.

## RESISTANT CAPITAL

Resistance is a complicated, contextual, and often contradictory set of phenomena. As evidenced by the field of resistance studies, there is no single conceptualization of what constitutes resistance.[8] Narrowing the focus to resistance within educational contexts still leaves one with a significant and conflicted range of definitions.[9] In this chapter, I draw upon a framing of resistance by Yosso which, as noted below, is widely cited in attempts to disrupt cultural deficit perspectives on, and recognize the strengths of, students from racially, ethnically, and linguistically minoritized backgrounds.[10] Along with its prevalence in educational circles, witnessing favorable responses to Yosso's work in my own classes and professional development sessions as a teacher educator further compels my engagement of her scholarship. By exploring BQY's resistance through a cogent and widely accepted framework in educational circles, I am inviting urban secondary educators to engage a provocative proposition—sensitivity to Black queer students who fight back—on more familiar and palatable terms.

What I refer to as Black queer resistant capital builds upon Yosso's conceptualization of the cultural wealth of communities of color. In contrast to the culturally deprived image of those communities implied by Pierre Bourdieu's popular theories of capital, Yosso defines community cultural wealth as the "array of knowledge, skills, abilities and contacts possessed and utilized by Communities of Color to survive and resist macro and micro-forms of oppression."[11] Six forms of capital—six modes of knowing, being, and navigating the world—are identified by Yosso to illustrate the cultural assets within communities of color. By aligning capital with the culturally derived knowledges of students, families, and communities of color, Yosso retains capital as a marker of value while concomitantly inviting educators to appreciate the assets for learning and thriving deposited throughout racially and ethnically minoritized communities. Its widespread uptake in teacher preparation and professional development illustrates the significant impact of community cultural wealth on anti-deficit pedagogical work in the United States.[12]

One of the six forms of capital comprising community cultural wealth, resistant capital is defined as "those knowledges and skills fostered through oppositional behavior that challenges inequality."[13] Yosso locates resistant capital in legacies of anti-oppressive struggle in communities of color, troubling in the process white supremacist misrepresentations of resistant capital as evidence of these communities' lawlessness. Mirroring Yosso's critique, I want to dispute the vilification of BQY who defend themselves against anti-queer violence. Reframing BQY's acts of self-defense as resistant capital exposes the white supremacist and cisheteronormative logics that punish these young people for refusing dehumanization. This, however, does not mean that BQY's resistant capital is beyond reproach. Citing work by Daniel Solórzano and Dolores Delgado Bernal, Yosso asserts that some forms of oppositional behavior can leave oppressive structures intact and may even have the unintended effect of reinforcing them.[14] For Yosso, a critical consciousness of, and a desire to transform, racially oppressive structures distinguish certain enactments of resistance as *transformative* resistant capital. This distinction will be examined later in this chapter's analysis of BQY's resistant capital.

Yosso's conceptualization of resistant capital has been widely cited in scholarly literature on racially and ethnically minoritized students, particularly those identifying as Latinx and/or Black. Included in this body of work are examinations of resistant capital as a tool for navigating and persisting in undergraduate, graduate, teacher preparation, and K–12 educational contexts.[15] Other offerings focus on the resistant capital of youth of color during the college selection process, as well as in out-of-school and informal learning settings.[16] While all of these works underscore the benefits of resistant capital for racially and ethnically minoritized students, only a small subset to date has explored resistant capital's queer potential. This includes Summer Pennell's analyses of queer cultural capital and Antonio Duran and David Pérez II's examinations of queer Latino male collegians' community cultural wealth.[17] Although the former accords relatively minimal space to resistant capital and the latter is set in the postsecondary context, both point to the affordances of resistant capital as a heuristic for queer students' negotiations of power and autonomy in anti-queer educational settings. This chapter builds upon the groundwork laid by those scholars to pose resistant capital as an appropriate lens for understanding Black queer students' maneuvers through queer-negative urban secondary schools.

## THE CULTURAL CONTEXT OF BLACK QUEER RESISTANT CAPITAL

Characterizations of certain knowledge and practices as resistant capital have more credibility when corroborated with evidence of their anti-oppressive function within a particular cultural experience. In this section, I cite scholarship and cultural productions on the lived experiences of Black queer communities to establish the cultural context of two forms of Black queer resistant capital: *reading* and *self-defense*. More compassionate interactions between urban secondary educators and BQY require, among other factors, the former's understanding of how cultural practices like reading and physical retaliation stem from and serve Black queer survival.

Several connotations exist to reading as a Black queer cultural practice.[18] To frame the significance of the youth narratives shared in this chapter, I use reading to describe a performative style of verbal assertion and truth-telling in Black queer culture, and I focus specifically on its use by Black queer individuals against non-Black queer antagonists.[19] As E. Patrick Johnson offers in his portrait of Black queer communicative practices, "To read someone is to set them 'straight,' to put them in their place, or to reveal a secret about someone in front of others in an indirect way—usually in a way that embarrasses a third party."[20] The competitiveness, performativity, and quick wit that characterize reading liken it to the dozens, signifying, and other variations of verbal sparring in Black culture.[21] However, its stylized use by Black queer individuals during discriminatory situations imbues reading-as-resistance with a uniquely Black queer cultural sensibility. A good *read*—a stinging, intimidating, and/or embarrassing verbal putdown or callout—is one strategy employed by Black queer folks to deter further harassment from cultural outsiders.

Countless examples of the type of reading explored in this chapter can be found in *Pose,* the FX television series depicting the queer Black and Latinx House Ball community in New York City in the 1980s and 1990s.[22] The central involvement of House Ball community members as writers, directors, and actors lends a unique level of authenticity to the series' depiction of Black and Latinx queer culture.[23] In one scene, Elektra, a Black trans woman, delivers the following read of a cis white woman who pressures Elektra and two other trans women of color to leave a restaurant, and who subsequently accuses them of being men dressed up as women: "God may have blessed you with Barbies, a backyard with a pony, and with a boyfriend named Jake, and an unwanted pregnancy that your father paid to terminate so that you could go to college and major in being a basic bitch *[Angel, one of Elektra's tablemates, snaps her fingers for emphasis]*. None of these things make you a woman."[24] With a stinging comeback that exposes the artifice of middle-class white cis female respectability, Elektra embarrasses the cis white woman harasser, intimidates her into returning to her table, and thwarts the attempt to expel the trans women of color from the restaurant. Praise for this scene underscores how reading not only functions, but is venerated, as a Black queer tactic of verbal retaliation against slights and threats.[25]

The restaurant scene from *Pose* is one of countless examples across Black queer scholarly and cultural productions of reading—along with its linguistic cousin, shade—as a purposeful Black queer cultural practice.[26] Some of those accounts specifically highlight the salience of reading for BQY. For instance, in her study of a community-based agency serving a mostly Black group of LGBTQ+ youth, Mollie Blackburn quotes Thunder, a young Black queer male participant, as he recounts a public transit interaction with some masculine-presenting, homophobic, male riders: "*Thunder:* And they [said], 'you faggot ass.' [And I said,] 'Is that all you can say, you cunt? Look at your Timberlands, they are leaning like the Eiffel Tower . . .'"[27] Just as Elektra's retort undermined her harasser's attempt to wield white cis female respectability against her, Thunder's use of "cunt" challenged the validity of his harassers' hypermasculinity and, subsequently, deterred further intimidation. That Thunder shared this anecdote to the delight and applause of his peers during a group discussion on Black queer literacy practices further casts reading as a revered Black queer cultural practice.

As a response to anti-queer harassment, reading, like in the examples described above, has the potential to prevent verbal taunts from escalating into physical assaults. When attacks cannot be avoided, physical acts of self-defense by Black queer individuals constitute another form of Black queer resistant capital. Critical here is an acknowledgment of the chance for brutal assaults across numerous domains—from K–12 schools and college campuses to bars, nightclubs, and other public spaces—as an enduring exigency of Black queer life in the United States.[28] When set against the systemic and pervasive threat of bodily harm, fighting back in self-defense against anti-LGBTQ+ violence can be understood as Black queer resistant capital.

One source for discomforting yet informative reflections on Black queer self-defense as a cultural practice is *Check It,* a 2016 documentary that follows the lives of several members of Check It, a group of Black LGBTQ+ young people in Washington, DC, who defended each other against anti-queer violence.[29] Founded in 2009, Check It defied popular stereotypes of queer weakness by responding brutally and decisively to would-be queerbashers, establishing itself in the process as a formidable presence on the streets of the nation's capital. Intermixed with the film's snapshots of physically violent encounters are interviews with Check It members like Skittles who, in the following excerpt, reinforces the purposefulness behind fighting back: "A lot of people think that gays are weak and that we can't fight, but I just got tired of it, like just letting people pick on me and say what they want to me. And so one day I just started fighting back, and ever since then I've been a fighter."[30] As a fighter, Skittles eschewed queer victimhood by striking back against his assailants. His sentiment is one that recurs in other documentations of Black queer lives in the United States.[31] When situated against the backdrop of anti-queer violence, fighting back—for Skittles, his Check It peers, and many other Black queer individuals—cannot be dismissed as indiscriminate violence. Rather, it emerges as a culturally lauded strategy for survival. In the case of Check It, the group's operation as a chosen family, yet another Black queer cultural practice, reinforces the shared commitment to self-defense as both a core community value and a form of Black queer resistant capital.[32]

While *Check It* focuses primarily on group members' lives outside of formal K–12 settings, other sources contextualize BQY's reliance on physical retaliation in schools. For instance, in its survey data on the experiences of Black LGBTQ+ middle and high school students, GLSEN has found that almost two-thirds of the respondents reported varying levels of victimization in schools—including physical assaults—based on sexual orientation, and over half reported victimization based on gender expression.[33] To make matters worse, a joint research venture by the GSA Network and the Crossroads Collaborative at the University of Arizona found that in addition to anti-queer harassment from both peers and school staff, LGBTQ youth of color experienced "increased surveillance and policing, relatively greater incidents of harsh school discipline, and consistent blame for their own victimization."[34] The brutality of these combined circumstances is painfully narrated in an account from Sage, a trans-identified participant in the National Black Justice Coalition's panel on Black LGBTQ+ schooling experiences.[35] In the following passage, Sage describes being disciplined by school staff for defending herself against anti-queer violence:

> In middle school, I was suspended seven times, a combination of out-of-school suspension and in-school suspension. I was, you know, always punished when violence was taken against me. I was suspended when I was attacked and called a faggot by six kids who told me I was too gay. They threw shoes at my head and beat me up, and I was caught on video telling them to get the fuck off of me, and I was suspended for using, you know, for using curse words, and nobody else was suspended. Nobody else was punished.[36]

Abhorrent experiences like those reported by Sage unfortunately resurface in the youth narratives presented later in this chapter. Like Sage, those youth narrators recall protecting themselves against anti-queer peer violence in schools and, in some instances, being subsequently punished for their attempts at self-defense by school officials. By proposing Black queer resistant capital as a framework for consideration by urban secondary schools, my hope is to encourage a more compassionate and just treatment of Black LGBTQ+ students who, in the absence of effective school protections, have to rely on physical violence to protect themselves.

Overall, drawing conceptually upon community cultural wealth affords my consideration of reading and physical acts of self-defense as resistance strategies, valued by and transmitted in Black queer culture, that counter the constellation of hostilities and violence that produce Black queer vulnerability. My singular focus on resistant capital is not meant to suggest that this form of capital operates discretely from others in Yosso's model. In fact, much of the scholarship on community cultural wealth explores minoritized students' concurrent and overlapping activations of two or more categories of capital.[37] There are, however, some scholarly analyses that delve deeply into a sole category from Yosso's model.[38] My specific attention to resistant capital is informed by the narratives analyzed in the next section of this chapter—narratives that detail retaliations against BQY who resisted anti-queer harassment in their schools. The potential repercussions faced by Black LGBTQ+ students who dare to disrupt their in-school victimization warrant concerted efforts to nurture more critical understandings of Black queer resistant capital among urban secondary educators. This chapter takes a step toward that end.

Before presenting the analysis of the Midtown AIDS Center (MAC) study data to follow, I want to reiterate that resistance is a complex and often contradictory phenomenon. Both resistance studies at large and its subfield within educational studies reveal how historical backdrops, nationalisms, political economies, identities, epistemologies, pedagogical orientations, and a host of other factors mediate varied perspectives on the constitution and evidence of resistance.[39] As previously suggested, the currency of Yosso's work in K–12 educational circles in the United States offers a cogent and familiar terrain for discussions of Black queer resistant capital with urban secondary educators. And yet even this does not eliminate the inherent complexities and conflicts at play. Namely, sympathies toward Black LGBTQ+ students who are forced to fend for themselves are understandable, as are concerns about the violent institutional cultures perpetuated by these young people's actions. To be clear, glamorizing how BQY fight back against in-school harassment and violence is not the aim of this chapter. Rather, my hope is that a sensitivity to the need for cultural practices like reading and fighting back in self-defense will help educators to consider a wider range of strategies in response. As resurgent anxieties toward school violence in the United States increase the appeal of zero tolerance policies that lump all disciplinary infractions together, it is especially urgent to provide schools with frameworks to differentiate BQY's acts of self-defense from the acts of anti-queer aggression that necessitate them.

## ACCOUNTS OF BLACK QUEER RESISTANT CAPITAL IN SCHOOL

The accounts of Black queer resistant capital explored below emerged in the narratives of youth participants in the MAC study, which I described in detail in chapter 1. As context for understanding their enthusiastic engagement with MAC as an educational space, youth study participants were asked to describe their K–12 schooling experiences. Incidentally, these data collection sessions coincided with the release of survey results of students' public schooling experiences in Midtown, the city in which MAC was located. Those results revealed that 35 percent of the city's students reported engaging in a physical fight in school in the month prior to the survey, and 13 percent reported carrying a weapon to school during the same timeframe.[40] Against that backdrop, two themes surfacing across MAC youth's narratives captured the anti-queer nature of their experiences with school violence: their encounters with anti-queer harassment, and their mobilizations of Black queer resistant capital. These two themes are discussed below. And as a reminder, Table 1.1 provides a demographic breakdown of the MAC study youth participants.

**School-Based Anti-queer Harassment**

Scholarly publications, advocacy organization reports, and news media coverage provide disturbing evidence of BQY's encounters with anti-queerness in American K–12 education.[41] Echoing those sources, eight of the ten youth participants in the MAC study described their own experiences with school-based anti-queer harassment and violence. Since the nature of anti-queer bullying has been widely documented, and since my goal in this chapter is to foreground considerations of resistance, I forego longer descriptions below in favor of keywords and brief summaries that convey the baleful tone of participants' queerphobic encounters.

Unsurprisingly, much of the anti-queer harassment reported by study participants came from other students in their schools. For instance, two participants, Aaron and 2, recalled getting into fights after being called "faggot" by peers. Another participant, Mystery Man, described hearing "fag alert" from a boy when entering a bathroom, and Twizzler reported being called "faggot" as well as "batty bwoy," the latter a Jamaican homophobic epithet. Reflecting how deeply anti-queer harassment could scar those who were targeted, peer threats of getting "bashed" led one participant, Levi, into an extended period of silence throughout middle and high school. Together, these and other incidents described by study participants confirmed the presence of anti-queer peer harassment in their schooling experiences.

Alarmingly, other students were not the only culprits behind school-based anti-queer encounters. Four of the MAC study youth participants described harassment from teachers, administrators, and other school personnel. One of those participants was Nicole. Despite distributing a letter to inform school personnel of her chosen name and female gender pronouns, Nicole reported being intentionally misgendered by transphobic teachers, administrators, and security guards. Another participant, Binky, remembered being called "you little faggot" by an adversarial math teacher, and a nonbinary youth named 2 recounted being teased in front of other students for their femininity by male gym teachers. For M, the cafeteria emerged as a site of anti-queer harassment when a cafeteria worker quoted homophobic Bible passages in front of students during his school's gay pride celebration. Sadly, all of these incidents evince the anti-queer bullying experienced by some Black LGBTQ+ youth at the hands of the school personnel entrusted with their care. Combined with the earlier descriptions of homophobic peer interactions, the anti-queer harassment from adults provides a graphic backdrop for examining study participants' enactments of Black queer resistant capital.

## Reading and Self-Defense as Black Queer Resistant Capital

In response to their queerphobic school cultures, six of the ten MAC study youth participants described moments when they and/or their Black queer peers resisted harassment through reading and/or self-defense. These practices, when situated against the backdrop of anti-queer victimization in schools, fall within Yosso's definition of resistant capital as the "array of knowledge, skills, abilities and contacts possessed and utilized by Communities of Color to survive and resist macro and micro-forms of oppression."[42] In this section, I present study participants' accounts of their responses to both peer and staff bullying in school with one major goal in mind: to replace oversimplified perceptions of unruly BQY with more sensitive depictions of their unfortunate yet understandable assertions of Black queer resistant capital.

*Resisting Peer Harassment.* Some of the most evocative accounts of enacting Black queer resistant capital were offered by 2, a study participant who recalled "kicking ass in 7th grade" to defend themselves from peer bullying. For 2, fighting back against anti-queer bullies served as a deterrent from further physical violence. "By 8th grade," 2 noted, "it was like, 'Okay, we're going to leave him alone 'cause he's not . . .' I let people know that I'm not a punk. Like, I will fight you and I'll hit first. So by that time, people would just talk about me behind my back." As the physical violence from peers shifted to anti-queer gossip and verbal taunts, 2 relied more heavily on reading as a resistive strategy, as detailed in the following passage:

> I fought more to survive and not physically. Like I can count on one hand and maybe a couple fingers how many fights I've been in in school. But it was more so just trying to survive 'cause I mean it was rough. Like, every which way I always had to have a comeback, just some smartass remark, and let me tell you, I said some pretty nasty things back then to people. Like I used to say, "I fuck your father when your mom's at work and you're at school." I said, "I'm happiest when I'm fucking your father up the ass." I used to say horrible stuff and it was so mean, but I just didn't know what else to do.

The tone of this passage provides an important starting point for this section. While stinging reads enabled 2 to stand up for themselves in the face of ongoing verbal harassment, they also left 2 feeling exasperated. Ideally, reading as a form of Black queer resistant capital should not have been necessary for 2's survival. The toll of standing up to anti-queer bullying in this manner is yet another layer of injustice, as conveyed poignantly in the following excerpt from 2's interview responses: "Lots of LGBT students are bright and talented but their education is interrupted because they're constantly on alert, and they're constantly in the state of anxiety of 'am I gonna have to slap the shit out of somebody today?' The danger is real."

2's modeling of Black queer resistant capital proved invaluable for another MAC youth, Binky, who attended middle and high school with 2 prior to her gender transitioning. Binky credited 2 with teaching her the necessity of self-defense when they explicitly told her, "'Bitch, you better stand up for yourself.'" Like 2, Binky started to fight back against queerphobic bullies. In her words, "Once they knew you were going to fight back, they would respect you. So you have to be like, 'If you touch me, I'm gonna beat your ass.'" For Binky, as with 2, the willingness to meet physical violence with her own retaliation deterred further attacks and thus functioned as an unfortunate yet effective form of Black queer resistant capital.

Another participant who recounted fights with homophobic peers was Aaron. Not only did Aaron fight back against anti-queer harassment, but he got suspended repeatedly for doing so. Looking back on his experiences as a ninth and tenth grader, Aaron recalled, "Anybody who called me a faggot or messed with me or, you know, did any stupid things to me that I didn't like, it's time to fight." In Aaron's case, the peer violence was exacerbated by teachers' disciplinary actions. He stated:

> I was disrespecting the teachers because I felt as though I was always getting, I was the one they were targeting. I would get suspended but what about the other person? Why are you coming at me when this man started with me? I didn't do anything, and I used to just hate it. I felt as though it was more favoritism, and I felt as though it was because of the fact that teachers, they have their favorites. And they would, just by them knowing me and they just assume that I'm gay—of course they know I'm gay—so they don't like me either. But they cannot say that because of their position, you know.

From Aaron's perspective, teachers unfairly punished him for defending himself against anti-queer harassment from other students. Suspensions for acts of self-defense added insult to the injury of queerphobic peer violence.

Two more study participants who recalled responses to anti-queer peers in school were Twizzler and Mystery Man. Twizzler described a gay friend who pulled out a knife when fellow students tried to bully him. This incident resulted in a resonant acknowledgment from straight boys at school—"'That's a faggot who can fight'"—and it taught Twizzler the importance of standing up to physical harassment. For Mystery Man, a homophobic encounter in the boys' bathroom at school led to a physical exchange with noteworthy consequences: "I was in the bathroom and this boy was like, 'Oh, fag alert, fag alert.' So I'm like, okay, so I didn't say nothing about it. So it was like when I was leaving out of the bathroom, he pushed me, so I just started beating him up. And then they escorted us to the dean's office, and then, like, I didn't get in trouble because it was like shocking to them for me to be in an office in trouble. So they just let me slide, but him, they suspended him." Mystery Man went on to state that the school contacted his mom to inform her of the bathroom incident. However, the principal, in Mystery Man's words, "stuck up for me more than they stuck up for him because, like, I don't, I was never like a trouble-worthy kid." Although I did not obtain the principal's own insights on the bathroom incident, the sympathy reported by Mystery Man suggests a response to BQY's acts of self-defense that deserves further consideration. This case will be revisited toward the end of this chapter.

Overall, the preceding accounts illuminate the types of circumstances that can lead Black LGBTQ+ students to rely on reading and fighting back in self-defense as forms of Black queer resistant capital. Left to fend for themselves, some MAC youth engaged these practices to navigate physically and emotionally violent anti-queer encounters with other students. Considering BQY's responses to peer-based bullying as potential enactments of resistant capital may be one important step toward more just resolutions of anti-queer harassment in secondary schools.

**Resisting Personnel Harassment.** Adding to their catalog of queerphobic encounters in schools, two MAC youth participants spelled out their resistance against harassment from school personnel. One of those participants, Binky, retraced a contentious relationship prior to her gender transitioning with a math teacher whom she characterized as "one of those white girls that thinks she hood." As the antagonism between the two increased, the teacher addressed Binky in front of other students as "you little faggot." Binky responded by calling the teacher an "ugly bitch" and subsequently hanging disparaging posters about the teacher in the hallways, for which she received an in-school suspension. Describing the aftermath, Binky stated, "Now she's crying, and I said, 'I don't care. She shouldn't have called me faggot.' So then she tried to apologize, and then we were cool from then on 'cause then I threatened to beat her up if she ever said it again."

Comparing Binky's reactions to her math teacher with her responses to peer bullies (described in the previous section) is instructive. As a reminder of the latter, Binky stated, "Once they knew you were going to fight back, they would respect you. So you had to be like, 'If you touch me, I'm gonna beat your ass.'" The same calculus was apparent in her reactions to her math teacher: Binky demonstrated her willingness to strike back against the teacher (echoing "Once they knew you were going to fight back . . ."); she received some signs of respect from the teacher in the form of an apology (echoing "they would respect you"); and she deterred future verbal attacks from the teacher through the threat of physical violence (echoing "If you touch me, I'm gonna beat your ass"). That the teacher addressed Binky as "you little faggot" in front of other students likely raised the stakes of the exchange by inviting peer harassment against Binky—that is, were the comment to remain unchecked. To be clear, I am neither applauding nor condemning Binky's actions during and after this incident. My aim here, as with the other anti-LGBTQ+ encounters chronicled in this chapter, is to help readers understand the conditions that make reading and fighting understandable and, at times, effective forms of Black queer resistant capital. Binky was already being targeted by other students for her queerness and emergent transness in a school district with troubling rates of peer-to-peer violence. Her pushback against the math teacher can be understood as, among other things, her resistance against even further marginalization and vulnerability.

The other study participant who described resisting the actions of school personnel was Nicole. In response to being repeatedly misgendered as "sir" by a transphobic school security guard, Nicole composed a letter in which she formally requested to be addressed as a girl, and she sent copies of the letter to all of her teachers. Disappointingly, she had to follow that letter up with a fierce, face-to-face read of a male teacher, as recounted in the following passage: "So, for example, today a teacher called me sir and I told them, 'Sir? Whoa.' I said, 'Ma'am, you called me a sir.' He said, 'Who are you calling ma'am?' 'I called you a ma'am because you called me a sir and not a ma'am. So either you reciprocate that or we can just call and play this game, you know what I mean?'" As her account continued to unfold, Nicole described the teacher's reaction to her read of him:

> He responded as if he was imperfect, like he didn't mean to. I sort of said, "I know we're imperfect but let's not do it again." Because it was in a room where no one was there, I didn't really get kind of upset, you know. But it is what it is. Sorry. Totally professional, and there wasn't anybody at the classroom. I didn't tell him in front of everybody to embarrass him and, like, make fun of his place. I told him, "We're out of the classroom." I told him, "You called me a sir. Either you call me a ma'am or I'm going to report you like I said I was going to do in that letter." And he said, "I'm sorry." I said, "No one is perfect. Just don't let it happen again." And I walked out.

Nicole's account of this incident offers yet another example of reading as a form of Black queer resistant capital. Confronted by a teacher who continued to misgender her, Nicole used reading—her fierce, snappy callout of the teacher's actions—to disrupt his transphobic harassment in the moment and deter his misgendering of her in the future. The absence of anyone else in the room when the interaction occurred further suggests that the presence of other students informed the heightened antagonism of Binky's incident with her math teacher. Perhaps most significantly, Nicole did not rely solely on reading as her source of Black queer resistant capital, nor did she resort to physical threats. Instead, she informed the teacher that she would report him—as stated in the letter she had distributed—if he continued to misgender her. Additionally, as she and Peggy Lee, a MAC staffer, reported in separate individual interviews, Peggy Lee ended up accompanying Nicole to a meeting with school administrators to discuss her letter.

Together, three of Nicole's strategic moves—writing the letter, inviting Peggy Lee to advocate for her during a school meeting about the letter, and warning the teacher that she would report future acts of misgendering—distinguish her account as an instance of *transformative resistant capital*. As noted earlier in this chapter, Yosso differentiates transformative resistant capital as modes of resistance informed by a critical consciousness of, and a desire to transform, racially oppressive structures. Nicole's approach to pushing for trans inclusion in this instance exemplifies how critical understandings of institutional hierarchies, along with trustworthy support from allies like Peggy Lee, can inform more strategic self-advocacy by Black queer and trans students. Reading and fighting back are understandable modes of Black queer resistant capital, but they need not be the only options available to Black LGBTQ+ youth. As this chapter comes to a close, I want to suggest some new options for Black LGBTQ+ students and urban secondary schools to consider together. It is my hope that these options produce more enriching schooling experiences for BQY.

## A QUEERLY RESPONSIVE SHIFT FROM VICTIMIZATION TO RESISTANCE

In chapter 2, I proposed queerly responsive pedagogy as a framework for supporting Black and other racially minoritized queer youth in urban secondary schools and youth-serving community-based organizations. The sensitivity to Black queer resistant capital for which I advocate in this chapter is a direct extension of that framework's first commitment: *Provide a critical ethic of care to queer youth of color through queer of color peer and community networks, as well as through connections with critically caring adults.* A queerly responsive critical ethic of care, as explained in chapter 2, acknowledges how white supremacy, anti-queerness, and other forms of domination dehumanize queer youth of color, and it supplies the compassion, protection, reassurance, and sociopolitical consciousness necessary for racially minoritized LGBTQ+ youth to heal, persevere, and ultimately thrive. The educational scholarship, news media accounts, and MAC youth narratives cited throughout this current chapter clearly illuminate how anti-queerness precariously positions BQY as targets of harassment and violence. Queerly responsive critical caring would require urban secondary schools to recognize the need for BQY's acts of self-defense, determine compassionate responses to those acts, and collaborate with these youth to strategically dismantle anti-queer institutional cultures. A queerly responsive critical ethic of care is essential when addressing Black queer resistant capital.

This chapter opened by identifying a critical oversight of the queer victimhood trope that pervades American K–12 education: the possibility of LGBTQ+ students fighting back. The BQY in my MAC study confirmed that, yes, they were targeted by anti-queer harassment in their schools. But some of them also described responses to victimization that disrupted popular presumptions of their helplessness. Unfortunately, many found themselves in schools where their right to protect their bodies and stand up for their humanity, if envisioned at all, was not consistently honored. As stated several times throughout this chapter, my reason for exposing this tangle of circumstances is to help readers understand why and how Black LGBTQ+ youth may defiantly stand up for themselves—sometimes verbally, sometimes physically—when confronted by homophobic peers and staff members in urban secondary schools. Culturally situating reading and fighting back as Black queer survival and protest practices seems a requisite step toward support strategies that respect and account for BQY's resistant capital.

Something else that bears repeating is the significance of the current state of American public education as a backdrop for discussing BQY's resistant capital. Two dilemmas mentioned elsewhere in this chapter inform the urgency of my analyses: the ever-expanding slate of anti-queer and anti-trans legislation and related efforts to intensify anti-LGBTQ+ school cultures; and the renewed appeal of zero tolerance approaches to discipline, informed by legitimate concerns over school safety, that can fail to differentiate BQY's acts of self-defense from other behaviors, especially anti-queer bullying. Having multiple policies and practices that intersect to undermine queer students' K–12 schooling experience is, of course, nothing new. That said, the recent intensification of these measures strengthens the warrant to think carefully about Black queer students' modes of resistance.

Building on Yosso's community cultural wealth model allows me to delimit some preliminary boundaries for Black queer resistant capital in urban secondary schools. For starters, not every defiant or disruptive act committed by a Black LGBTQ+ student qualifies as resistant capital. I expressly took excerpts from MAC youth's narratives that mirror Yosso's classification of "knowledges and skills fostered through oppositional behavior that challenges inequality."[43] Identifying Black queer resistant capital requires clarity around how oppositional behaviors like reading and fighting back in self-defense defy anti-queerness in urban secondary schools. That clarity can then inform how we support Black queer students' enactments of their resistant capital. Of the cases cited in the findings section of the chapter, Nicole's stands out as the most premeditated, multipronged approach to challenging anti-LGBTQ+ harassment in school. Her attention to the structural barriers to trans inclusion makes Nicole's the one reported response to school-based harassment that clearly rises to Yosso's distinction of transformative resistant capital. As urban secondary educators work to improve the schooling experiences of Black LGBTQ+ youth, Nicole's case can serve as an exemplar for what students' strategic self-advocacy—that which rises to the level of transformative Black queer resistant capital—looks like.

Along with the self-advocacy demonstrated by Nicole, the sympathetic administrative response to Mystery Man's bathroom incident seems worthy of deeper consideration. Since my study design did not include opportunities to gather insights from the principal who responded to the incident, it is not clear if that principal's leniency (i.e., to not suspend Mystery Man for fighting back) was solely because he was seen as a "good student" in the school, or if being the target of homophobic bullying also informed the principal's seemingly sympathetic decision-making. Either way, the bathroom incident presents an opportunity to consider the following question: how can an awareness of Black queer resistant capital guide an administrator's response when a Black queer student fights back against anti-queer harassers? Responding to questions like this might prepare urban secondary schools to push back against zero tolerance logics that equate Black queer students' acts of self-defense with the aggressions of their attackers.

## IMPLICATIONS FOR URBAN SECONDARY EDUCATION

As with any attempt to innovate educational practices, this chapter's implications for supporting BQY in urban secondary schools will vary based on contextual factors like established disciplinary policies and procedures, leadership sensitivities and/or biases, institutional and regional attitudes toward LGBTQ+ issues in schools, and the size and visibility of the Black queer student population. I implore readers to keep that caveat in mind as they consider the four recommendations outlined below. Additionally, I encourage readers to consider how these recommendations might inform efforts to create safer schools for other LGBTQ+ students as well.

1. *Investigate disciplinary alternatives:* While this chapter highlights BQY's bouts with insensitive disciplinary procedures, a larger body of work has documented the deleterious impact of zero tolerance policies and other punitive modes of school disciplinary systems on racially and ethnically minoritized youth more broadly.[44] Students of color, including those who identify as LGBTQ+, will continue to be policed and dehumanized as long as carceral approaches to urban school discipline persist. Supporting the ongoing movement for restorative justice and other alternatives to punitive disciplinary cultures is one way to make room for more compassionate institutional and interpersonal responses to BQY's resistant capital.
2. *Provide professional development:* The combination of punitive disciplinary policies and cultural deficit perspectives in schools works against critically conscious and compassionate considerations of why and how Black queer students engage certain forms of resistant capital. Urban secondary schools will likely need professional development on Black

queer resistant capital to establish a shared understanding of its significance. Strategically, including Black queer resistant capital as one piece in a professional development session on an already familiar topic—perhaps on LGBTQ+ issues or positive behavioral supports and student engagement—may help educators to see its connection to the overarching mission of supporting and caring for their students.

3. *Maintain incident logs:* During data analysis for the MAC study, I realized that the findings contained an unofficial record of MAC youth's encounters with anti-queer harassment in schools. A more formal log of such incidents within urban secondary schools could support advocacy by and on behalf of Black queer students against punitive disciplinary measures. It could also help administrators identify trends that need to be addressed in order to effectively disrupt anti-queer harassment. A GSA or similar student organization within a school could provide an ideal setting for generating and maintaining this type of incident log, with the added benefit of centering youth as agents of change.

4. *Promote teacher intervention:* The lack of adult intervention during incidents of anti-queer harassment and violence is a recurrent theme across the accounts featured in this chapter. Echoing anti-bullying recommendations elsewhere, a clear implication for urban secondary educators is to intervene when Black queer students are being targeted and harassed.[45] This includes moments when other adults in the school are the harassers. In my professional development sessions on LGBTQ+ issues in schools, I place teachers in small groups to role play ninety-second responses to anti-LGBTQ+ scenarios unfolding in classrooms, hallways, and teachers lounges. Rehearsing the wording and tone of those responses is one way to give teachers the confidence to interrupt anti-queer harassment in their schools.

CHAPTER 4

# Trans Fugitivity in a Black Queer Youth Space

*Thinking Beyond Safety*

When I initiated my research of the Midtown AIDS Center (MAC) as an alternative pedagogical space for Black queer youth (BQY), I did so with the presumption that MAC, an HIV/AIDS prevention and support services agency serving a predominantly Black population of LGBTQ+ youth, was a safe space.[1] Fostering safe spaces for queer youth has always been one of my biggest passions as an openly queer educator, and nothing that I witnessed during my pre-study visits to MAC gave me pause about the agency's safe space status. It would take a blowup between youth participants during a brainstorming activity at MAC to disabuse me of that presumption. That critical incident, along with subsequent interviews and observations, revealed that MAC was not a safe space for some of the Black trans female youth (BTFY) who participated in its programming. My first attempt to make sense of this finding produced a co-authored book chapter with Tomás Boatwright that described the challenges to, and presented strategies for, creating safe and inclusive spaces for trans youth of color.[2] Taking for granted that safe spaces were possible, my response to the lack of safety for trans youth at MAC was to identify ways to fix it.

Since then, I have become increasingly aware of the fraught nature of safe spaces for LGBTQ+ youth. Critiques of safe spaces from both academic and activist circles have illuminated how any given space is constituted by a particular set of power relations that threatens the safety of some potential participants.[3] Similarly, another body of work has surfaced internal divisions across factors like race and gender that confound the safety of spaces specifically intended for queer youth.[4] In light of anti-queer hostilities that LGBTQ+ youth can face in contexts like families, schools, churches, health care, and any number of public spaces, the rhetoric of safety has understandably defined social, political, and educational movements to support queer youth for at least the past three decades. Unfortunately, that rhetoric belies the contentious power dynamics—and in some cases, the harm—that can rattle a purportedly safe space for young queer people.

This chapter marks my attempt to wrestle with the institutional and identity politics that can fracture and compromise the safety of queer youth spaces. In what follows, I revisit my co-authored account of BTFY's experiences at MAC through the analytical lens of *fugitivity,* a framework from the field of Black studies that explores how the precarity and liminality of Black life in the United States informs the ways in which Black people produce knowledge, read the world, and develop strategies for survival and resistance. Combining previously shared study findings with some data that are published here for the first time, I use fugitivity to pose new interpretations of BTFY's experiences at MAC. These interpretations consider how to make sense of these young women's actions when transmisogyny—the contempt and suspicion toward, and the pathologization and marginalization of, trans girls and women—is understood as endemic to their lived experiences, even in spaces designated as safe for LGBTQ+ youth.[5] While not wholly abandoning the hope of supportive spaces for BTFY, this chapter searches for the insights and strategies that emerge when the presence of transmisogyny is anticipated in BQY spaces. The potential implications of my analysis for work with BTFY and potentially other groups of queer youth as well are considered at the end of the chapter.

Before proceeding further, I want to name a dilemma that this chapter generates. By spotlighting youth negotiations of transmisogyny at MAC, this chapter speaks to the third core commitment of queerly responsive pedagogy—*Address any tensions that challenge a respect for and inclusion of variously identi-*

*fied queer youth of color*—which I discussed in detail in chapter 2. In efforts to establish spaces for LGBTQ+ youth, respect and inclusion, both of which are featured in that third commitment, are often aligned with safety. My attempt to trouble our assumptions about safety in such spaces may, at times, feel in conflict with my queerly responsive pedagogical call to attend to the respectfulness and inclusivity of these spaces. I believe that the difficulty of resolving this tension is precisely what makes it generative. As I assert in this chapter, discourses on safe spaces underestimate the complex identity politics and power relations that define these spaces. Fugitivity as a conceptual paradigm acknowledges those complexities and offers a more nuanced lens for engaging them. My hope is for readers to leave with potential strategies for supporting BTFY that are informed by a more sophisticated, and perhaps conflicted, rendering of their experiences in queer youth spaces.

Finally, this chapter presents a reckoning with my own biases and limitations as a scholar who studies the educational perspectives and experiences of Black LGBTQ+ youth. For over a decade, my work has predominantly engaged young people who present and/or identify as Black queer cis males. This population, as explained in chapter 1, was prioritized in HIV/AIDS prevention and supports funding at the time of both of the studies featured throughout this book. My research relied on and/or was heavily influenced by those funding streams, thus skewing my study samples toward Black queer cis males. That said, I also recognize that I have not challenged myself enough to create research opportunities that reach more gender-diverse populations of BQY. My attempt in this chapter to center BTFY brings my queer cis male oversights as a researcher into view. Though uncomfortable, it is always important as a researcher and educator to identify current shortcomings and areas for future growth. I attempt to model that reflexivity in this chapter while also considering the possibilities for future work that centers and values the lives of BTFY.

## FROM SAFETY TO FUGITIVITY: A PARADIGM SHIFT

The questions we ask about the lives of BTFY, along with the answers we subsequently seek, stem from the paradigms through which we try to understand their experiences. This chapter features my attempt at a paradigm shift from safety to fugitivity. The nature of and reasons for that shift are outlined below.

## Safety

Despite the seismic increase in LGBTQ+ visibility over the past thirty years, along with precarious yet transformative queer political gains, growing up queer in the United States still presents its share of challenges. Verbal and physical harassment in K–12 schools, anti-queer violence across myriad out-of-school contexts, structural determinants of violence like housing insecurity and health disparities, and legislative attacks on queer-inclusive curricula and gender-affirming medical procedures collectively enact physical, psychological, and spiritual harm on LGBTQ+ youth.[6] It is because of these enduring threats that efforts to support LGBTQ+ youth have focused heavily on the provision of safe spaces—sites that affirm queer identities, provide queer youth with a sense of connectedness to others, and protect those youth from the anti-queer hardships that abound.

In K–12 schools, extracurricular student organizations like gay-straight alliances (GSAs) have become recognizable formats for safe queer spaces. Research has confirmed a number of benefits to queer students' access to GSAs, including an increased sense of safety, a more queer-accepting school climate, higher attendance rates and academic achievement, improved mental health and well-being, increased social connectedness, and a site for LGBTQ+ advocacy.[7] GSA-related resources provided by advocacy organizations like GLSEN and Lambda Legal underscore the perception of GSAs as a safe space in schools for queer students.[8] In some cases, alternative educational programs offer more affirming options for queer students who leave or get pushed out of conventional, and often anti-queer, K–12 schools.[9] Beyond schooling, community-based and advocacy organizations that serve queer youth, as well as queer familial and cultural networks like the House Ball community, seek to create safe, nurturing, and empowering spaces for queer youth's personal and political development.[10] Together, these examples reflect the provision of safe spaces for LGBTQ+ youth as a fundamental commitment of queer educational, political, and community organizing in the United States.

Though the concern for queer youth's safety responds to a particular constellation of anti-queer structural and ideological conditions, its prominence in queer advocacy initiatives reflects a much broader cultural logic about the nature of safe spaces. With the proliferation of diversity and inclusion discourses over the past three decades, educational institutions, community-based organizations, and advocacy-oriented sites are among the numerous settings to promise safe spaces for dialogues on and community-building across cultural differences and social injustices. With ground rules in place to guide interactions, participants are encouraged to delve vulnerably and honestly into risky conversations with the assurance that their safety—from physical and emotional harm, academic retribution, peer judgment, etc.—will be protected. The concept of safe spaces has since come under fire by conservatives who, in their resistance to critical analyses of the status quo, cast it as a mechanism for politically correct censorship.[11] From the opposite end of the political and intellectual spectrum comes another set of concerns about safe spaces that are more relevant to this chapter. In his work on recentering Indigenous paradigms in K–12 classrooms, Timothy San Pedro quotes the following personal communication from Leigh Patel about *truth spaces:*

> Learning is not often safe as it involves such profound transformation. And what facilitates learning for one person is often unproductive or even harmful for another. The white centeredness of education is what has led to consistently harmful spaces for racially minoritized and Indigenous populations. Truth would involve reckoning with that history and the less than polite reality of learning. The danger with calls for safe spaces is that they are fueled more by logics of identity politics than learning and architectures of harm.[12]

This quote conveys an important critique of the concept of safe spaces. Whether in classrooms or elsewhere, what Patel characterizes as "the less than polite reality of learning" entails the uncomfortable collective reckoning with the settler-colonialist, white-supremacist, cisheteropatriarchal legacies that value and protect the identities, histories, bodies, beliefs, and emotions of some participants over those of others. The promise of safe spaces denies the unavoidable riskiness of addressing power when some in the room possess that very power over others. Echoing Patel, critical scholars like Zeus Leonardo and Ronald Porter, as well as Cheryl Matias and Robin DiAngelo, have traced power dynamics along race that turn safe spaces into sites of risk and retribution for participants from historically minoritized backgrounds.[13] In effect, these scholars respond to the promise of safety in such spaces with an urgent question: *Safe for whom?*

Critiques of the concept of safe spaces have important implications for practitioners within and beyond urban secondary schools who work with Black LGBTQ+ youth. Although GSAs, as noted earlier, pose several benefits to LGBTQ+ students, scholarly works by Mollie Blackburn, Cris Mayo, Lance McCready, and Jon Wargo document racial divides between white and Black group members that undermined the latter's participation and sense of belonging.[14] Furthermore, in chapter 2 of this book, as I presented the case for queerly responsive pedagogy's third commitment—*Address any tensions that challenge a respect for and inclusion of variously identified queer youth of color*—I cited a range of tensions that have complicated the safety of certain populations of queer youth of color in spaces designed to serve and affirm them. The marginalization of trans youth by their cis queer peers was one source of these tensions.[15]

Although oversimplified claims about safe spaces in schools and other pedagogical settings persist, more nuanced understandings of the limitations of safety as a framework for sensitive, collective deliberations have gained noticeable popularity. Perhaps the most recognizable departure from safe spaces are *brave spaces,* a framework that acknowledges the riskiness and discomfort associated with critical discussions of identity, culture, power, and the like.[16] Rather than promising an uninterrogated notion of safety, brave spaces name the need for courage as groups learn about and confront the legacies of white supremacy, cisheteropatriarchy, and other systemic forms of domination. In this chapter, I seek to step even farther away from safe spaces by not only considering the need for courage, but also exploring the maneuvers that account for and work around the risks that invariably remain. It is in this vein that I now turn to fugitivity.

## Fugitivity

Alongside abolition, fugitivity is one of Black studies' more fecund conceptual paradigms over the past two decades, deployed by noted scholars in the field to avow slavery's persistent reverberations throughout Black life in the United States.[17] These reverberations are what Saidiya Hartman has termed the afterlife of slavery, or the "skewed life chances, limited access to health and education, premature death, incarceration, and impoverishment" that Blacks in the United States have inherited from the nation's slavery-dependent birth.[18] Analyses of fugitivity do not simplistically equate contemporary Black suffering to that of the historically enslaved. Rather, they trace slavery's indelible imprint on the American experience to explore the ever-present shadow of Black containment, the precarity of Black humanity, and the resultant strategies for Black survival and resistance, all of which mirror the remnant contours of an enslaved past. As racial capitalism in the United States is deeply rooted in slavery, so too are the fugitive exigencies of Black life within that political economy's present.[19]

The afterlife of slavery provides the sociohistorical and intellectual contexts for scholarship on fugitivity. Citing Tina Campt's definitive work, Damien Sojoyner explains fugitivity as follows:

> My conceptualization of Black fugitivity is based on the disavowal of and disengagement from state-governed projects that attempt to adjudicate normative constructions of difference through liberal tropes of freedom and democratic belonging. It builds on Tina Campt's (2014) argument that "the concept of fugitivity highlights the tension between the acts or flights of escape and creative practices of refusal, nimble and strategic practices that undermine the category of the dominant." These practices of refusal, operating alongside practices of disengagement, are central to Black fugitivity and extend beyond common understandings of resistance.[20]

Here, Sojoyner expresses a cynicism toward "liberal tropes of freedom and democratic belonging" ever defining Black life in a nation state founded on—and still driven by—anti-blackness.[21] That cynicism informs a repertoire of fugitive strategies to escape the American condition, disengage from it, refuse its corrupt values and dictates, and/or find "nimble and strategic practices" to undermine it. Fugitive strategies for Black survival and resistance signal two underlying pillars: a recognition of the persistent, state-sanctioned investment in Black suffering; and the mix of cunning, determination, and defiance required by the fugitive Black subject to wrangle freedom regardless.

Building on the intellectual groundwork from Black studies, critical educational scholars have articulated what fugitivity does and could look like in educational spaces and practices.[22] At the core of this body of work is the following question posed by Jarvis Givens: "What does it mean for Black education to be in service to freedom dreams within the American schooling project, a project that is inherently anti-Black?"[23] From the prohibitions against and brutal consequences for Black education from slavery's inception to today's disproportionate disciplinary referrals, in-school physical harassment from security officers, curricular misrepresentations and erasure, and other modern-day transgressions against Black students, Black education in the United States is understood as a deeply anti-Black state endeavor in the critical educational scholarship on fugitivity.[24] This premise is what distinguishes fugitivity from safety as a paradigm for thinking about schools. As with the fugitive sensibilities needed to navigate the afterlife of slavery, Black students must hone fugitive maneuvers to survive American schooling, an institution that Michael Dumas has characterized as a "site of Black suffering."[25] The endemic anti-blackness of American schools undermines their potential as safe spaces for Black students. With safety sidelined, fugitivity demands an attention to risk and harm while concurrently striving for more empowering educational experiences. These analytic properties make fugitivity a nuanced lens for interrogating Black education.

To date, Black trans youth have not been accorded a substantive presence in educational scholarship on fugitivity. I contend that fugitivity presents a new opportunity to outline the intersecting oppressions that make schools and perhaps other pedagogical spaces in the United States persistent sites of Black trans suffering, and to investigate the nuanced strategies that Black trans youth must nurture to navigate those spaces. To illustrate these potential analytical affordances, I pay particular attention in this chapter to three themes in the extant educational scholarship that seem worth attending to in studies of Black trans fugitivity:

1. *Subjectivity:* Mirroring enslaved Blacks' encounters with fugitive subjectivity—the criminalized existence imposed on them by slavery-era legislation, economics, and policing—critical educational scholarship on

fugitivity has explored Black students' negotiations of selfhood in the face of anti-Black constructions of them.[26] Jamila Lyscott, for instance, describes her search for self as a Black girl at the intersection of familial messages about her hair and the anti-Black policing of her hair in schools and society at large.[27] For BTFY like the ones I met at MAC, how might fugitivity illuminate the sense of self that emerged for them as they wrestled with transmisogynist and anti-Black dehumanization? This question presents a new lens through which to consider data from the MAC study.

2. *Space:* Casting American schools and the sociopolitical contexts in which they reside as endemically anti-Black and, thus, harmful for Black students, critical educational scholarship on fugitivity has considered how Black students carve out spaces in the margins and/or outside of schools. For instance, kihana miraya ross describes her search for a Black educational fugitive space—"a space of rage, of melancholy, and of a bitter sweetness"—that can provide an escape from anti-blackness and a place for Black healing.[28] Grace Player and colleagues call for fugitive spaces in schools that bring survival strategies and out-of-school knowledges to bear on the learning experiences of youth of color.[29] These and other examples lead me to wonder about the spaces that BTFY at MAC inhabited and/or foraged for themselves—namely, whether these spaces, in the shadows of transmisogynist and anti-Black harm, were able to foster the collectivity, resistance, and knowledge production ascribed to other instances of fugitive space. I take up this wondering as I revisit my MAC study data.

3. *Practices:* If Black students must develop fugitive practices to survive anti-Black schooling contexts, then what do those practices actually look like? Karen Zaino offers one set of responses as she describes how a racially mixed population of high school students evaded and pushed back against the surveillance of their technology use, surreptitiously shared controversial texts with each in defiance of a standardized curriculum, and found "weak spots" in their tightly monitored schedules to determine their own use of time.[30] In the literacy realm, Esther Ohito, casting fugitivity as "myriad modes of resistance to and refusal of

bondage vis-à-vis slavery," presents multimodal essay composition as a fugitive literacy practice that refuses the logics and dictates of whiteness and anti-blackness.[31] The attention to fugitive practices modeled by Zaino, Ohito, and others informs my re-examination of MAC study data. Figuring out what fugitive practices were developed by BTFY at MAC may help practitioners determine if, when, and how to support them.

Drawing upon my explanation of fugitivity above, I now revisit my prior analysis of the experiences of BTFY at MAC. This new engagement, which includes some previously unpublished data, considers what we might learn if we understand the endemic nature of transmisogyny, and if we focus on the fugitive maneuvers that BTFY must generate as a result.

## FUGITIVE REINTERPRETATIONS

When I conducted my study of MAC, the provision of safe spaces drove my work with and for Black LGBTQ+ youth. Fugitivity as a frame for academic analysis was not on my radar. Were I to conduct the study today, I would surely probe for participants' fugitive sensibilities directly. In the absence of such probes, what I offer here is a reinterpretation of data snippets that, in retrospect, suggest the fugitive nature of BTFY's experiences at MAC. Despite some limitations, a few emergent themes do point to the potential affordances of fugitivity as a prism for understanding these young women's lives.

### Social and Institutional Contexts

Scholarly works on fugitivity explore the exigencies of the present-day Black condition within the milieu of the afterlife of slavery. Following that lead, the social and institutional contexts of the lives of BTFY at MAC provide an important backdrop for considering these young women's fugitive sensibilities. For starters, decades of deindustrialization and white flight had taken their toll on Midtown. At the time of my study, with unemployment at a thirty-year high, Midtown also had the highest childhood poverty rate in its state and one of the highest among comparably sized cities in the United States.[32] Poverty was a viciously racialized phenomenon in Midtown, with stark divides between predominantly white, middle- and upper-middle-class enclaves and the city's more expansive, economically depressed, predominantly Black and Latinx neighborhoods. Sadly, violence was an ongoing challenge for the city, with violent crime and murder rates that were over two and three times higher than the national rates, respectively. As revealed by a survey of Midtown students at the time of the study, the city's violence at large had seeped into its schools, with 35 percent of students reporting they had engaged in a physical fight in school in the month prior to the survey, and 13 percent reporting they had carried a weapon to school in that same timeframe. The city's school district also had one of the highest dropout rates in the state, especially for youth of color. Together, these are just a few of the indices that capture the bleaker aspects of the racial, socioeconomic, and educational contexts of Black life in Midtown.

That Midtown was enduring tough times is crucial to keep in mind throughout this analysis, for the living conditions described above posed particular dilemmas to BTFY. Trans women, particularly trans women of color, often experience high rates of unemployment and housing insecurity, ostracism from familial and communal networks, pathologizing medical discourses, and physical violence, all of which exacerbate their social and economic precarity.[33] When job discrimination and other life hurdles leave little to no viable employment options, some trans women of color turn to sex work to support themselves financially.[34] Such was the case for a handful of BTFY at MAC. In a city where multiple, intersecting structural inequities already placed Black youth on the social, economic, and educational fringes, the additional hardships faced by BTFY pushed some of them to take on tough measures for survival. It is important to stress that any urge to pathologize these young women for engaging in sex work relies on an intentional and intellectually lazy disregard for the intersecting social injustices that conscribed their lives. A responsible examination of their experiences must account for the intersecting structural inequities at play.

Complementing the dire aspects of life in Midtown were some institutional circumstances at MAC that contributed to the marginalization of BTFY. Out of the 148 programs and services listed on MAC's events calendars during a six-month period that overlapped with the study, only six had a specific focus on trans issues. While all six of these programs were open to trans youth, only two were part of the 108 youth-oriented programs and services offered over that period. One reason for the scarcity of trans-specific programming was MAC's reliance on restrictive governmental funding. As one senior staff member explained, because of the erosion of federal funding streams, around 90 percent of MAC's funding was comprised of state grants that supported HIV/AIDS prevention efforts specifically targeting young Black men who have sex with men (MSM), a population that had recently seen severe spikes in HIV infection rates throughout the state.[35] Under strict state surveillance of grant implementation, MAC staff members were obligated to rigidly tailor state-supported programs toward young Black MSM.

The narrow focus that typified MAC's advertised programs and services did not go unnoticed by trans youth. As one trans youth study participant, Binky, stated during her one-on-one interview, "I saw that when I came here, a lot of the funding was just for MSM and didn't include transgender. To me that's a sign of loopholes, and I don't believe that's fair, because transgender groups are only on Saturdays now. So I definitely saw a problem and I want to fix it." While retaining a belief in her ability to remedy this dilemma, Binky still understood that funding for young Black MSM HIV prevention initiatives had produced lopsided programming at MAC and had pushed trans issues increasingly to the margins. Binky's criticism, along with the senior staff member's explanation of funding stream constraints and the lack of trans-specific events on MAC's calendars, pointed to the center's programming as a backdrop for BTFY's fugitive navigations.

On a final note, at the time of the study, MAC released its own assessment of the health needs of the local LGBTQ+ community of color, with a specific focus on topics other than HIV. Three concerns reported by trans participants are worth highlighting: (1) many trans women reported being misgendered as cis males by government agencies and large health-care providers, in effect misrepresenting their experiences as those of queer cis men; (2) interactions with police left many trans women respondents feeling disrespected and unsafe; and (3) many trans women reported experiencing discrimination from queer cis males. The appearance of these themes, especially the third one, in MAC's own agency report reaffirms their salience in the lives of trans women of color in Midtown and provides an important backdrop for the dilemmas discussed in the next section of this chapter.

## Transmisogyny, Sex Work Stigma, and Trans Fugitivity

The relative scarcity of trans-specific programming meant that the trans female youth who spent time at MAC often found themselves sharing space with their predominantly cis-presenting queer male peers.[36] The interactions that ensued became, at times, sites of transmisogynist identity politics that targeted a subset of BTFY who were involved in sex work. When these particular young trans women were present, some of the young queer cis-presenting males, or "butch queens" as they were commonly referred to at MAC, engaged in transmisogynist discourses about trans female sex work that undermined the safety of the space for some trans youth. That transmisogyny, along with trans youth's fugitive responses, is the focus of this section.

Two quick notes: Binky and Nicole, the only trans youth who were interviewed for this study, were not involved in sex work. Some of the young trans women who were involved agreed to participate in the activity described below, but none of them signed up for study interviews—a fact that I will return to later.

The most animated example of the opprobrium for trans female involvement in sex work emerged during a brainstorming activity that my graduate research assistant and I facilitated at the beginning of the study. During the session, we invited MAC youth to discuss, unpack, and question the meaning of the LGBTQ acronym. To elicit youth perspectives, we posted large sheets of paper on the walls of a meeting room. Each sheet had one of the LGBTQ identity labels written at the top of it ("Lesbian," "Gay," and so on), and youth were asked to write whatever came to mind when they saw each identity label. The sheet for the "T" in the acronym started off with familiar and benign terms for individuals who might fall under the trans moniker, including "Transexual," "2 Soul People" (referring to two-spirit), and "T-girls" and "Fem Queen" (friendly colloquialisms). As the brainstorming activity progressed, some of the queer cis-presenting males wrote pejorative references to trans female sex work on the list. These included "Prostitutes" as well as demeaning descriptors of sex acts like "Givin head in the Alley" and "gaping hole." Two more additions, "Broadway" and "Broadway bitches," named a local street where trans female sex workers were known to meet clients, while "Craigslist Whores" and "backpage" named websites where some trans female sex workers advertised their services. The mischievous giggles accompanying the appearance of these terms signaled a shared knowledge of and delight toward their slanderous intent among some queer cis-presenting males in attendance.

Responding to the derogatory references on the trans identity sheet, the BTFY who engaged in sex work took to the list for "Gay" identity, which had started off with benign descriptors like "2 men," "Butch Queen," "Janet" and "Gaga" (references to Janet Jackson and Lady Gaga's popularity among queer cis males), and the underlined self-identification, "Me." Those terms were subsequently followed by comments like "Suck dick for nothing," "Suckin 'Dick' IN The Alley," "yong butt lovers!," and "**Do the same things trannies do**," all of which called out the queer cis-presenting males in the room for engaging in sex acts resembling the ones appearing on the trans list.[37] Other descriptions like "Vogue everyday" and "will always be a faggot" depicted queer cis-presenting males' obsessions with seemingly frivolous activities. The antagonism behind the terms on both the trans and gay lists became apparent as my graduate research assistant and I attempted to facilitate a whole-group discussion on the responses. A vicious and intense shouting match erupted between the trans female youth seated on one side of the room and the group of mostly queer cis-presenting males seated across from them. Each group accused the other of ill intentions, wrongdoings, and indecent acts. After ten minutes, several youth walked out, and a few more were asked to leave by MAC staff to prevent further conflict. The entire episode underscored the sharp animosity between some of the trans female youth and their queer cis-presenting male peers.

The friction that disrupted the LGBTQ identity brainstorming activity became evident during other moments of the MAC study. For instance, Binky—a trans participant who, once again, was not involved in sex work—disparaged her sex work–engaged peers during an interview:

> No shade, they've gotten beat up by almost every youth in here 'cause [the transgender girls] have a lot of mouth . . . I'm not saying all the transgender girls, the main group. There's about six, and . . . they have a lot of mouth, and

they think that butch queens are disgusting and all that. But I'm like well, you used to be a butch queen and you used to do the same things. You used to be in the back room of MAC voguing, so why are you all high and mighty? You're women now, okay I respect that, but don't forget where you came from. You used to be here with us, chilling and everything, and because you became a girl and now you are "working women," you're all high and mighty. News flash, you can't claim your job on your taxes if it's illegal. So I feel that they need a reality check and they need help—not mental help, maybe—but you know, there's something in them that they're unhappy about and they're taking it out on anyone else. So there's a lot of tension between the girls [the butch queens] and the T-girls that aren't humble.

Binky's references to prior physical altercations between the trans female youth with "a lot of mouth" and queer cis-presenting males underscored the severity of the tensions between the two groups. Additionally, her remark about "working women" who could not claim their "illegal" labor on their taxes echoed the disdain toward sex work–engaged trans female peers that arose during the brainstorming activity. Aaron, a queer cis-presenting male study participant, expressed a similar sentiment during his interview: "I think the transgenders, they set a bad name for the gay community because of the way they come out of the house looking, the way they carry themselves overall . . . Say, for example, I walk down the street with a transgender who gets around and who is a whore; they're going to look at me the same way." In addition to Binky's and Aaron's comments, Peggy Lee, a MAC staff member, lamented that the tensions on display during the brainstorming activity were affecting attendance patterns at MAC events, as some trans female youth tried to avoid running into the queer cis-presenting males. While the brainstorming activity was my first glimpse of the conflagrant dynamics surrounding trans sex work at MAC, those dynamics preceded and extended beyond the exchange that unfolded that evening.

Looking back at these MAC experiences through the lens of fugitivity, I am struck by the fraught nature of safety for BTFY who had to rely on sex work. Given their minoritized identities and criminalized survival strategies, these young women likely had to contend with overlapping structural inequities that threatened to push them even further toward Midtown's fringes. At MAC, they faced ostracism from some of their queer cis-presenting male peers while seeing fewer agency-sponsored programs and supports that targeted their specific needs. In what was intended as a safe space, these young women still could land in the institutional margins, cast (out) as trans fugitives.

Engaging fugitivity as an analytical lens not only directs our attention to the forces that produced these young women's fugitive status, but it also begs us to think critically about their responses to how they were being positioned. During the brainstorming activity, the BTFY who relied on sex work were outnumbered by the queer cis-presenting males in the room, some of whom had allegedly been in physical altercations with them. Echoing scholars like Ohito, Ashley Woodson, and ross who characterize Black refusal of anti-Black rhetorics as fugitive resistance, the young trans women's responses during the brainstorming activity could be read as acts of Black trans refusal.[38] These young women arguably refused to cower to the transmisogynist hostility that surrounded them, and they refused to comply with the anti–sex work construction of their subjectivities, even if their refusals required a readiness for confrontation. This reading is not to suggest that these acts of refusal were beyond reproach; after all, these young women did reproduce the very anti-sex rhetorics that were being used against them. Nevertheless, bringing fugitivity to bear encourages us to account for the BTFY's marginality and vulnerability during that activity. Rather than framing all the participants' actions that evening as equally disruptive and disrespectful, fugitivity pushes us to distinguish how we might weigh the queer cis-presenting males' behavior from the responses of their trans female peers. If we recognize that these young women, in that moment, were fugitive subjects—navigating a hostile space with their backs against the wall—then we can appreciate the necessity of their resistance.

Ultimately, gauging the validity of this reinterpretation of events would require the input and voices of the BTFY who took part in the brainstorming activity confrontation. As previously noted, those young women chose not to participate in the one-on-one interviews conducted during the MAC study. Moving forward, my intention is to find new opportunities to learn from young people like the trans youth who stood up for themselves that night at MAC. Revisiting the brainstorming activity in this chapter helps me to consider how fugitivity might inform those future opportunities. In particular, fugitivity leads me to wonder about the insights that might emerge if transmisogyny and other forms of domination are understood as endemic in the lives of BTFY, and if queer youth spaces are consequently interrogated as sites of anti-trans risk. My hope is that more nuanced perspectives on these matters may surface if we are willing to begin from the sobering premise that safe spaces for LGBTQ+ youth, in reality, are not safe.

### The Fugitive Search for Supports

MAC's lack of trans-specific youth programming, along with its intermittent bouts of peer-based transmisogyny, did not produce absolute barriers to trans youth supports. However, emerging across the data on trans youth experiences at the agency is a discernible pattern: the importance of private interactions and trans-only spaces. Although Binky and Nicole were visible trans participants in programs predominated by queer cis-presenting male youth, discreet moments of trans youth disclosures, out of the queer cis-presenting male majority's view, took on a special significance in trans youth experiences at MAC. In this section, I want to pose the pursuit of less visible, trans-serving interactions and spaces as a trans fugitive practice—one that was informed by the transmisogynist aspects of MAC's institutional culture and illustrative of trans youth's savvy navigations to fulfill their needs in spite of the challenges at play.

When it came to supporting trans youth at MAC, one person's name repeatedly came up: Peggy Lee, a white, pansexual, genderqueer/female staffer who played a pivotal role in addressing trans youth's needs. Binky and Nicole, the two trans female youth who were interviewed for the study, attested to the value of Peggy Lee's one-on-one support. Reflecting on her search for trans-specific information about puberty, Nicole stated the following:

> MAC offered help [during] my process, my mental process of my gender role and identity, I guess, and also therapy sessions with Peggy Lee helped me a lot. For example, I recently had a session with Peggy Lee about puberty 'cause I was going through a lot of stuff. I didn't know what it was, and she was somebody I could relate to. She kind of gave information about what I was going through and kind of helped me with it—young female puberty . . . Like if I had a mother, I would ask my mother, but I have a sister, but she wasn't

here at the time, you know. But it's information which I could get anywhere, but I'd rather get it from Peggy Lee.

This excerpt was one of several across Nicole's interview that pointed specifically to Peggy Lee as a reliable source of support for her around trans-specific issues. Likewise, Binky identified Peggy Lee as an especially supportive MAC staffer in several interview responses, including the following:

> I came back to MAC right before my transition. I met Peggy Lee, and I poured my heart out to her for some reason. Like I told her that "yeah I'm transgender," and then we were like sitting there talking about it. And I'm like, "Well I don't know this bitch and she don't know me, but I was sitting here telling you my life story because I'm enjoying you," and she became my mom. And like I became a core group member like two weeks later. I started attending events regularly. I started throwing events and really becoming an active member.

For both Nicole and Binky, Peggy Lee's responsiveness positioned her as a go-to person on MAC's staff for trans-sensitive supports. For Binky, Peggy Lee even became a mother figure for her at MAC. Strategically testing the waters during private moments of trans disclosures, Nicole and Binky were able to identify Peggy Lee as someone who could be trusted to support and care for them as young trans women.

For her part, Peggy Lee was aware of her status as a go-to person at MAC for youth who were questioning their gender identity. In this interview exchange, she describes her interactions with one of those youth:

PEGGY LEE: Recently I had a youth come to me and say, "I've always wanted to be a woman," and this person you would not ever think would be a woman. I mean very butch queen, but . . . he'll be in pumps, but like he'll be in skinny jeans, not a skirt, you know what I mean?
INTERVIEWER: Mmm-hmm.
PL: And he wants to be a woman, and he sat in my office and he cried about it because no one took him seriously. So now . . .
INT.: No one?
PL: No one he's ever spoken to, even at MAC, has really taken him seriously because, you know, he's kind of seen as like a very kind of butch, you know, he's cute.

INT.: He's a butch queen.

PL: He's a butch queen, you know, it's what they do. They walk in pumps sometimes and sometimes they don't. But for him, he explained to me what it meant for him to put on pumps, just that simple act, and I was allowed to really understand that . . . and we were allowed to have this conversation.

In the same interview, Peggy Lee went on to describe another young person who presented as a queer cis male but, in private conversations with her, disclosed "that he's neither male or female," and that "he just feels sort of lost because he can hang out with this group of people and that group of people," referring to the cis/trans social divide at MAC, "but he doesn't feel like he's a part of anything."[39] With transmisogynist politics at play among MAC youth, private sessions with Peggy Lee, away from the gaze of others, emerged as a help-seeking strategy engaged by trans and possibly gender nonbinary youth. Its discretion, reminiscent of the discretion required by fugitive Black subjects, suggests this strategy as a fugitive trans practice.

Peggy Lee was not the only adult within MAC's programmatic orbit who was identified as supportive of trans youth. Importantly, both Binky and Nicole connected with (slightly) older trans women of color as mentors and role models. Binky described how Symone, a trans former member of MAC's peer leadership group, had helped her to present more realistically as female as she began transitioning (an important strategy for avoiding anti-trans harassment) and advised her on where to access trans health care. Nicole recalled her own aspirations being reaffirmed after meeting a successful Black trans woman professional with a Ph.D. at a MAC-sponsored forum. Neither of these connections demonstrated the level of discretion reflected in the previous examples of support-seeking strategies, but they underscore the importance of access to trans women of color role models and, thus, deserve mention.

Besides Binky and Nicole's one-on-one connections with older trans women of color, there were two trans-specific spaces that did, in fact, unfold out-of-view from the majority of MAC's youth and adult populations. The first was the Black Queens Collective, a meeting led by Black trans adult women from the local community that was open to trans female youth. This meeting was held on alternating weekends, a time when there usually were few other events scheduled at MAC, over the first two months of the study. The other space was a series of workshops offered by Peggy Lee for the BTFY who were involved in sex work. During these workshops, Peggy Lee reviewed sex work safety precautions while also offering exit strategies from the sex work industry. Given the discreet nature of these spaces, neither my research assistant nor I (both of us were queer cis males of color) attended them or elicited specific details about them. In addition to these two discreetly facilitated trans female spaces, both Binky and Peggy Lee reported that some trans female youth would avoid MAC on days when they knew that antagonist queer cis-presenting males would be there.

Together, these two strategies—the provision of discreet spaces for BTFY and the avoidance of MAC by some of those youth on certain days—present another potential set of fugitive practices. Just as trans youth's private sessions with Peggy Lee suggested a fugitive awareness to maintain a low visibility within a sometimes hostile space, so too did the Black Queens Collective and Peggy Lee's trans sex work workshops. The latter's explicit focus on a criminalized activity makes a fugitive preference for caution all the more understandable. That these support-seeking strategies unfolded in MAC's institutional margins, beyond the direct reach of the transmisogynist identity politics that riddled youth's peer interactions, provides further cause to consider fugitivity as a framework for BTFY's experiences in recurrently unsafe queer spaces.

## SAFE SPACES FOR "GOOD" TRANS KIDS

The more I employ fugitivity as an analytical framework, the more I am haunted by the absent voices of the BTFY at MAC who were engaged in sex work. The clamor surrounding their lives was sometimes deafening at the agency, and yet they chose, for whatever reasons, to withhold their versions of their stories from this study. Rereading my previously published, co-authored book chapter on the politics of trans inclusion at MAC, I am struck by more than just the paradigmatic limitations of my preoccupation at the time with safe spaces for LGBTQ+ youth (and since I was the lead author and the co-author's faculty advisor, I want to claim those limitations as my own). Now, I see a respectability politics in that previous analysis that foregrounded Binky and Nicole as model trans youth with promising educational futures. I also see how the idealization of Binky and Nicole depends in part on the voicelessness of their sex work–involved peers. And after revisiting early drafts of that co-authored book chapter, I am reminded of the publishers' instructions to remove sexually explicit language from the description of the brainstorming activity, thus contributing in their own way to the erasure of trans female sex work and the emphasis on the "good" trans kids. Why do BTFY who rely at times on sex work rarely appear in educational scholarship on and representations of safe spaces for LGBTQ+ youth? With fugitivity as an analytical guide, I am starting to wonder if the "bad" trans kids are among the outcomes that safe spaces seek to prevent.

In chapter 3, I noted how queer victimhood has dominated representations of LGBTQ+ youth in both educational scholarship and popular media representations, and how the victimized queer student has served as justification for school-based anti-bullying initiatives.[40] Here, I want to add an important qualification: not all queer victims are created equal. As Susan Talburt observes in her work on public discourses about youth sexualities in the United States, white, middle- and upper-class children have historically been the ones deemed sexually innocent and, thus, deserving of protection, while "the African American youth, for example, is always already sexual and has no access to the category of innocence."[41] Additionally, in their content analysis of US news coverage of victims of fatal anti-trans violence, Max Osborn notes that Black trans women of color are routinely depicted as hypersexual, aggressive, untrustworthy, and likely criminal.[42] News media emphasis on their involvement in sex work serves to cast these women as "ultimately to blame for their own victimization."[43] These factors may help to explain the general absence of sex work–involved BTFY in school-based narratives on queer youth victimhood and the need for safe spaces. As fate would have it, unsympathetic views of these young women were held by some of their peers at MAC as well, contributing to transmisogynist hostility within the space.

A consideration for everyone who reads this chapter and works with BQY in urban secondary schools and/or community-based settings is how to create spaces that thoughtfully negotiate the presence and needs of BTFY who rely at times on sex work. It is also important to determine how to bring their voices to the fore while avoiding the essentialization of sex work as *the* BTFY experience. If anything, MAC study data suggest the need for further investigation of the diversity among and divides between BTFY. As noted earlier, Binky and Nicole, the only two trans youth who agreed to be interviewed for the MAC study, were not involved in sex work. Yet despite the absence of interview data from the young trans women who did rely on sex work, Binky's friction with that group became quickly evident. At the beginning of the MAC brainstorming activity, Binky aligned herself with the sheet of paper with "Queer" written at the top, claiming that identity as her own rather than trans. She subsequently sat next to some queer cis-presenting male peers, joining their side in the verbal confrontation that ensued with the trans female youth who engaged in sex work. In the following excerpt, Binky elaborated on her own tensions with other trans female youth at MAC:

> Unfortunately, the older girls—I wouldn't say older, the generation before me of T-girls, maybe in their twenties—don't like me or the other new girl, Nicole. They don't like the newer girls because they feel that we're competition to them, and it's like the crab-in-the-barrel effect. They're going to pull you down so that you won't go ahead of them, and unfortunately when I try to help them, they don't like me. So I can't reach out to them for help or even helping them, and they feel that I have to pay homage to them because they came before me. Like you're only a couple years older than me, girl. Don't give all that. So and then I've always tried to give a helping hand, whether it's name change, food help, clothing, doing hair, if you need help with school. I always try to help, and they feel I'm being stuck up because I'm trying to help you. "Oh, you got your name changed, you think you're all that." No, it was for me, not for you all. I don't care. So a lot of them don't like me and that's a relationship I wish I could mend. I don't care if they don't like me, but I do. As a person you don't have to like me, but I'm here to help you. So I wish I could mend that relationship.

As she mentioned in this excerpt, Binky had managed to complete the legal process for changing her name to align with her gender identity. This process was a major step toward trans self-affirmation, but, unfortunately, it could be lengthy, costly, and thus inaccessible to those without sufficient means. Elsewhere in her interview, Binky also noted that she had managed to secure a job, enroll in community college, and rent an apartment with a few of her queer cis-presenting male friends. By contrast, some of her slightly older trans female peers—the ones engaged in sex work—had not achieved some of Binky's accomplishments. With employment status, educational access, and other factors protecting her from a reliance on the sex industry, Binky found herself at odds with some trans female peers on the other side of the sex work divide.

Her educational and professional trajectories, housing security, and visibility as a youth leader at MAC arguably positioned Binky as one of the agency's success stories. She was a young trans woman managing to defy the odds of living on the sex work margins. Looking back, I cannot help but contemplate the role of MAC, and perhaps other institutions shaping the lives of trans female youth in Midtown, in validating a young person like Binky as exceptional and, in the process, solidifying the divide between her and some of her trans female peers. To be clear, *I am not critiquing or slighting Binky;* she worked hard to overcome a number of barriers and deserved every and any success that came her way. Rather, I am questioning the ideological forces that may pose her story as more respectable than the fugitive stories of her sex work–involved peers. How might fugitivity help us to understand institutional and cultural investments in exceptionalizing some trans female youth while demoting others to the fugitive margins? What is the impact on how these young women see themselves individually and on how (if at all) they nurture community and allyship with each other? And what impact do these processes have on young people who are still wrestling with their gender, for example the MAC youth who sought private counsel with Peggy Lee while avoiding public disclosures of their emergent trans or gender nonbinary identities? These questions underscore the need to acknowledge and support the diversity among BTFY. Fugitivity, as I explore further in the closing section of this chapter, seems an ideal lens for doing so.

## FUGITIVE IMPLICATIONS

> Everyone else can be free only when transgender women of color—especially black transgender women—are free.
> —Julian Glover, "Representation, Respectability, and Transgender Women of Color in Media"

Earlier in this chapter, I referenced a body of literature that has chronicled examples of discord and alienation within sites designated for LGBTQ+ youth. Together, the dynamics detailed in that scholarship complicate the often oversimplified rhetoric of safe spaces for young people who situate themselves along the rich spectrum of queer identities. Although this chapter has focused specifically on the experiences of BTFY, its findings can serve as a case study for more broadly framed deliberations over marginality and harm in queer youth spaces. Despite intentions to the contrary, these spaces are not immune to cisgenderism, whiteness, and other forms of domination pervading the social contexts that surround them. The more we name this dilemma, the easier it will hopefully become to strategically address it. Fugitivity, I contend, is uniquely capable of serving this end as an analytical lens.

My engagement of fugitivity allowed me to grapple more critically than before with the transmisogyny that emerged at MAC. That said, this analysis does not invalidate the many successes of MAC's efforts to serve the needs of Black LGBTQ+ youth in Midtown. Nor is this analysis meant to suggest that my snapshot of MAC's institutional culture would be forever set in stone. The visibility of Black trans women and their activism increased substantially in just a few years of my study, and that visibility has galvanized more strident assertions of Black trans women's voices in grassroots and community-based spaces across the United States.[44] And yet, the brutal persistence of structural and physical violence against Black trans women bears witness to the longevity of transmisogyny and anti-blackness. My hope is for spaces serving Black LGBTQ+ youth to anticipate the inevitable spillover of the risks facing BTFY in America at large.

Revisiting my MAC study data through the prism of fugitivity has helped me to name the transmisogyny that placed BTFY in potential harm's way. This process has also forced me to think more critically about my role as a researcher. Of the several revelations to come more clearly into focus is the possible risk that my research—an act that seeks to raise the visibility of participants' life experiences—poses to young people engaged in a criminalized activity like sex work. Educational scholars like Cindy Cruz and Sam Stiegler offer examples of research methodologies that have enabled them to successfully include the voices of LGBTQ+ youth who are involved in sex work.[45] Their studies, however, have been situated outside of traditional K–12 schools. Generating a stronger research base for urban secondary in-school supports for sex work–involved trans youth, and doing so discreetly given the ever-intensifying anti-trans surveillance of K–12 schools in the United States, are crucial tasks for those of us in the educational research field.

With the shift from a focus on safe spaces to an engagement with fugitivity comes new considerations for practice. I conclude this chapter with three recommendations that will hopefully guide practitioners' fugitive-informed approaches to creating and negotiating spaces with, by, and for BTFY and other LGBTQ+ young people:

1. *Accommodate fugitive spaces:* Whether within or outside of urban secondary schools, groups or organizations that serve BTFY might benefit from being nimble enough to accommodate the fugitive spaces that these young people request and/or create. The separate, lower-profile, trans-only spaces at MAC are one set of examples. These fugitive spaces could align with the third commitment of queerly responsive pedagogy—*Address any tensions that challenge a respect for and inclusion of variously identified queer youth of color*—by affording opportunities for participants to build strategies for addressing frictions with other LGBTQ+ youth and/or among themselves. Private, one-on-one interactions with critically caring adults—similar to the fugitive support that trans youth at MAC received from Peggy Lee—is another option for consideration.

2. *Address power and privilege:* Whether for queer cis-presenting males at MAC, white middle-class students in a GSA, or another applicable constituency, school- and community-based spaces that serve BTFY must be prepared to facilitate reflections on power and privilege among participants who engage in transmisogynist identity politics and other forms of discrimination within these spaces. Much like racial consciousness spaces where white participants engage each other in critical analyses of whiteness—thus relieving people of color from the burden of teaching white people about whiteness—spaces for LGBTQ+ youth

need in-house resources that call members to task pushing BTFY to the margins, and that do not rely on BTFY to do this work.[46]

3. *Provide professional development on trans sex work:* Since the lives of BTFY who engage in sex work are complex, practitioners who serve these young people need professional development on what compassionate and thoughtful supports for them look like. Though not necessarily ideal, knowing organizations and resources to recommend to this group of young people is an alternative to consider in spaces where anti-trans surveillance and anti-sex stigma prevent this form of professional learning.[47]

CHAPTER 5

# Queerly Responsive Sex Education for Young Black Queer Males

During the 2010s, as my research on the learning experiences of Black queer youth (BQY) started to increasingly center access to queer-affirming sex education, I became palpably anxious about sharing my work on such a taboo topic with K–12 educators and fellow university-based educational studies scholars. Fortunately, my university department colleagues at the time agreed to serve as a sounding board. Toward the end of one of our meetings, I screened a short scene from a film titled *The Skinny,* a fictional depiction of five Black queer college friends who attend New York City's gay pride weekend together.[1] In this particular scene, one of the cis male characters helps another to prepare physically and emotionally for what will be his first gay anal sex encounter.[2] After presenting my analysis of the characters' exchange as an example of sex-positive, culturally responsive sexuality education among young Black queers, I asked my white, cishetero-presenting colleagues for their reactions.[3] One response, to this day, still resonates: "Where can I find the version of this for a 40+ heterosexual white woman?"

My colleague's question conveys an unfortunate truth: Many of us raised in the United States in the twentieth century—across regions, identities, and other differences—were inadequately prepared by schools and other institutions in our lives for sex. Beyond mechanistic overviews of reproductive penile-vaginal intercourse and stark warnings against doing it too soon, K–12 schools in the United States often did little to equip those of us of a certain age with the requisite skills and knowledge to develop healthy sexual identities and informed sexual practices, forcing us to rely instead on peers and popular culture to fill in the blanks if family members were not up to the task. Realistically, I know this chapter's focus on sex education for BQY increases its chances of being skipped by some and deplored by others. But for those who choose to engage this chapter's subject matter thoughtfully, I encourage you to consider if and how my "40+ heterosexual white woman" colleague's question speaks to your own experiences. Namely, what anxieties, omissions, and silences shaped your sex education experiences? What sexual dilemmas, confusions, and harms did you face as a result, and what information and supports could have improved your sexual identity development and decision-making? Your own answers to these questions will likely underscore the shared urgency for all of us, including BQY, to have access to sensitive, comprehensive sex education.

To that end, this chapter draws upon findings from two empirical research projects, the Midtown AIDS Center (MAC) study and the Sexual Engagements with Networked Technologies (SENT) study (described in detail in chapter 1), to respond to the following questions: How do young Black queer males (YBQM) who identify and/or present as cis learn about sex outside of K–12 schools, and what are the implications of their experiences for sex education within and beyond urban secondary education?[4] Like so many of their LGBTQ+ peers nationwide, the YBQM who participated in my research projects relied heavily on out-of-school resources to learn about queer sexual practices and explore their own queer sexual identities and desires.[5] Doing so presented a mix of affordances and challenges that deserve more frequent and nuanced scholarly investigations. By wedding the voices of the youth participants in my studies with my conceptualization of queerly responsive pedagogy (QRP) from chapter 2, my goal is to advance efforts to envision and provide queerly responsive sex education that respects, protects, and empowers YBQM and possibly other LGBTQ+ young people as well.

Ideally, sex education programs and curricula should cover several topical domains. According to the National Sex Education Standards (NSES), a set of guidelines and frameworks constructed through a collaboration between three leading national sex education organizations, sex education should provide students with medically accurate and equity-driven perspectives on subjects such as "consent and healthy relationships; puberty and adolescent development; sexual and reproductive anatomy and physiology; gender identity and expression; sexual identity and orientation; interpersonal and sexual violence; contraception, pregnancy, and reproduction; and HIV and other STDs/STIs."[6] Since an exhaustive treatment of these and other potential domains is beyond the scope of this chapter, I consider the implications of my research findings primarily for two topics: *sexual identity and orientation,* with an attention to how YBQM determine their queerness and learn about the mechanics of queer sex; and what the NSES refer to as *functional knowledge and skills*—that is, the information and strategies that enable safe, thoughtful, and autonomous sexual decision-making.[7] The research findings presented in this chapter underscore the urgency of supporting YBQM's learning in these two domains. Hopefully, this chapter will lay the foundation for future examinations of YBQM's experiences with additional sex education topics.

Before proceeding further, I want to offer three important notes about this chapter. First, I focus on queerly responsive sex education solely for YBQM because that population comprised the overwhelming majority of participants in the MAC and SENT studies, the two data sources for this chapter. As I mentioned in chapter 1, the skewed demographic profiles of my research samples were due in no small part to the funding landscape at the time of both studies. The shifting locus of the HIV/AIDS epidemic to YBQM's sociosexual networks in the 2000s spurred funding streams for HIV/AIDS-related research and services targeting that population. Consequently, community-based public health agencies like MAC found themselves increasingly reliant on funding for YBQM-centered initiatives, and research like the SENT study became more fundable if it, too, targeted that demographic. On the plus side, I can now combine data from two studies to explore how YBQM learn about sex. However, the lack of study sample diversity is a clear limitation, leaving ample room for future educational research that includes a panoply of BQY voices and experiences.

Second, given its subject matter, this chapter, primarily in the study findings sections, contains sexually explicit language, including frank descriptions of queer sexual acts. Ensuring relevant and empowering sex education for LGBTQ+ youth requires a willingness to model open, direct, and thoughtful discussions of topics of interest to them, including—and especially—queer sexual practices. Those who are discomforted by sexually explicit language generally and/or discussions of queer sex specifically may want to read this chapter together with colleagues who feel more comfortable with its subject matter. Doing so could allow those readers to rely on colleagues for less graphic summarizations of the study findings sections while still participating in considerations of the chapter's aim to make queerly responsive sex education accessible to YBQM and possibly other LGBTQ+ youth, too.

Lastly, it is important to be upfront and strategic about the risks associated with the work discussed in this chapter, especially for readers who work in urban secondary schools. To state the obvious, school-based sex education is a powder keg in the United States. The current conservative backlash against abortion and LGBTQ+ rights has intensified the already contentious backdrop for discussions of sexuality in K–12 schools. Those of us who advocate for sex education, especially queer-inclusive approaches, face vilification as "groomers" and, in some cases, job insecurity. To be frank, even I, a tenured university professor, found myself worrying about harassment and other repercussions in response to this chapter, particularly given the demonization of queer educators like me as pedophiles. While we cannot ignore these risks, we also cannot overlook the harm inflicted on queer youth who are denied access to queer-affirming sex education. Thus, after presenting examples of how YBQM sought out and engaged information on queer sexualities, I conclude this chapter with implications for strategically navigating anti-queer and anti-sex backlash as we attempt to provide the kind of sex education that all queer youth rightfully deserve.

## SEX EDUCATION AND QUEER YOUTH

Sex education in the United States has always been about more than just sex. Historical analyses of sex education policy and curricula reveal efforts to valorize a hegemonic form of white middle-class heterosexuality that is situated in the nuclear family, propagated through monogamous marital intercourse, and in service of a white-centered vision of America.[8] Present-day struggles over the aims and scope of school-based sex education reveal ongoing attempts to promote marriage-based cisheteronormativity. According to the Guttmacher Institute, as of September 1, 2023, thirty-nine states and Washington, DC, required instruction on abstinence in sex education classes—with twenty-nine states requiring an *emphasis* on abstinence—and nineteen states mandated "instruction on the importance of engaging in sexual activity only within marriage."[9] These mandates have persisted despite compelling evidence of the ineffectiveness of sex education curricula that stress abstinence only until marriage (AOUM), specifically heterosexual marriage.[10] By contrast, only ten states and Washington, DC, required "inclusive content with regard to sexual orientation" in school-based sex education.[11] Additionally, in its 2021 national survey of LGBTQ+ students' schooling experiences, GLSEN reported that only 7.4 percent of respondents had received sex education that addressed LGB and trans/nonbinary experiences.[12] Some queer youth have encountered sexuality-related content in subject areas outside of sex education, namely literature.[13] These encounters do not compare, however, to examinations of sex-related content in a robust, comprehensive sex education curriculum. Together, these data points illuminate a political and pedagogical campaign to privilege cisheteronormativity and marriage through sex education in American K–12 schools.

Scholarly analyses of LGBTQ+ students' learning experiences further corroborate the cisheteronormative bias that undermines queer inclusion in school-based sex education in the United States. Queer informants across a number of these works recount sex education curricula that focused solely or overwhelmingly on heterosexuality and cisnormativity, leaving them feeling silenced, overlooked, or erased.[14] Similar feelings emerge in accounts of queer students' encounters with AOUM curricula.[15] As several scholars have noted, the exclusion of queer-oriented content in school-based sex education robs queer students of important opportunities to explore and understand their own sexual and gender identities.[16] That exclusion also prevents the acquisition of crucial knowledge on the how-tos of queer sex, leaving many queer students alarmingly unprepared for their first sexual encounters.[17]

Given the scarcity of queer-inclusive sex education in K–12 schools, LGBTQ+ youth often orchestrate their own search for knowledge on queer sexualities. In doing so, these young people must precariously sift through informational sources of varied factual accuracy and pedagogical sensitivity. For many, their journeys begin on the internet vis-à-vis unvetted sexual information on social media platforms like Instagram and YouTube, dating and hookup apps like Tinder and Grindr, and the endless array of sites generated through Google searches on topics like "what is transgender" and "how to have anal sex."[18] Much like their non-LGBTQ+ peers, LGBTQ+ youth frequently turn to online porn, namely to learn about the mechanics of queer sex, while navigating porn's often problematic representational tropes.[19] Some queer youth learn nothing about queer sex until their first sexual encounters, when their lack of sexual knowledge leads to increased chances of STI exposures and other sexual health risks.[20] Across all of these strategies, LGBTQ+ youth demonstrate impressive bravery and resourcefulness in their self-directed quests for information on queer sexualities. Nonetheless, the absence of consistent, reliable, queer-oriented content in school-based sex education programs forces queer youth down risky pathways in search of information that is vital to their sexual identities and health. Against this backdrop, the exclusion of queerness from sex education in K–12 schools must be understood as an act of harm against queer youth.

The preceding review of the existing scholarship on queer youth's sex education experiences clearly reveals the cisheteronormative shortcomings of school-based curricula, as well as queer youth's determined yet risky searches elsewhere for resources on queer sexualities. Unsurprisingly, a number of queer youth have expressed interest in more formal online sex education resources, particularly those that address the mechanics of queer sex.[21] While the existing literature surfaces important insights, two of the gaps that remain are especially relevant to this chapter's focus on YBQM's experiences with sex education. First, this body of work stems overwhelmingly, and in some cases solely, from the perspectives of white informants.[22] Just as influential bodies of scholarship in cultural studies have documented the gender and sexual politics of blackness that mediate Black sexual identities and experiences, analyses of YBQM's encounters with sex education must engage the intersections of blackness, gender, and queer sexualities.[23] Second, sex education researchers have repeatedly noted the field's struggle to foreground analyses of pleasure.[24]

As Eva Goldfarb and Lisa Lieberman observe in their extensive review of sex education scholarship, the persistent framing in American culture of sex among youth as a maladaptive behavior to be prevented "eliminates the opportunity for young people to explore and experience normal, healthy, safe, and pleasurable sexual activity."[25] And yet, amidst the deluge of sexual storytelling in American popular culture, the silence around youth sexual pleasure understandably does little to forestall young people's attempts to imagine that pleasure—and if possible, to explore it.

With those two scholarly gaps in mind, I pay close attention in the next sections of this chapter to the significance of blackness and pleasure as I examine how YBQM learn about sex. Findings from two research projects, the MAC study and the SENT study, illustrate the resonance of these topics for YBQM as they forge their sexual identities and navigate their sexual desires. Creating sex education opportunities that authentically serve the needs of YBQM demands an honest reckoning with the conditions and yearnings that shape their experiences with sex. Throughout the remainder of this chapter, I try to model that reckoning.

As a reminder, Tables 1.1 and 1.2 list the pseudonyms and demographic descriptors of MAC and SENT study participants, respectively.

## WHAT'S MISSING FROM SCHOOL: FINDINGS FROM THE MAC STUDY

When I first started volunteering at the MAC, an urban, community-based HIV/AIDS services agency in the northeastern United States, HIV infection spikes loomed heavily over its work with BQY. At the time, the Centers for Disease Control and Prevention reported a 48 percent increase in HIV infection rates nationwide among young Black men who have sex with men, or MSM (a label used in public health to identify the behaviors under consideration).[26] That same year, the health department for the county in which MAC was located reported a staggering 91 percent increase in HIV infection rates among young Black MSM, which meant that some MAC youth were already HIV-positive while others were at heightened risk of infection. Because of these circumstances, MAC's original mission to improve health and wellness among queer communities of color assumed a primary focus during the 2010s on HIV/AIDS prevention education and health services for YBQM. During my time at MAC, I saw staff members apply constantly for grants to support youth sexual health programs; meet with city and state public health stakeholders to collaborate on youth sexual health initiatives; and advocate for nonpathologizing, culturally sensitive HIV prevention messaging from state and national agencies. In what follows, I describe how the programs and services that resulted at MAC created unique opportunities for sex education with MAC's YBQM attendees. As a reminder, the research findings sections of this chapter contain frank and explicit descriptions of queer sexual acts.

Weekly workshops on safer sex practices were the centerpiece of MAC's sex education programming for YBQM. Four workshops appearing on consecutive weeks of one of MAC's monthly events calendars exemplified the focus and tone of this programming. The first workshop, "You've Got a Mouth: Use It!," addressed oral sex. This session included instruction on how to use one's mouth to apply a condom on a penis—a savvy strategy for eroticizing condom usage when engaging a condom-aversive sexual partner. Next was "Ride 'Em Cowboy," a workshop on the mechanics of anal sex co-facilitated by a Black trans woman who, as a former sex worker, drew upon her real-world expertise on sexual safety and pleasure. Rounding out the calendar, "From Head to Toe" and "Touch Me Here, Touch Me There" focused on the use of fetish toys and erotic massage, respectively, as safer yet enjoyable alternatives to oral and anal sex. Peggy Lee was the MAC staff member in charge of these workshops, and she underscored why these workshops were so important to offer:

> All of these things [are important], especially the fetishism and the massage. Even oral sex and anal sex. We talk about foreplay a lot because foreplay, you get to inspect your partner, you know, and if you don't know your partner's body, you don't know what you're sleeping with. Also it gives them ideas of what they can do until they find out another person's HIV status and they know it for sure, and they know what their [own] status is. So if I can have fun in all these different ways, and I know how to give head good with a condom or without, but I can do it with a condom and I feel confident in that, then we've given them an outlet.

In addition to recounting frank conversations about topics like foreplay, condom use negotiation, and oral sex, Peggy Lee described other pedagogical tactics and tools for sex education at MAC during her one-on-one interviews. For instance, she recalled showing an instructional video on tantric genital massage during one workshop that enabled youth to see how this technique could be used as a safer sex strategy. During another workshop, she had youth cover their palms with dental dams and then instructed them to lick their hands; this simple activity allowed youth to discover that dental dams would not prevent the sensation of intimate touch, thus helping to eroticize the use of dental dams for anilingus and cunnilingus. For youth who were at least eighteen years old, Peggy Lee would organize field trips to a local adult video store to show them how to select and purchase safer sex paraphernalia. Together, these examples illustrated the types of pedagogical strategies that Peggy Lee employed to deliver sex education to YBQM.

Two important characteristics of MAC's sex education programming surfaced in the examples provided by Peggy Lee. First, the agency's programming offered functional knowledge and skills, a sex education topical domain identified earlier as a key concern of this chapter. Whether led by trained agency staffers or community members with real-world expertise, MAC's workshops provided explanations, and in some instances low-intensity simulations, of specific strategies for safer sex encounters that covered a range of erotic practices. This stood in dramatic contrast to the limited sex education provided by the Midtown School District which, as noted in its curriculum guidelines, covered condom usage for heterosexual penile-vaginal intercourse while encouraging abstinence. From offering tips on how to erotically apply a condom to presenting erotic massage as a strategic alternative to anal or oral sex, MAC's workshops presented youth with specific and practical functional knowledge and skills for negotiating safer sexual encounters.

The second characteristic of MAC's sex education programming worth highlighting here is its attention to pleasure, a topic identified earlier in this chapter as a major gap in the scholarship on sex education. MAC's workshops were grounded in sex-positive perspectives that valued erotic pleasure as an outcome of safer, consensual sex. Not only did this stand in contrast to the tentative coverage of sex in the local school district's abstinence-oriented sex education curriculum, but it also diverged from the tendency of HIV-related messaging in the public health sphere to pathologize Black queer males' sexual networks and practices.[27] From playful workshop titles to an acceptance of sex as enjoyable, the sex-positive framework of MAC's workshops eschewed fear-based discourses on queer sex with deliberate attempts to make safer sex strategies not only accessible to, but pleasurable for, YBQM.

MAC's weekly workshops on safer sex practices were complemented by other programs and services on sexual health for YBQM. For instance, in their individual interviews, TJ and Travis, adult volunteers with professional backgrounds in sexual health, each described being invited on separate occasions to lead workshops on STI prevention during outbreaks among MAC youth. As with the weekly workshops described by Peggy Lee, TJ's and Travis's sessions provided functional knowledge and skills, or specific strategies for safer sex practices, to empower youth attendees to protect themselves and prevent further STI transmissions. In another instance, Armando, a university-based health researcher who volunteered at MAC, developed specific strategies to support HIV prevention efforts among MAC youth by involving them in his research. As he noted in a one-on-one interview, his efforts included two separate projects with MAC youth as collaborators that resulted in HIV prevention curricula tailored specifically toward YBQM. Along with STI prevention workshops and research-based HIV interventions, fliers and posters for campaigns like "I Love My Boo" adorned MAC's walls to reinforce safer sex messages in a sex-positive and culturally responsive fashion.[28] In all, these examples further evidence MAC's engagement of YBQM as recipients—and with Armando's projects, as co-creators—of practical and authentic sex education experiences.

The significance of MAC's sexual health programming was underscored by several youth study participants during individual study interviews. Two youths, Levi and Twizzler, described how MAC's sex education curricula empowered them to provide safer sex information to their younger siblings and cousins. Two more youths, Concerned Activist and M, critiqued their high schools for not offering the safer sex education that they were receiving at MAC. As M stated in his interview, "I wish that the things that we learn here at MAC we would learn in our health class because a lot of stuff that I've learned here I didn't learn in school, and it's helped me out. It's helped me stay safe as far as I am. I get tested every three months for HIV, not because I have sex that often, which I don't—which is kind of sad, no I'm just kidding!—but a lot of people at school don't know to get tested every three months." Together, M and the rest of his peers referenced above attested to the value of the sex education they received at MAC—an education that, for some, was noticeably absent in their urban schooling experiences.

MAC's independence from the local school district was one factor that enabled its dynamic approach to queer-affirming sex education. That said, two potential avenues for MAC to challenge the cisheteronormative restrictions on sex education *within* Midtown's secondary schools became apparent during the study. First, Midtown teachers with personal connections to MAC staffers and volunteers would occasionally invite those individuals to deliver sex education presentations in their classrooms. Much like my visit to a high school gay-straight alliance (GSA) that I recounted in chapter 1, these queer-inclusive presentations were not part of the mandated curriculum and, thus, reached limited numbers of Midtown students. Nevertheless, by flying under the radar of anti-queer surveillance from administrators, these presentations were one strategy for discreetly making queer-inclusive information about sex accessible to at least some Midtown secondary-level students.

Another potential strategy became apparent when I brought a cohort of predominantly cishetero-presenting women preservice teachers to MAC for a youth-led workshop on LGBTQ+ issues in schools. At the workshop's conclusion, MAC youth invited the preservice teachers to help stuff condoms and lubricant into safer sex packets that would be distributed later outside of local queer nightclubs. Along with being the only exposure to queer sexual knowledge during their teacher preparation program, the workshop marked the first time that most of the preservice teachers learned about female condoms. Since I did not follow-up with these teachers about this experience, I cannot speak to if and how they brought knowledge from the workshop into their preservice teaching in Midtown schools. Still, their receptiveness suggested that such workshops could provide an avenue for organizations like MAC to increase urban secondary educators' queer sex knowledge base.

As an organization with strong ties to local queer communities of color, along with committed staff and volunteers with expertise in serving those communities, MAC capitalized on its unique capacity to provide YBQM with the kind of sex education they longed for. With young people's right to sexual autonomy as a given, MAC's workshops equipped youth attendees with functional knowledge and skills to smartly and agentively navigate their sexual decision-making. Furthermore, the agency's sex education programming countered fear-based discourses on queer sex with unapologetic validations of sexual pleasure. Guided by a desire to practically and joyously support the youth attendees' sexual well-being, MAC modeled a valuable alternative to the cisheteronormative, AOUM frameworks that have constrained much of the school-based sex education curricula in the United States. The implications of MAC's programming for queerly responsive sex education for YBQM will be considered at the end of this chapter.

## FIGURE IT OUT ON YOUR OWN: FINDINGS FROM THE SENT STUDY

The MAC study provided a unique opportunity to see approaches to sex education that were guided by qualified and critically caring practitioners, and that were situated in settings deeply committed to BQY's sexual safety, empowerment, and pleasure. Unfortunately, not all BQY have access to spaces like MAC. That realization became one warrant for the SENT study. Twenty-two YBQM across four cities in the northeastern United States enrolled in this research. During one-on-one data collection sessions, each participant was provided an iPad or tablet and asked to demonstrate how he navigated internet pornography sites, geolocation hookup apps, and social media platforms like Tumblr, Snapchat, and Facebook, all for sexually oriented purposes. The navigation of these sites and platforms, in stark contrast to the sex education delivered at MAC, occurred without the assistance of caring adults, thus offering glimpses into what can happen when YBQM are forced to search for sex-related resources on their own.

In this section, I consider SENT study participants' engagements with sexually explicit content on porn sites and social media platforms as informal yet influential sex education experiences. Two affordances of these informal, self-directed learning experiences became evident during data analysis: participants' discoveries of their queer sexualities, and their exposure to the mechanics of queer male sexual encounters. In what follows, I describe how these two affordances were articulated and demonstrated by study participants, and I then discuss the dilemmas posed by the prevalent depictions of Black men as thugs in the online pornographic content preferred by many study participants. As a reminder, the research findings sections of this chapter contain frank and explicit descriptions of queer sexual acts.

## Pedagogical Affordances: Self-Discovery and Mechanics

As noted in this chapter's introduction, sexual identity and orientation, with an attention to how YBQM determine their queerness and learn about the mechanics of queer sex, is one of the topical domains of sex education to which my research findings speak. Drawing upon SENT study data, eleven of the twenty-two participants described how their engagement of sexually explicit online content facilitated their process of sexual self-discovery by sparking and/or solidifying realizations of their queerness. This queer self-discovery, in some instances, resulted from exposure to explicit heterosexual content. For example, a participant named Chris recalled paying attention to the men in straight porn videos that an older male cousin showed him around the age of sixteen or seventeen. Another participant, Eros, described a similar experience with straight porn when he was thirteen: "So like I said, I thought I was straight up until then. But when I was watching straight porn, I noticed myself looking at the guy more and getting aroused . . . So I'm like, 'Whoa, what's going on here?' So that's when my mind started racing and thinking like, 'What? What is this? Am I . . .' I don't even think I knew what gay was back then, but yeah, I noticed that I was liking gay porn more than straight porn." Although both Chris and Eros went on to describe regular viewings of gay porn, it was straight porn videos that first aroused their queer sexual wonderings.

Unlike Chris and Eros, some participants bypassed straight porn and sought out queer online content more directly. In the following passage, a participant named Stitch recounts perusing informational websites on queer sexuality at fifteen or sixteen, which subsequently led him to gay online porn: "But then my question was always like, 'Alright, cool, I think I'm gay. How does that work?' . . . I just was very interested about, like, how gay sex worked. I had no clue, I really wanted to know, so I was like, 'Okay, cool, alright.' I guess I'm reading, like, how to prevent diseases and stuff. I'm reading that part, okay. And then I guess one day I was just like, "Gay porn, it's so simple.

Why didn't I think of that before?'" After identifying gay porn as a resource for figuring out his own sexual orientation, Stitch also realized the importance of race in his unfolding process of self-discovery:

> I realized very early on I only liked watching videos with Black men. Like I just, I could not watch anything that didn't just have Black men in it. I think that's because like, again, as I was understanding my identity race-wise, like I only could sort of, you know, I could only see them as attractive. Like I couldn't see anyone else as attractive [when] watching those videos. So I guess that kind of like pretty much set [me] up for how I consumed porn to the present.

Stitch's initial suspicion—"Alright, cool, I think I'm gay"—reflects a common adolescent reckoning with identity and desire that launched his search for online resources on sexuality. The pervasiveness of gay online porn made it a logical and easily accessible resource during this moment of Stitch's sexual identity exploration. That he restricted himself to online videos with Black men underscores the racial dimension to porn's role in facilitating his self-discovery as a Black queer male teenager. In all, Stitch's comments convey the practicality behind many young people's choice to seek information about sexuality through porn, and they illuminate how porn can aid YBQM's process of queer self-discovery.

Other participants who spoke about the sexual self-discovery facilitated by sexually explicit online content included Adonis, who recalled frequenting a website that featured queer male erotic stories at age twelve or thirteen; and Batman, who described how online porn helped him discover his attraction not only to other men but to trans women as well. In all of these cases, these YBQM had to make sense of their sexual self-discoveries on their own. One account offered by a participant named Blue poignantly captures a downside of that isolation:

> I remember this day, as clear as day, crystal clear. I was sitting at the computer watching male-and-male porn, and I was just touching myself. And I felt this sensation, and something had came out, came out of me and I ejaculated. And it looked weird, I didn't know what it was. I was scared. My heart was beating fast. I was terrified, I was petrified, and it smelled like raw eggs. It did, it smelled like raw eggs to me, and I was just so completely scared.

Thirteen years old at the time, Blue's lack of sexual knowledge made his first ejaculation a terrifying experience. Gradually, he recognized ejaculation as a moment of pleasure, and he continued to watch gay porn in order to achieve it and to further explore his queer desires. Still, his isolation during this time produced frightening conditions for his sexual awakening.

Along with the process of self-discovery that was conveyed in the preceding accounts, exposure to the mechanics of queer male sexual encounters emerged as an affordance of participants' engagements of porn sites. Explaining the benefits of watching online porn videos, one participant, Batman, characterized queer sex as something that was difficult to learn "hands-on," thus making opportunities for "visualizing" beforehand even more important. Other participants who echoed the educative value of watching porn included Kai, who said that it taught him about "penetration, getting head, all that . . . I'm gonna say all the basics"; Bobby, who reported that watching porn enabled him to "learn how to suck dick properly" and "learn how to ride"; and Will, who shared that he learned "different positions and different methods during sex" from watching online porn videos, including "how to give head, I would say. How to be on top." Given the lack of information about queer male sexual practices in school curricula and other potential resources, online porn videos provided participants with a unique avenue for learning some of the specifics about queer male sex.

By allowing them to learn some of the mechanics of queer male sex, watching porn equipped some participants with a sexual self-confidence. Such was the case for Bobby, who credited porn with building his confidence as a bottom, the receptive partner in penile-anal intercourse. A similar sentiment was offered by Will, who reflected, "It seemed like when I started having sex with guys, everybody else was more experienced than I was. So I felt kind of behind and it's like, 'Oh, [here's] what to do now.' So [watching porn] kind of helped me out." Along with fine-tuning their skills, some participants credited porn with introducing them to new and innovative sexual practices. AJ, for instance, offered the following response when asked about the educative value of watching sexually explicit content on Tumblr and Instagram, as well as gay porn videos:

INTERVIEWER: Okay. Has using the apps helped you learn anything about sex?
AJ: Mmm hmm *[emphatically]*.
INT.: Okay.
AJ: Yeah, oh I'm sorry.
INT.: That was a very visceral reaction.
AJ: Yeah, 'cause if you watch some, you want to know how to do something, or you just want to be more extra, you want to be more freaky or whatever. You see yourself and you're like, "Oh, I want to try that" or "I'm interested in it" or whatever.

Importantly, AJ's emphatic "Mmm hmm" reflected the connection between sexual knowledge and pleasure. Discovering new practices through online porn furthered AJ's capacity to enjoy his sexual encounters. Other participants like Adonis, Eros, Michael, and Stitch echoed AJ's sentiment, noting with delight how they learned "new tricks" from porn videos to bring into their sex lives. Together, the participants cited throughout this paragraph attested to sexual self-confidence and pleasure as outcomes of their engagements with sexually explicit online content.

To be sure, viewing porn videos and other sexually explicit online material was not without its complications. One set of dilemmas associated with the pornographic images consumed by SENT study participants—gay porn's representation of Black men as thugs—is the focus of the next section of this chapter. Nonetheless, through their self-directed perusal of sexually explicit online content, the young men cited above created opportunities to explore their queer sexualities and learn about the how-tos of queer male sexual encounters. As stated earlier, these opportunities are hard to come by in cisheteronormative, AOUM approaches to school-based sex education. Discussions of porn's deleterious impact on YBQM (and on other groups of young people) must also consider what to make of its potential affordances. I take up this very task at the end of the chapter.

### The Dilemmas of Black Thuggery

Dominant representations of Black men in the United States have a dubious structural and ideological legacy. The trope of the Black brute—which, on the one hand, justifies racial disparities in the policing and imprisonment of Black men—also drives the American fascination with Black males' athletic performance, sexual prowess, and cultural productions.[29] In this regard, gay porn in the United States is certainly a product of its environment. Within its cross-racial slate of over-the-top characterizations, pornographic content marketed to queer male audiences regularly casts Black men as the ghetto thug. Emerging from the tough streets of urban Black America, the ghetto thug wears baggy jeans and du-rags and speaks in urban Black slang as he seeks emotionless sexual gratification. For the YBQM in the SENT study, depictions of Black thuggery provided a frequent and problematic backdrop to their porn-mediated sexual explorations.

As study participants demonstrated how they navigated a variety of sites to find desired content during data collection sessions, fifteen of them confirmed their distinct preference for sexually explicit images and videos of Black men, at times articulating their specific desire for the thug trope. Kai and Lionel were among those who, when asked to identify the types of videos they watched online, selected content with "Black thug" or "DL thug" as descriptors.[30] Likewise, Kris chose content with Black men whom he labeled as "trady trady," meaning masculine, and Stitch pulled up "Beat It Up Like a Drummer," a video clip with a title that signaled, in Stitch's words, "very aggressive fucking."[31] Even Adonis, who critiqued dominant representations of Black men in porn for their savagery early on in his interview, subsequently identified a video clip titled "Black Thugs on Bareback Action Compilation" as the type of video he liked to watch.[32] For these four YBQM, as well as eleven other study participants—Batman, Blue, Bobby, Chris, Eros, Sean, Sora, Stitch, T, Tommy, and Will—characterizations of thuggish Black male sexual aggression marked the terrain on which they explored their sexual desires vis-a-vis online porn.

Lengthy one-on-one interviews during the SENT study revealed that participants' desires for Black thugs were informed by the trope's pervasiveness throughout American popular culture. However, online porn sites played a unique role in cultivating those desires through platform features and algorithms. As eleven of the participants demonstrated how they navigated porn sites, predetermined content classifications directed their selections of videos featuring Black men. Choosing "Black" or "Ebony" in category menus at the top of the screen, or hitting tag filters like "Black thugs" beneath individual videos, led participants to site-determined curations of Black male content. After selecting a video, site algorithms generated thumbnails of additional videos based on participants' previous choices. The result was a steady stream of content compiled by the sites that reinforced the desirability of sexually aggressive and thuggish representations of Black men.

The data collection session with the participant Adonis illustrated the importance of porn site curation. Using an iPad, Adonis pulled up Pornhub, the world's largest porn site, which contains free sexually explicit content. He then selected the webpage's link for the "Gay" content category, followed by the link for the "Black" subcategory. These actions generated a list of thumbnails for videos with the same, limited depiction of Black men as brutish sexual aggressors. Thumbnail titles like "Thugs, Big Pistons," "BASKETBALL PLAYA FUCK," "Terrorized by Big Black Cock," and "Get That Black Cock in His . . ." reinforced stereotypes of a tough, thuggish Black masculinity culminating in a savage sexual prowess. For Adonis and other study participants who sought Black male representations on PornHub, MyVidster, XVIDEOS, and similar porn sites, predetermined content classifications, navigational tools, and algorithmic recommendations produced a thug-centered viewer experience.

The Black thug, for better or worse, is but one of many stock characters in the exaggerated and farcical lineup of contemporary pornographic storytelling. Its prominence in the online porn viewing of SENT study participants does, however, beg the following question: What are the potential repercussions of Black thug pornography—with its eroticization of a domineering Black masculinity and insatiable sexual aggression—on YBQM's sexual sense of themselves and on their sexual and romantic relationships with others? As noted in this chapter's introduction, healthy sexual and romantic relationships are an important topical domain of sex education, but they are not analyzed in this chapter due to space constraints. As for YBQM's sexual sense of self, an interview exchange with Stitch speaks to the importance of questioning the impact of Black thug imagery in porn. In what follows, Stitch reflects on a small number of videos that he saved for their depictions of more intimate connections between Black queer men:

STITCH: I think I'm more attracted to the intimacy that I'm seeing there on the screen than the actual sex that happens.

INTERVIEWER: Okay.

S: I think that's really what it is. And I noticed even with the little stash of porn that I have on my PlayStation ... they're all videos of people who in the scene, in the moment, are like having this really passionate sex. And it's like, you can tell there is real chemistry between them.

INT.: Uh huh.

S: I think that is ... the turn on for me and why I watch the porn that I watch. And I think it's important at least for me to see that intimacy between Black gay men 'cause I feel like I don't see it in real life. I guess that might be [a] thing or at least ... *[voice trails off]*.

INT.: Oh, say more.

S: I feel like I don't get to see it in real life as much or, like, play it out in real life as much. But I see it in porn where it could be fictional, it could not be fictional, but to me that's arousing to me. That is what I wanna see. And I guess ... oh wow, and I guess it's also what I don't have in my own life. Oh, just mind blown. Yeah, like that's, that's yeah ...

INT.: What was that mind blown moment?

S: That it's, like, that's what I kinda wanna see in my life, and I guess that's why I like watching it in porn. Yeah, because I feel I don't get to see that sort of, like, same intimacy shown out-and-about in the real world as much. Or not to say that it isn't there 'cause I know it's there, but I don't get to see it as much as I feel like I would like to, as people just being Black gay men, just being intimate with one another. Not even so much in a sexual sense.

Stitch's reflection helps to contextualize one reason to be concerned about the ubiquitous Black thug trope in online porn. In reproducing barbarous depictions of Black male sexuality, the trope leaves little-to-no room for emotional intimacy (as well as thoughtful communication between partners and negotiations of desires and consent). YBQM like Stitch—who see few if any examples of Black queer male sexual and romantic intimacy around them, and who rely on free online porn to imagine their own sexual lives—are provided scant models for how their encounters can incorporate intimacy and emotional connectedness. Other study participants like Adonis, Blue, Bobby, and Eros echoed Stitch's desire for more intimate depictions of Black queer male sexual encounters in porn and/or critiqued the dearth of such depictions. After noting that "Black videos are usually aggressive," Bobby shared the following lamentation: "The only time I look for videos when I really need something [with] intimacy—this may go against what I like—is when I go to white videos. That's the only time." Despite repeatedly asserting his attraction only to other Black males throughout his interview, Bobby admitted turning to online videos with white men for depictions of intimacy, as he struggled to find them in the "Black videos" curated by porn sites.

In summary, the data shared in this section attests to the significance of race as a mediator of SENT study participants' queer sexualities. As noted earlier in this chapter, the existing scholarship on queer youth's experiences with sex education is based overwhelmingly on insights from white informants. SENT study participants' perspectives suggest that any examinations of how YBQM learn about sex will be incomplete if they fail to center the salience of blackness. Focusing especially on interactions with online porn sites, study data revealed that while porn had the capacity to facilitate study participants' queer self-discoveries, those experiences relied heavily upon depictions of Black thuggery that reduced Black men to hypermasculine sexual aggressors. Additionally, the design features and algorithmic decisions of online porn sites played no small part in cultivating participants' repeated encounters with thug-based content. While many study participants were turned on by online porn videos featuring Black men, the ever-present Black thug trope offered scant representations of Black queer male intimacy and limited possibilities for Black queer male sexual identities. What these findings mean for sex education with YBQM are considered in the next and final section of this chapter.

## QUEERLY RESPONSIVE SEX EDUCATION FOR YOUNG BLACK QUEER MALES

The purpose of this chapter was to draw upon findings from two empirical studies to respond to the following questions: How do YBQM learn about sex outside of K–12 schools, and what are the implications of their experiences for sex education within and beyond urban secondary education? These are big questions, and developing robust answers to them will require multiple, ongoing, and well-informed collaborations between multiple stakeholders, including researchers, school- and community-based practitioners, and of course YBQM. The findings that comprise this chapter are intended not as exhaustive and conclusive examinations of the issues at hand, but as critical contributions toward sex education approaches that more authentically, compassionately, and effectively address YBQM's learning needs.

Collectively, the chapters in this book render queerly responsive pedagogical possibilities for BQY's learning experiences. Those possibilities are guided by the four core commitments of QRP that I detailed in chapter 2:

- Commitment 1: Provide a critical ethic of care to queer youth of color through queer of color peer and community networks, as well as through connections with critically caring adults.
- Commitment 2: Pair intersectional analyses of oppression with opportunities for queer youth of color to affirm and explore their identities, desires, and agency.
- Commitment 3: Address any tensions that challenge a respect for and inclusion of variously identified queer youth of color.
- Commitment 4: Advocate for educational and social justice with and for queer youth of color.

To wind down this chapter, I draw upon QRP's four commitments to consider the MAC and SENT studies' implications for queerly responsive sex education for YBQM and, when it makes sense, for other LGBTQ+ youth as well. I then present some closing thoughts on sex education for queer youth.

### Implications of the MAC Study

In a previous version of my analysis of MAC study findings, I propped up the agency as a model for how urban secondary schools might support queer youth of color. Revisiting those study findings through the lens of QRP leaves me more convinced of the unique value of MAC's work, especially its approach to sex education for YBQM. MAC's sex education programming exemplified three of QRP's core commitments. First, MAC's adult staffers and volunteers clearly embodied the first commitment of providing an ethic of critical care. Through a variety of sex education programming, staffers and volunteers critically responded to the structural determinants of YBQM's sexual health risks out of a deep concern for MAC youth's welfare. Second, the strategies that youth learned for safer and pleasurable sexual practices align with QRP's second commitment, as those strategies empowered MAC youth to affirm and explore their sexual identities and desires. Third, the agency's role in HIV/AIDS prevention and support services positioned staffers and volunteers to pursue the fourth queerly responsive pedagogical commitment—advocacy with and on behalf of youth—through strategies ranging from Armando's HIV prevention research projects to staffers' efforts to influence state policy on HIV services funding. The agency's skewed gender demographics—a predominantly queer male youth population, a smaller group of trans female and gender nonbinary youth, and few if any regular attendees who identified as cis female queer youth—significantly reduced opportunities to see the third queerly responsive commitment enacted. This marks an important limitation of the MAC study that demands deliberate attention in future research. Nevertheless, MAC's programming offers some instructive examples of what queerly responsive sex education can look like for YBQM.

While I remain excited about the examples offered by MAC's sex education programming, I am now more skeptical about the possibility of bringing MAC's practices into urban secondary schools. Supported by state and federal funding for HIV/AIDS-related services in queer communities of color, MAC staff members belonged to a network of public health agency staffers, policy-makers, medical providers, researchers, and community advocates who regularly engaged in frank conversations—with each other and with the clients and communities they served—about queer sexual health. Its status as a community-based organization freed MAC from the more virulent anti-LGBTQ+ surveillance of sexual discourses within K–12 schools. By contrast, school-based sex education, as noted several times in this chapter, remains under the stranglehold of cisheteronormative, AOUM doctrines. That predicament promises to get worse before it gets better based on the ever-expanding wave of anti-LGBTQ+ legislation across the United States. Consequently, the three recommendations below are posed with the constraints against queerly responsive school-based sex education in mind.

1. *Create partnerships:* Developing partnerships with queer youth-serving organizations like MAC, sexual health organizations like Planned Parenthood, local hospitals with community education departments, and agencies like local health clinics is one way for urban secondary schools to make queerly responsive sex education more available to YBQM and their LGBTQ+ peers. Staff members at these organizations may have expertise in queer-inclusive sex education, and their independence from school districts can grant them a relative buffer from the repercussions of anti-LGBTQ+ surveillance in schools. Partnerships with these organizations can supply the foundation for (a) professional development sessions for school personnel on the basics of queer sexual health; (b) the in-school delivery of queer-inclusive sex education by partner organizations (potentially lessening the professional risk for school personnel); and (c) referrals to local, queer-affirming sexual health resources that are accessible to youth. Similarly, partnerships with organizations like MAC, with clear expertise in YBQM's needs and experiences, can prove fruitful for other out-of-school organizations that want to offer queer-inclusive sex education resources to YBQM and other queer youth as well.
2. *Consider strategically located in-school support:* Urban secondary educators might consider identifying informal and discreet queer-inclusive sex education resources that YBQM and other LGBTQ+ students can access within schools. When available, nurses, guidance counselors, health educators, sex education instructors, and GSAs are a few possible sources for LGBTQ+ sex education resources that are located outside of core curricula and, thus, may be further from view of retributive anti-queer surveillance. When offering direct support to students is too professionally perilous for school personnel, having a pre-vetted list of suggested out-of-school resources for students to access on their own is a possible alternative. Along with relevant and accessible local

organizations, this list could include websites, TikTok channels, and content on other currently popular online platforms that have reliable, queer-affirming information on sex.[33] Lowering the visibility of informal, in-school information and resources, while not without its risks, could prove a practical option for at least a modicum of support for YBQM and other LGBTQ+ students.

3. *Develop cross-curricular content:* Since some queer youth have reported encountering sexuality-related content outside of sex education curricula—namely in literature courses—cross-curricular nods to queer sexualities may be an option for urban secondary schools that still have some leeway on queer-inclusive content. Monique Perry's work offers innovative insights on cross-curricular approaches to sexuality education on the middle school level.[34] GLSEN's 2021 High School Booklist, the HistoryUnErased website, and similar resources can also help urban secondary educators create space for YBQM and their LGBTQ+ peers to see their own identities and self-discovery processes reflected in and validated by school curricula.[35]

**Implications of the SENT Study**

The inveterate hostility toward queer-inclusive sex education in K–12 schools has led many LGBTQ+ youth to comb through porn sites for information on queer sexual identities and practices. The insights featured in this chapter from SENT study participants provide a warrant for more intentional examinations of blackness in YBQM's engagements of pornography. When viewed through the prism of QRP, SENT study participants' experiences with online porn align partially with the framework's second commitment: *Pair intersectional analyses of oppression with opportunities for queer youth of color to affirm and explore their identities, desires, and agency.* Though intersectional analyses of the forces shaping Black male-themed gay porn content were often missing, participants' interactions with porn did allow them to affirm and explore their identities and desires. In fact, exposure to porn was, for some of these YBQM, the catalyst for their queer sexual self-discovery, as well as an avenue to learn about the mechanics of queer sex and build their own sexual confidence. That said, porn's affordances for SENT study participants were coupled with the seemingly ubiquitous presence of Black thug imagery that equated Black queer masculinity and sexuality to domination and aggression. That equation unfolded at the expense of readily available depictions of Black queer male intimacy, which were identified by some as a crucial dimension of their queer sexual identity development. The prevalence and impact of the Black thug trope underscore the need for QRP's commitment to intersectional analyses of identity and power, and they also point to the potential value of critically caring adults who can help YBQM make sense of the images and messages they consume during their porn viewing.

The omnipresence of porn and other online content as alternative sites of sex education begs for future research on how to potentially capitalize on these resources' affordances while managing their shortcomings. Unfortunately, as Paul Byron and colleagues note in their review of scholarship on youth's porn literacies—their ability to make sense of the forces and ideas shaping pornographic content and determine their own terms of engagement with porn—empirical work on the subject is still in its relative infancy.[36] Additionally, much of the effort to date on young people's relationship to porn tries to emphasize the genre's detrimental effects and deter youth's consumption.[37] With these factors in mind, the recommendations below target YBQM's critical engagements with a range of online resources on queer sex, and they identify concerns related to YBQM's porn consumption that warrant considerations in burgeoning attempts to hone this population's porn literacy. Further studies will hopefully explore the relevance of these recommendations for other groups of LGBTQ+ youth.

1. *Incorporate online sex education resources:* Given YBQM's reliance on porn and other online content as alternatives to the widespread absence of queer-inclusive sex education in K–12 schools, online sex education resources deserve close attention from practitioners who work with YBQM. Recent years have seen a proliferation of content on platforms like YouTube, Instagram, and TikTok by sex educators who deliberately address questions about LGBTQ+ sex.[38] Additionally, a number of websites and podcasts—some by individual sex educators, others by organizations committed to sex education access—offer queer-inclusive

information about sex.[39] These potential resources present an opportunity for critically caring practitioners in youth-serving spaces like MAC to vet online content for accuracy, gauge its attentiveness to the forces that shape YBQM's intersecting identities, and develop curricula to guide YBQM's engagement. Ideally, practitioners would directly engage YBQM as they learn how to sift through online sex education resources, and they would center questions about Black queer male sexual identities, desires, and intimacies. Alternatively, community-based practitioners and possibly urban secondary educators as well could create a vetted list of reputable online sources, perhaps accompanied by framing questions, to guide YBQM's self-directed explorations of online content.

2. *Foster Black queer male porn literacy:* The complicated role of porn in the sexual wonderings and desires of SENT study participants suggests the need for porn literacy research and practice targeted specifically to YBQM. Specifically, the pervasiveness of Black thug imagery begs for structured learning opportunities for YBQM to engage critical scholarship from Black masculinity studies and Black queer studies that provides frameworks and language for unpacking porn's dominant messages about Black queer male sexualities, and for thinking through YBQM's own queer identities and desires.[40] The impact of porn site design features and algorithms on SENT study participants' experiences underscores the need for opportunities to join YBQM in considering their navigation of those factors as well. Once again, exploring these topics with guidance from knowledgeable, critically caring practitioners—especially in out-of-school settings that may have more freedom and flexibility to engage YBQM in this kind of work—would be preferable. Within schools, critical media literacy curricula might not be able to address porn directly, but they could make indirect contributions like helping YBQM to unpack dominant images of Black masculinity in American culture at large.

## A Closing Thought: "That Was Me"

This chapter marks my first published analysis of the combined insights on queer sex education from the MAC and SENT studies. It is not, however, my first time sharing these joint study findings with others. During the early phases of data analysis for the SENT study, I started receiving invitations from colleagues to deliver research talks at public health convenings and on college and university campuses. On multiple occasions, I was approached privately after the audience Q&A by young queer folks—usually entry-level staffers from community-based organizations at the convenings and undergraduate students at the campus talks—who voiced variations of the same theme: "That was me. I was that queer kid who didn't have access to queer sex education, and then this happened." The disclosures they shared of their sexual health histories initially caught me off guard. I was, after all, a stranger. And in many cases, despite my focus on YBQM, the young queer folks who approached me were not even Black males. Yet some combination of my approachability and their longing for a sympathetic queer ear sparked impromptu confessions of their most intimate and jarring sexual tribulations.

I opened this book with a nervous question that I received about sex between girls during a visit to a high school GSA. There is a clear throughline from that nervous question to the sobering exchanges that have repeatedly followed my research talks. The vulnerability that LGBTQ+ youth can experience around queer sex is soul-deep, marking the conflicted convergence of their desire for connection and the foreboding silence around queer sexual practices. American K–12 schools can establish anti-bullying policies to ostensibly protect queer kids from getting beat up, but the refusal to support queer sexual autonomy still places LGBTQ+ youth in harm's way. For some of the young people who have participated in my research projects or approached me after my research talks, their harms will follow them for the rest of their lives. While some K–12 educators have courageously and creatively found ways to incorporate queer sex education content into classroom lessons, the obstacles to replicating that intervention in schools across the United States are severe. However, through my interactions with, research on, and advocacy for queer youth, I can see that K–12 schools are not our only option. A sincere commitment to queer youth's humanity and well-being demands providing, with critical care, the functional knowledge and skills that are necessary for safe and fulfilling queer sexual lives. If American K–12 schools continue to balk at this commitment, then those of us who care about queer youth will have to proceed accordingly.

CHAPTER 6

# A Pedagogy of the Closet

During one of my favorite lessons from my years as a high school history teacher, I nervously screened a short documentary clip on the life of Michael Wigglesworth, a seventeenth-century Puritan cleric and writer whose poem, "The Day of Doom: or, A Poetical Description of the Great and Last Judgment," became one of New England's earliest bestsellers.[1] The title says it all; this poem is full-throttled fire and brimstone, forecasting the merciless demise of sinners on the furious day of godly reckoning. Not as apparent, however, was Wigglesworth's own bouts with sin and shame. In private diaries, Wigglesworth castigated himself for his sexual desires for other men. The self-loathing in his secret confessions was torturous and all-encompassing. By putting Wigglesworth's life narrative in conversation with the eighteenth-century theologian Jonathan Edwards's hellfire sermon "Sinners in the Hands of an Angry God," my official goal was to establish the connection between the surveillance of difference and discourses on American exceptionalism.[2] Unofficially, I wanted to ease into critiques of anti-queerness as an American injustice—a risky move on my part as an openly queer teacher who could end up being accused of proselytizing. None of my students openly rejected or resisted the lesson, and no parental complaints to school administrators ever materialized. Nevertheless, I had an explanation of the nonqueer intent of my lesson on deck, just in case my job security depended on it.

Maybe a week or two after the Puritan unit, resurgent speculations about Abraham Lincoln's sexual orientation appeared in a magazine article with a campy illustration of Lincoln in the cis gay male clone attire of the present day—a white tank top with biceps a-blazing, faded blue jeans, and a tiny hoop earring in one ear.[3] Spotting the article, which just happened to be sitting on my desk (wink), a student asked me, "So . . . did Lincoln 'get his Wigglesworth'?" Once the other students finished giggling, I reiterated the historiographical challenge of studying identities and relationships from centuries' past through present-day constructions of categories like masculinity and queerness. Nevertheless, for the remainder of the semester, "did so-and-so get their Wigglesworth" became an ostensibly lighthearted yet efficient shorthand for students' inquiries about queerness in American history.

Despite coming out to my school community during my second year of teaching, mostly to undercut some students' homophobic speculations about me, my initial attempts at raising LGBTQ+ topics in my classroom were tentative. As stated above, I knew that being an openly queer teacher could raise suspicions about my motives for incorporating queer content in the curriculum. Additionally, I had no models to draw upon, as none of my more established colleagues were addressing LGBTQ+ issues in their classrooms; or, if they were, they certainly were not advertising it. For five-plus decades, bringing representations of queer communities, heroes, struggles, and triumphs front and center has been a central tactic in social, political, and educational campaigns to secure rights for and increase the acceptance of LGBTQ+ people in the United States.[4] Uncertain about the repercussions of such tactics for me as an anxious young teacher, I opted at times for more discreet routes with built-in off-ramps: "I was teaching about power and surveillance, not queerness," or "I didn't realize that the magazine article was on my desk." Rather than pride flag–waving assertions of queer identity or commitment, I engaged in what I would classify as closeted pedagogical maneuvers—tactics for speaking queerness into existence while falling under the radar of anti-queer suspicions. Given the ongoing and insidious surveillance of queer students, families, educators, and curricula in American K–12 schools, closeted modes of knowledge production are one set of strategies that may warrant (re)consideration.

Throughout this book, I have tried to account for the professional risks and institutional limitations that can complicate practitioners' efforts to support Black queer youth (BQY), particularly within schools under strict anti-queer surveillance. This chapter focuses more directly on the noxious present-day milieu for school-based initiatives on LGBTQ+ issues by presenting *a pedagogy of the closet* as a framework for educators' queer-inclusive classroom practices in decidedly anti-LGBTQ+ times. Drawing on a conceptualization of the closet as shifting degrees of queer visibility and invisibility, I pose a pedagogy of the closet as a possible set of maneuvers for discreetly and strategically delivering queer-inclusive curricula to BQY and other LGBTQ+ students. My goal here is to consider how dimming the brightness of queer inclusiveness in classroom instruction may afford varying levels of student exposure to queer content while providing some cover for teachers from political and professional backlash.

The impetus for this chapter stems from my interactions with K–12 educators over the past few years, primarily during professional development sessions and speaking engagements, and to some extent in my teacher education courses. Repeatedly, my suggestions for addressing LGBTQ+ issues in classrooms have been met with some variation of "but how do I do this without getting in trouble?" This chapter presents my attempt to tease out my response to that question—a response mirrored in the efforts of a few brave educators who have confided to me their similar approaches to this dilemma in their schools. The urgency to support teachers has motivated me to share some ideas in this chapter without first investigating them through empirical research, marking a distinction from the preceding chapters. But as a tenured university professor, I know that I can think out loud about discreet strategies for queer-inclusive curriculum and instruction without the same level of job insecurity that looms over an ever-increasing number of classroom teachers. My hope is that this chapter's think-aloud will contribute to the creativity, ingenuity, and resolve of K–12 educators who want to do right by their LGBTQ+ students.

In what follows, I define *a pedagogy of the closet* and offer examples of how it might shape measured approaches to curriculum content and classroom instruction on Black queer experiences in history and English language arts (ELA) classrooms. I then conclude with lingering concerns about and future possibilities for supporting the learning experiences of Black-identified and other LGBTQ+ youth in the United States.

## DEFINING A PEDAGOGY OF THE CLOSET

Casual references to the closet can discount the complexities of the phenomenon they represent. In this chapter, I want to emphasize two salient characteristics of the closet that inform my pedagogical engagement of it. First, it is imperative to frame the closet as a set of survival strategies necessitated by anti-queer domination. A substantial body of scholarship has compellingly, and sometimes painfully, detailed the structural and ideological arrangements of power in the United States that have defined queerness as a moral perversion, a medical pathology, a legal violation, and a cultural, educational, and existential threat.[5] Amidst an assemblage of anti-queer abuses, ranging from job loss and incarceration to physical violence and social exile, the closet is the aggregation of strategies for obscuring and disavowing queerness. Cisheteronormative gender presentations, furtive locations for social interactions, and silence about one's intimate life are but a few of the tactics that can allow one to remain "in the closet." In making decisions about if, when, where, and how to deploy such tactics, queer people still exercise some agency while negotiating their vulnerability in anti-queer contexts. Nevertheless, *it is the systemic nature of anti-queer oppression, not the dishonesty or cowardice of queer individuals,* that is ultimately responsible for the closet. My reason for emphasizing this is to counter discourses that demonize closeted queer people as sneaky, deceitful, and responsible for their own misery.[6] These accusations rely on a denial of the anti-queer social, cultural, economic, and political factors that force queer people at times to hide or deny their queerness. As I discuss later, stressing how the closet is an essential response to anti-queer repression provides a key warrant for a pedagogy of the closet.

The second characteristic of the closet that is critical for this chapter is its negotiability. Scholarship in the field of queer studies has troubled the fixity of binaries like secrecy/disclosure and invisibility/visibility that undergird references to being either *in* or *out* of the closet.[7] Citing Diana Fuss's seminal work, that familiar rhetoric fails to acknowledge that "most of us are both inside and outside at the same time"—that is, one's queerness can be known or detected by some while simultaneously obscured from others.[8] This concurrence of inside and outside, of invisible and visible, is key to my deployment of the closet in this chapter. As I explained in a previously published conceptualization of the closet:

> By making queer aberration a consequential phenomenon, the arrangements of power that orchestrate the closet have produced a heightened awareness, or "spectacle" (Sedgwick, 1990), of queer secrecy, allowing them to enforce the suppression of queerness while concurrently shining a taunting spotlight on the act of queer hiding. Even if the closet door is ostensibly and dutifully closed, the queer subject is not necessarily immune to external campaigns to acknowledge the door's presence and function. Consequently, in addition to marking the sociohistorically produced pressures to conceal queerness, the closet functions as a contested site where the impulse for queer secrecy and disavowal coexists and collides with attempts to make queerness visible and, thus, more accessible to homophobic surveillance and derision. Instead of absolute distinctions between "in" and "out," the closet is constituted at once by degrees of silence and disclosure, degrees of ignorance and knowing (Sedgwick, 1990). Furthermore, as socially produced nodes of power, the degrees of secrecy and exposure that constitute the closet can be modified by multiple actors within a given social context, making the negotiation of the closet a collective social enterprise.[9]

An understanding of the closet as degrees of queer concealment and exposure, negotiated by queer individuals and other actors in a given social context, underscores the burden of anti-queerness in the lives of LGBTQ+ people. Importantly, this conceptualization also creates opportunities to explore the closet as an agentive space. One example, as mentioned above, is how queer individuals who are navigating the closet exercise varied measures of agency by choosing tactics for managing their queer (in)conspicuousness. Another example—and one of particular significance to this chapter—is how the closet has enabled LGBTQ+ individuals to discreetly exchange queer knowledge. Historically, queer spaces like bars, private home gatherings, and other congregation sites, relatively hidden from and/or unknown to those outside of queer communities, have relied on levels of invisibility to foster information exchange and community building.[10] Similarly, coded communicative strategies that are unrecognizable to nonqueer bystanders have afforded queer knowledge transmission in cisheteronormative spaces.[11] In all of these cases, the possibility of exposure looming in the background produces the need to maintain queer discretion; the closet is, after all, still patrolled by anti-queer risk. Nonetheless, the closet can also be understood as a strategic and agentive space for the exchange of queer knowledge, and it is here that we find the closet's pedagogical implications.

Like Eve Kosofsky Sedgwick's treatment of the closet as a site of knowledge production in her seminal text, *Epistemology of the Closet*, I want to propose the closet as a mode for K–12 educators' pedagogical work.[12] This mode, a pedagogy of the closet, is an engagement with queer content that modulates how openly or subtly queerness is named based on contextual factors like teacher and student identities, subject matter, school culture, the intensity of anti-queer surveillance, and the strength of teachers' and students' protections from that surveillance. More than simply the site of queer silence and despair, the closet, I contend, can operate as a pedagogical space that enables maneuvers for discreetly delivering queer-inclusive curricula. This definition differs from the one other substantive attempt I have found at conceptualizing a pedagogy of the closet: the one advanced by Rogério Diniz Junqueira.[13] For Junqueira, the closet remains the site of anti-queer oppression, as he casts a pedagogy of the closet as the maintenance of heteronormativity in schools by the policing of queer sexualities and gender expressions. My formulation relies on an understanding of the closet's capacity to function at once as a site of anti-queer repression *and* an agentive space for exchanging queer knowledge. Pedagogically, a careful management of the visibility and intensity of queer inclusiveness in classroom instruction may afford varying levels of student exposure to queer content while providing some cover for teachers who are operating under anti-queer surveillance.

An important similarity between my conceptual engagement of the closet in this chapter and my use of fugitivity as an analytical lens in chapter 4 is worth mentioning here. Regarding the latter, I discussed how scholars in the field of Black studies—and subsequently, critical educational scholars who study Black educational experiences—have taken up fugitivity to recognize the persistent, state-sanctioned investment in Black suffering, along with the mix of cunning, determination, and defiance required by the fugitive Black subject to survive and thrive in the afterlife of slavery.[14] Fugitivity's imbrication in antebellum Black resistance in the United States presents historically rooted perspectives on contemporary Black struggles for freedom. In similar fashion, the closet's status as the marker of LGBTQ+ suffering in the United States provides a sociohistorically authentic backdrop for analyzing ongoing struggles to name, affirm, and explore queerness while simultaneously dodging the anti-queer spotlight. This specific connection to legacies of anti-queer oppression is what distinguishes a pedagogy of the closet from other frameworks for describing teachers' resistance to restrictive curricular mandates and other attacks on their autonomy and expertise.[15] Aligning low-profile, queer-inclusive pedagogical maneuvers with navigations of the closet serves two purposes: it keeps the presence and power of anti-queerness front and center; and it honors pedagogical discretion under these circumstances as a valid act of resistance.

Finally, though the closet is associated with the experiences of LGBTQ+ people, its impact extends beyond those who identify as such. For instance, cishetero-identified children of LGBTQ+ parents, as well cishetero-identified allies of LGBTQ+ communities, have described navigating the closet in order to evade anti-queer backlash for their pro-queer loyalties.[16] Whether queer or not, teachers who engage a pedagogy of the closet are taking on the professional risk that the closet presents. Obdurate cultural perceptions of queer teachers as threats to children may amplify that risk especially for them—a likelihood I would encourage cishetero-identified allies to take into consideration—but some measure of risk, regardless of their sexual orientation, will face teachers who attempt strategically low-profile approaches to queer inclusion in times of intensified anti-queer surveillance in schools. Gauging that level of risk and shaping one's plans accordingly must precede enactments of the strategies presented in the sections that follow.

## APPLYING A PEDAGOGY OF THE CLOSET

The goal of this chapter is to help teachers think more intentionally and strategically about ways to create opportunities to explore queer-related content, especially within increasingly anti-queer political and educational milieus. In the examples below, I draw upon Black queer-related topics to illustrate how the closet might guide teachers' inclusion of queer content and knowledge in their classrooms.

### An Example for History Curriculum: Bayard Rustin

Curriculum is a multifaceted phenomenon, unfolding over multiple spaces with input and pushback from multiple stakeholders. Recent attacks on the inclusion of racial justice and LGBTQ+ topics in American K–12 schools signal, among other things, an attempt to bound, script, and oversimplify the malleable and multilayered nature of students' curricular encounters.

To help teachers dodge those attacks, I want to name two concepts from the field of curriculum studies that can inform their strategic engagements and enactments of queer-related curriculum: the *formal curriculum,* defined as the topics and learning objectives that are identified in state and district curricular standards and included in official curricular materials (also referred to as the explicit, official, or intended curriculum); and the *taught curriculum,* defined as the version of the formal curriculum that is taught in the classroom and mediated by a teacher's individual adaptations and instructional choices.[17] Ideally, both of these curricular sites should facilitate queer-inclusive pedagogical work. However, given the hostility expressed by a growing number of state legislatures and local school districts across the United States toward LGBTQ+ inclusion in schools, one reason for naming both the formal and taught curriculum is to strategically direct our attention to the latter when anti-queer measures obstruct the former. To be clear, it is certainly, and sadly, not impossible for anti-queer surveillance to extend into the classroom and affect teachers' enactments of the taught curriculum.[18] But in cases where that surveillance has not completely infiltrated every moment and interaction within every individual classroom, a pedagogy of the closet could inform teachers' queer-inclusive negotiations of the taught curriculum.

To illustrate this possibility, I will now propose two sets of guiding questions for a potential history class lesson on Bayard Rustin, the Black queer political organizer, lifelong pacificist, and onetime communist who was a lead organizer of the 1963 March on Washington for Jobs and Freedom. Despite being a close advisor to Dr. Martin Luther King Jr., reservations among Black civil rights leaders in the 1950s and 1960s toward Rustin's queerness relegated him to a behind-the-scenes role in the movement and, at times, pushed him toward the fringes of the movement's leadership.[19] In schools and districts where history curriculum and instruction have not been completely decimated by attacks on racial justice in the classroom, the Black civil rights movement can provide a backdrop for strategic analyses of queerness vis-a-vis the life of Bayard Rustin.

Even when attempting to raise queer issues through the taught curriculum, the curricular standards that comprise the formal curriculum are still a crucial starting point for a pedagogy of the closet. Aligning queer-related curriculum additions to official curriculum standards provides rational justification for this pedagogical move. The following is a state standard for US history instruction in secondary-level social studies classes in Pennsylvania, the state where most of my work as a teacher educator is currently situated: "8.3.9.A. Compare the role groups and individuals played in the social, political, cultural, and economic development of the U.S."[20] Since analyses of the Black civil rights movement of the 1960s can align with this standard, those analyses offer an opportunity to consider Rustin's role as an openly queer organizer within the movement (thus addressing both individuals and groups, as stated in the standard). Teachers situated in relatively queer-tolerant school settings might design learning experiences guided by the following questions:

1. What role did Bayard Rustin play in 1960s Black civil rights organizing, and why was that role significant?
2. How did stakeholders within and opponents outside of the Black civil rights movement respond to Rustin's queerness, and why were those responses significant?
3. How was Rustin's subsequent participation in the gay rights movement similar to and/or different from his participation in the Black civil rights movement?
4. What similarities and/or differences exist between Rustin's role in the 1960s Black civil rights movement and the roles of Black queer organizers in the 2010s Black Lives Matter movement? Is the latter a sign of progress? Why or why not?

Collectively, these guiding questions address the 8.3.9.A US history curriculum standard by exploring Rustin's role as an individual political organizer, comparing that role across two sociopolitical movements (and in the process, comparing those movements), and comparing the roles of Black queer organizers across time in Black sociopolitical organizing. Aligning the study of Rustin to state curriculum standards thus uses the formal curriculum to justify an attention to Black queerness. Regarding classroom enactment, building lesson plans around these questions would allow teachers to demonstrate the significance of Black queerness for understanding key dilemmas in the study of US history (e.g., who sets agendas within political movements, how do political movements contend with diversity and divisions within their ranks), thus marking an important departure from cursory and tokenistic incorporations of queer topics that often occur through less critical approaches of multicultural curricular inclusion.[21] For teachers in relatively queer-tolerant secondary schools, these guiding questions could facilitate rigorous interrogations through the taught curriculum of both the tensions surrounding Black queer political participation and the agency of Black queer organizers in the face of anti-Black and anti-queer resistance. In the end, not only could Black queerness be foregrounded, but it could be explored in a manner that encourages anti-deficit lenses on Black queer difference.

Unfortunately, the open and rigorous approach to Black queer curricular inclusion outlined above may be impractical for secondary social studies and history teachers working under palpable anti-queer surveillance of curriculum and instruction. For those teachers, a pedagogy of the closet could help them to consider how to acknowledge the presence and importance of Black queerness more subtly. For instance, a more closeted pedagogical approach to studying Rustin might take on the following guiding questions:

1. What role did Bayard Rustin play in 1960s Black civil rights organizing, and why was that role significant?
2. How did stakeholders within and opponents outside of the Black civil rights movement respond to Rustin's politics, and why were those responses significant?

Unlike the first set of proposed guiding questions, these questions do not explicitly name Rustin's queerness. And yet, they do not foreclose attention to it in student responses, particularly if Rustin's queerness is mentioned in any curricular materials. Additionally, while the wording of the second question could lead to considerations of Rustin's role as a gay rights activist, it also affords analyses of his involvement in pacifist and/or communist activism. *This maneuver is key:* planning ahead to ensure non-queer-related learning goals to veer toward if challenges emerge to queer-inclusive content.

Together, the second set of guiding questions above allows for Rustin's Black queerness to surface in the taught curriculum while not foregrounding it as an explicit curricular focus. This closeted pedagogical approach grants space for teachers in potentially queer-resistant settings to inch their way into Black queer curricular inclusion, determine how much room (if any) exists for further inclusion in the taught curriculum, and shift to nonqueer content if need be to avoid, or at least lessen the blow of, anti-queer repercussions for their instructional practices. While obviously not as ideal as the more open and rigorous study of Rustin detailed earlier, a pedagogy of the closet offers a safer route for teachers who want to explore the possibilities for Black queer-inclusive curricula, but who must do so with the professional repercussions of anti-queerness in mind. In this way, a pedagogy of the closet acknowledges the constraints of—while also guiding teachers' practical decision-making within—school climates that are resistant to queer curricular inclusion.

### Rustin Continued: Queerly Responsive Curriculum Guiding Questions

While discussing curriculum in chapter 2, I recommended five *queerly responsive curriculum guiding questions* to help educators assess the validity and value of possible curriculum resources. To fill out this chapter's consideration of a lesson on Bayard Rustin, I want to briefly revisit those guiding questions and illustrate their potential application. As a reminder, here are those five questions:

1. *Authorship:* Is the resource from someone, queer of color-identified or otherwise, with track records of sharing authentic insights into queer of color communities and demonstrating a commitment to queer of color justice?
2. *Corroboration:* Do other resources from credible authors or creators corroborate the claims within this resource?

3. *Intersectionality:* How (if at all) does this resource afford intersectional analyses of power that may speak to the lives of queer youth of color?
4. *Curricular standards:* In what ways does this resource align with the curriculum standards that guide classroom content?
5. *Adjustments:* What aspects of the resource should be foregrounded, de-emphasized, excluded, or replaced to make it manageable for and relevant to particular groups of students?

The affordances of these questions are evident when applied to a potential curricular resource like the *Making Gay History* podcast's episode on Bayard Rustin.[22] Below is a summary of the questions' application to the podcast.

1. *Authorship:* The podcast was created and hosted by Eric Marcus, a queer author with a notable track record of publications on gay history in the United States. Those publications, along with the podcast, feature multiple examples of Marcus's critical attention to the lives and contributions of Black queer individuals.
2. *Corroboration:* The podcast episode presented perspectives on Rustin's life and career that are echoed in reputable and compelling sources like the GLAAD media award-winning documentary, *Brother Outsider: The Life of Bayard Rustin,* and noted queer historian John D'Emilio's biography, *Lost Prophet: The Life and Times of Bayard Rustin.*[23]
3. *Intersectionality:* The podcast episode describes how Rustin's life was shaped by, and how he sought to push back against, white supremacy and homophobia from multiple sources across multiple contexts of his life. This facilitates analyses not only of intersecting forms of domination acting upon him as a Black queer man, but of what his agency looked like under different circumstances.
4. *Curricular standards:* See the earlier example of the alignment with a Pennsylvania state curriculum standard for US History.
5. *Adjustments:* Depending on the amount of available instructional time and the desired instructional goals, a teacher might consider focusing on the one-on-one interview portion of the podcast episode, and perhaps crafting questions that address specific comments made by Rustin. Additionally, taking a pedagogy of the closet into consideration, episode

excerpts that focus less on his queerness could prove strategic alternatives to the more queer-centered snippets.

Note the direct attention to a pedagogy of the closet in my response to the fifth guiding question. As I suggested earlier in this chapter, having non-queer-related learning goals to veer toward if challenges emerge to queer-inclusive content is a key maneuver for a pedagogy of the closet. The fifth guiding question can serve as a reminder for teachers to plan accordingly for that maneuver. Additionally, the attention in the other guiding questions to curriculum standards and the quality and validity of potential curriculum resources can be cited to illustrate the thoughtfulness behind the incorporation of Black queer-related content. Under severe objections to queer-inclusive content, the preparatory rigor and care reflected in the five guiding questions admittedly may prove unpersuasive. But in schools and districts where anti-queer surveillance of classrooms has yet to reach a fever pitch, these guiding questions may provide teachers with talking points to support closeted pedagogical approaches to addressing LGBTQ+ topics in their classrooms.

### Black, Queer, Women: Examples for English Language Arts Classrooms

While not an expert in this area, I collaborated on occasion with ELA colleagues on curriculum units as a middle and high school history teacher, and I have continued to advise ELA pre-service teachers on their lesson plans and instruction as a teacher educator. Drawing on those experiences, I offer brief sketches in this section of how a pedagogy of the closet might inform ELA curriculum and instruction with works by and / or about Black queer women. As with all of the examples and recommendations posed throughout this book, applications of the ideas shared below must be further developed and adapted based on teacher expertise, student interest, school culture around queer curriculum content, and other factors that affect pedagogical possibilities within specific learning environments.

Poems by Black lesbian authors Pat Parker and Audre Lorde illustrate how a pedagogy of the closet might inform negotiations of ELA curriculum and instruction. In her 1978 poem, "Where Will You Be?," Parker insistently challenges other LGBTQ+ people to consider their readiness to take a stand in the face of anti-queer oppression, asking in the closing stanza, "They will come for / the perverts / and where will / you be / When they come?"[24] The poem's progression bears a striking resemblance to Pastor Martin Niemöller's "First They Came," about the failure to speak up against the Nazis.[25] Analyzing the poems together could generate interesting comparisons of the writers' marginalized backgrounds and writing conventions. However, Parker's poem is overtly queer, with no clear off-ramp for teachers who may need to veer toward a non-queer-centered reading of the text. By contrast, Lorde's 1973 poem, "Who Said It Was Simple," presents both queer-inclusive and queer-evasive options for classroom discussion.[26] Opening with "There are so many roots to the tree of anger / that sometimes the branches shatter / before they bear," the poem bears witness to those "many roots" as Lorde meditates on the frustrations she experienced as a Black queer woman participating in, and feeling marginalized by, multiple political movements. Queerness is never explicitly stated, thus enabling non-queer interpretations of the text if need be; but it certainly can be elevated in intersectional analyses of Lorde's somber reflection. Placing Parker's and Lorde's poems side by side helps to emphasize how a pedagogy of the closet might guide the selection and analysis of texts in a secondary-level ELA classroom.

In addition to Parker's and Lorde's poems, Nella Larsen's 1929 book *Passing* is another option worth considering for ELA classrooms.[27] Set in 1920s Chicago and New York, the book follows Irene Redfield, a fair-skinned and middle-class Black woman married to a successful Black male doctor, who unexpectedly runs into Claire Kendry, a mixed-race childhood friend who is passing for white and married to an overtly racist white man. As Redfield's and Kendry's lives become re-entwined, the novel surfaces the tensions, fears, and fantasies associated with racial passing. But as literary scholars have asserted, there is also a queer subtext to the relationship between Irene and Claire.[28] Their fascination for each other can be read racially and sexually, imbuing the book's title with double meaning. Ideally, the novel could afford rich discussions on the legacy and politics of queerness existing as subtext in Western literature, the similarities and differences of racial and sexual passing, and the book's messages about the (im)possibility of Black queer womanhood. However, the closeted nature of the text itself affords nonqueer readings if circumstances demand such. As with the Rustin and Lorde examples, classroom lessons on *Passing* have the capacity to pass as something other than queer. It is this flexibility that makes a pedagogy of the closet a strategic avenue for queer curricular inclusion.

## ADD THEM TO YOUR ARSENAL

Earlier in this chapter, I rationalized my invocation of the closet by contending that its association with the oppression of LGBTQ+ people poses two pedagogical affordances: it illuminates the anti-queer social, political, and educational conditions that necessitate low-profile treatments of queer content in the classroom, and it frames instructional discretion under these circumstances as an act of resistance. These affordances are critical amidst the present-day, multipronged political agenda of academic censorship and anti-queer harm behind bans against LGBTQ+ content in schools. By opposing campaigns to exclude any acknowledgment or affirmation of queer and trans existence in K–12 schools, a pedagogy of the closet reflects what I described in chapter 2 as the fourth commitment of queerly responsive pedagogy (QRP): *Advocate for educational and social justice with and for queer youth of color.* Sometimes advocacy for educational and social justice justifiably coalesces in loud and disruptive acts of public protest. But through a pedagogy of the closet, it is the subtle (semi)private classroom moves that can enable teachers to resist anti-queerness, engage in queerly responsive advocacy, and provide enriching learning opportunities for their students, queer and otherwise.

Not centering my empirical research on BQY presented an opportunity in this chapter to consider the implications of a pedagogy of the closet for queer-inclusive educational work more broadly. That said, I want to make sure that my overall mission to foreground BQY does not get lost as this book comes to a close. I have expressed a number of times over the previous chapters that BQY's lived experiences unfold at the intersections of multiple, systemic forms of subjugation that can complicate their pursuit of learning opportunities in varied pedagogical spaces. This observation served as the backdrop for my analyses of BQY's perspectives on their educational experiences in urban secondary schools, in an urban and queer youth-serving community-based organization, and across online platforms containing sexually explicit content. With QRP as my undergirding lens, my explorations of the experiences so generously shared by youth study participants surfaced insights that have not been consistently and rigorously engaged in existing bodies of educational scholarship. Looking back at the previous chapters, my primary hopes at this point are threefold: for practitioners who attend to BQY's learning experiences to consider this book's implications for queerly responsive practices in their respective spaces; for these practitioners to explore potential queerly responsive collaborations across their respective domains; and for researchers who examine BQY's learning experiences to build an even deeper empirical foundation for queerly responsive pedagogical work with BQY and their non-Black LGBTQ+ peers. Those of us who support BQY can surely enhance our impact by committing ourselves to these next steps.

Although this book makes exciting contributions to our understanding of BQY's learning experiences, it has its limitations. For starters, the young people whose insights are featured throughout the preceding chapters were located in the northeastern United States when they shared their stories. Though placing my book in conversation with other educational scholars' work on BQY produces some geographically diverse perspectives, I still look forward to including that diversity in my own scholarship in the years to come. Additionally, while the accounts offered by youth study participants traversed multiple social and educational contexts, they did not include data collection within urban secondary schools. As my research increasingly centers questions about BQY's experiences with sex education, I find myself pondering the practicality of attempting school-based projects as an openly queer man on queerly responsive sex education, especially if current efforts to purge queer content and people from American K–12 schools persist. Ultimately, if I am not a good fit for Black queer-focused research in secondary schools, then I will search for ways to support those who are. I encourage others to do so as well.

Gender and sexual diversity is one more limitation of this book that I want to revisit. As I have noted elsewhere, my study participants were predominantly Black queer cis males. While I am committed to including more gender and sexual diversity in my future work with BQY, I am also eager to recognize analyses by educational studies scholars who are already engaging these populations, specifically outside of higher education. Examples include Mara Johnson and monét cooper's exploration of Black queer girls' epistolary writing practices; Torie Wheatley's work on culturally relevant mindfulness practices for Black queer womxn and girls in the educational and criminal justice sectors; Savannah Shange's account of Black queer girls and Black stud/femme politics in an alternative high school; Latrise Johnson's gender-diverse analysis of BQY's literacy practices in an afterschool writing club; Sam Stiegler's work on Black queer and trans youth navigating New York City; Lance McCready's scholarship on Black gender nonconforming students' schooling experiences; Tomás Boatwright's gender-diverse account of BQY's zine-based storytelling; and Jon Wargo's gender-diverse work with Black and other racially identified LGBTQ2 youth.[29] My own writing is informed by these authors' scholarly interventions in the study of BQY, and I encourage anyone who reads my book to also read the works of these incredible scholars.

As I bring this chapter to a close, I find myself thinking a lot about the departure that this book represents. For about eight years, I held off on publishing my emergent research findings—particularly those on sex education—limiting myself instead to scholarly presentations at academic conferences and during campus talks. These presentations were primarily without livestreaming and always in places that were liberal enough to invite me to speak. With anti-trans bathroom bills, bans on queer content and discussions in classrooms, and attacks on gender-affirming medical care blooming into a full-fledged assault on queer-inclusive schooling and LGBTQ+ youth, I tried to avoid more public and unmonitored venues for disseminating research findings, opting instead for lower-profile and carefully facilitated opportunities to talk about BQY in person or to a selected Zoom audience. In effect, I was enacting a pedagogy of the closet well before writing about it.

The ability to test the waters, especially with my work on queer-inclusive sex education, was a huge affordance of research presentations in relatively friendly, insular settings. The downside, of course, was the short reach of research shared solely with smaller audiences. With anti-queer political and educational campaigns running amok, it is imperative for those of us who support BQY and their non-Black LGBTQ+ peers to have multiple advocacy strategies at the ready, from speaking up and fighting back at contentious school board meetings to deploying closet pedagogical maneuvers in queerly responsive classrooms. To those who see utility in the ideas presented in this book, I encourage you to add them to your arsenal.

# Notes

## Chapter 1

1. Throughout this book, I use pseudonyms for research sites and participants to protect the identities of the latter.
2. Pat Griffin and Mathew Ouellett, "From Silence to Safety and Beyond: Historical Trends in Addressing Lesbian, Gay, Bisexual, Transgender Issues in K-12 Schools," *Equity & Excellence in Education* 36, no. 2 (2003): 106–14; Matt Lavietes, "'Groomer,' 'Pro-Pedophile': Old Tropes Find New Life in Anti-LGBTQ Movement," *NBC News,* April 12, 2022, https://www.nbcnews.com/nbc-out/out-politics-and-policy/groomer-pedophile-old-tropes-find-new-life-anti-lgbtq-movement-rcna23931.
3. *Men who have sex with men* (MSM) is the nomenclature used in public health. I employ it when citing public health discourses. For the nationwide increase in HIV infections among young Black cisgender MSM, see Centers for Disease Control and Prevention, "New Multi-Year Data Show Annual HIV Infections in U.S. Relatively Stable," August 3, 2011, http://www.cdc.gov/nchhstp/newsroom/2011/HIVIncidencePressRelease.html. To protect the anonymity of the Midtown individuals who participated in my research, I do not cite sources on Midtown-specific data.
4. I use *minoritized* as a synonym for *marginalized* to describe groups that have been pushed to the institutional or societal fringes by structural and ideological forces that disadvantage them while advantaging others. For a further explanation, see I. E. Smith, "Minority vs. Minoritized: Why the Noun Just Doesn't Cut It," *Odyssey,* September 2, 2016, https://www.theodysseyonline.com/minority-vs-minoritize.
5. Cassi Pittman, "'Shopping While Black': Black Consumers' Management of Racial Stigma and Racial Profiling in Retail Settings," *Journal of Consumer Culture* 20, no. 1 (2020): 3–22; Gretchen Sorin, *Driving While Black: African American Travel and the Road to Civil Rights* (New York: Liveright Publishing, 2020).
6. Keith Boykin, *For Colored Boys Who Have Considered Suicide When the Rainbow Is Still Not Enough: Coming of Age, Coming Out, and Coming Home* (New York: Magnus Books, 2012); Michael C. LaSala and Damien T. Frierson, "African American Gay Youth and Their Families: Redefining Masculinity, Coping with Racism and Homophobia," *Journal of GLBT Family Studies* 8, no. 5 (2012):

428–45; Lance T. McCready, *Making Space for Diverse Masculinities: Difference, Intersectionality, and Engagement in an Urban High School* (New York: Peter Lang, 2010); Kai Wright, *Drifting Toward Love: Black, Brown, Gay, and Coming of Age on the Streets of New York* (Boston: Beacon Press, 2008).

7. Meredith Dank et al., *Surviving the Streets of New York: Experiences of LGBTQ Youth, YMSM, and YWSW Engaged in Survival Sex* (Washington, DC: Urban Institute, 2015); Myeshia Price-Feeney, Amy E. Green, and Samuel Dorison, "All Black Lives Matter: Mental Health of Black LGBTQ Youth," The Trevor Project, 2020, https://www.thetrevorproject.org/research-briefs/all-black-lives-matter-mental-health-of-black-lgbtq-youth/; Wright, *Drifting Toward Love*. Survival sex is "exchanging one's body for basic subsistence needs, including clothing, food and shelter" (Mike Marini, "Exchanging Sex for Survival," *The Atlantic*, June 26, 2014, https://www.theatlantic.com/health/archive/2014/06/exchanging-sex-for-survival/371822/). This term, in contrast to *sex work* or *prostitution*, emphasizes survival under dire living conditions as the motive for this category of sexual encounters.

8. Hilary Burdge, Adela C. Licona, and Zami T. Hyemingway, *LGBTQ Youth of Color: Discipline Disparities, School Push-Out, and the School-to-Prison Pipeline* (San Francisco: Gay-Straight Alliance Network and Crossroads Collaborative, 2014); McCready, *Making Space for Diverse Masculinities;* Therese M. Quinn, "'You Make Me Erect!': Queer Girls of Color Negotiating Heteronormative Leadership at an Urban All-Girls' Public School," *Journal of Gay & Lesbian Issues in Education* 4, no. 3 (2007): 31–47; N. L. Truong, A. D. Zongrone, and J. G. Kosciw, *Erasure and Resilience: The Experiences of LGBTQ Students of Color: Black LGBTQ Youth in U.S. Schools* (New York: GLSEN, 2020); Sabina Vaught, "The Talented Tenth: Gay Black Boys and the Racial Politics of Southern Schooling," *Journal of Gay & Lesbian Issues in Education* 2, no. 2 (2004): 5–26.

9. Joseph Kosciw, Caitlin Clark, and Leesh Menard, *The 2021 National School Climate Survey: The Experiences of LGBTQ+ Youth in Our Nation's Schools* (New York: GLSEN, 2022); Cris Mayo, *LGBTQ Youth and Education: Policies and Practices* (New York: Teachers College Press, 2022); Janelle T. Scott et al., *Law and Order in School and Society: How Discipline and Policing Policies Harm Students of Color, and What We Can Do About It* (Boulder, CO: National Education Policy Center, 2017); Kimberlé Crenshaw, Priscilla Ocen, and Jyoti Nanda, *Black Girls Matter: Pushed Out, Overpoliced and Underprotected*, African American Policy Forum, 2015, https://www.aapf.org/_files/ugd/b77e03_e92d6e80f7034f30bf843ea7068f52d6.pdf.

10. See n. 4 above.

11. Tamar Mendelson et al., "Opportunity Youth: Insights and Opportunities for a Public Health Approach to Reengage Disconnected Teenagers and Young Adults," *Public Health Reports* 133, no. 1, suppl. (November–December 2018):

54–64; Social Science Research Council, "Youth Disconnection," July 23, 2020, https://www.ssrc.org/programs/measure-of-america/youth-disconnection/.
12. For more on the meaning of *queer,* see Jessica A. Weise, "Queer," in *Encyclopedia of Queer Studies in Education,* ed. Kamden K. Strunk and Stephanie Anne Shelton (Boston: Brill, 2022), 484–89.
13. For an example of the pairing of queer and trans, see Darla Linville, "Resisting Embodied Failure: Queer and Trans Adult Allies Welcoming Queer and Trans Youth," *International Journal of Qualitative Studies in Education* 35, no. 9 (2022): 993–1006. For an example of the use of LGBTQIAS2, see Capacity Building Center for States, "Get to Know the Person in Front of You: LGBTQ-IA2S+ Youth and Families," Children's Bureau's Child Welfare Capacity Building Collaborative, 2022, https://capacity.childwelfare.gov/states/resources/know-the-person-in-front-of-you-lgbtqia2s.
14. Roderick A. Ferguson, *Aberrations in Black: Toward a Queer of Color Critique* (Minneapolis: University of Minnesota Press, 2004).
15. Cherríe Moraga and Gloria Anzaldúa, eds., *This Bridge Called My Back: Writings by Radical Women of Color,* 2nd ed. (New York: Kitchen Table: Women of Color Press, 1983); Barbara Smith, ed., *Home Girls: A Black Feminist Anthology* (New York: Kitchen Table: Women of Color Press, 1983).
16. D. L. Eng, J. Halberstam, and J. E. Muñoz, "Introduction: What's Queer About Queer Studies Now?," *Social Text* 23, nos. 3–4 (2005): 1–17; Annamarie Jagose, *Queer Theory: An Introduction* (New York: NYU Press, 1996).
17. Edward Brockenbrough, "Queer of Color Agency in Educational Contexts: Analytic Frameworks from a Queer of Color Critique," *Educational Studies* 51, no. 1 (2015): 28–44; Lance T. McCready, "Conclusion to the Special Issue: Queer of Color Analysis: Interruptions and Pedagogic Possibilities," *Curriculum Inquiry* 43, no. 4 (2013): 512–22.
18. Tomás Boatwright, "Flux Zine: Black Queer Storytelling," *Equity & Excellence in Education* 52, no. 4 (2019): 383–95; Shamari Reid, "Exploring the Agency of Black LGBTQ+ Youth in Schools and in NYC's Ballroom Culture," *Teachers College Record* 124, no. 6 (2022): 92–117; Susan Talburt, Eric Rofes, and Mary Louise Rasmussen, "Introduction: Transforming Discourses of Queer Youth and Educational Practices Surrounding Gender, Sexuality, and Youth," in *Youth and Sexualities: Pleasure, Subversion, and Insubordination In and Out of Schools,* ed. Mary Louise Rasmussen, Eric Rofes, and Susan Talburt (New York: Palgrave Macmillan, 2004), 1–13.
19. Boni Wozolek, "'It's Not Fiction, It's My Life': LGBTQ Youth of Color and Kinships in an Urban School," *Theory Into Practice* 60, no. 1 (2021): 94–102.
20. Ed Brockenbrough, "Becoming Queerly Responsive: Culturally Responsive Pedagogy for Black and Latino Urban Queer Youth," *Urban Education* 51, no. 2 (February 1, 2016): 170–96; Ed Brockenbrough, "Further Mothering: Reconceptualizing White Women Educators' Work with Black Youth," *Equity &*

*Excellence in Education* 47, no. 3 (July 3, 2014): 253–72; Ed Brockenbrough, "'We Don't See a Lot of People Like You': Black Queer Men Mentoring Black Queer Male Youth," in *Youth Sexualities: Public Feelings and Contemporary Cultural Politics,* vol. 1, ed. Susan Talburt (Santa Barbara, CA: Praeger, 2018), 229–54; Ed Brockenbrough and Tomás Boatwright, "In the MAC: Creating Safe Spaces for Transgender Youth of Color," in *Cultural Transformations: Youth and Pedagogies of Possibility,* ed. Korina Jocson (Cambridge, MA: Harvard Education Press, 2013), 165–82.
21. See Matthew R. Beymer et al., "Sex on Demand: Geosocial Networking Phone Apps and Risk of Sexually Transmitted Infections Among a Cross-Sectional Sample of Men Who Have Sex with Men in Los Angeles County," *Sexually Transmitted Infections* 90, no. 7 (2014): 567–72; Nicholas A. Grosskopf, Michael T. LeVasseur, and Debra B. Glaser, "Use of the Internet and Mobile-Based 'Apps' for Sex-Seeking Among Men Who Have Sex with Men in New York City," *American Journal of Men's Health* 8, no. 6 (2014): 510–20; Kimberly M. Nelson et al., "Sexually Explicit Online Media and Sexual Risk Among Men Who Have Sex with Men in the United States," *Archives of Sexual Behavior* 43, no. 4 (2014): 833–43.
22. danah boyd, *It's Complicated: The Social Lives of Networked Teens* (New Haven, CT: Yale University Press, 2014).
23. Mitchel J. Wharton, "Identifying Factors That Protect HIV Sero-Negative Status in Young Black Men Who Have Sex with Men" (PhD diss., University of Rochester, 2013).
24. Rodrigo Velezmoro, Charles Negy, and Jose Livia, "Online Sexual Activity: Cross-National Comparison Between United States and Peruvian College Students," *Archives of Sexual Behavior* 41, no. 4 (2012): 1015–25.
25. Tara J. Yosso, "Whose Culture Has Capital? A Critical Race Theory Discussion of Community Cultural Wealth," *Race Ethnicity and Education* 8, no. 1 (2005): 69–91.
26. Brockenbrough and Boatwright, "In the MAC."
27. Future of Sex Education Initiative, *National Sex Education Standards: Core Content and Skills, K-12,* 2nd ed. (Washington, DC: American School Health Association, 2020).

## Chapter 2

1. Ed Brockenbrough, "Becoming Queerly Responsive: Culturally Responsive Pedagogy for Black and Latino Urban Queer Youth," *Urban Education* 51, no. 2 (2016): 170–96.
2. Latrise P. Johnson, "Writing the Self: Black Queer Youth Challenge Heteronormative Ways of Being in an After-School Writing Club," *Research in the Teaching of English* 52, no. 1 (2017): 13–33; Jon Wargo, "Queer, Quare, and [Q]ulturally Sustaining," in *Critical Concepts in Queer Studies and Education:*

*An International Guide for the Twenty-First Century,* ed. Nelson M. Rodriguez et al. (New York: Palgrave Macmillan, 2016), 299–307; Jon M. Wargo, "'Every Selfie Tells a Story . . .': LGBTQ Youth Lifestreams and New Media Narratives as Connective Identity Texts," *New Media & Society* 19, no. 4 (April 2017): 560–78; Jon M. Wargo, "Lights! Cameras! Genders? Interrupting Hate Through Classroom Tinkering, Digital Media Production and [Q]ulturally Sustaining Arts-Based Inquiry," *Theory Into Practice* 58, no. 1 (2019): 18–28; Jon Wargo, "'I Don't Write So Other People Notice Me, I Write So I Can Notice Myself': Locating Queer at the Intersection of Rhetoric, Resistance, and Resource-Based Pedagogy," in *Queer, Trans, and Intersectional Theory in Educational Practice Student, Teacher, and Community Experiences,* ed. Cris Mayo and Mollie V. Blackburn (New York: Routledge, 2021), 50–63.

3. Mollie V. Blackburn and Lance T. McCready, "Voices of Queer Youth in Urban Schools: Possibilities and Limitations," *Theory Into Practice* 48, no. 3 (2009): 222–30; Durell Callier, "Gendered Violences and Queer of Color Critiques in Educational Spaces: Remembering Sakia, Carl, and Jaheem," in *Encyclopedia of Educational Philosophy and Theory,* ed. Michael A. Peters (Singapore: Springer, 2017): 914–19; Ramin Setoodeh, "Young, Gay and Murdered in Junior High," *Newsweek,* July 18, 2008, https://www.newsweek.com/young-gay-and-murdered-junior-high-92787.

4. Examples include Edward Brockenbrough, "Queer of Color Agency in Educational Contexts: Analytic Frameworks from a Queer of Color Critique," *Educational Studies* 51, no. 1 (2015): 28–44; Kia Darling-Hammond, "Queeruptions and the Question of QTPOC Thriving in Schools—An Excavation," *Equity & Excellence in Education* 52, no. 4 (2019): 424–34; Luis A. Leyva, R. Taylor McNeill, and Antonio Duran, "A Queer of Color Challenge to Neutrality in Undergraduate STEM Pedagogy as a White, Cisheteropatriarchal Space," *Journal of Women and Minorities in Science and Engineering* 28, no. 2 (2022): 79–94; Lance T. McCready, "Queeruptions, Queer of Color Analysis, Radical Action and Education Reform: An Introduction," *Equity & Excellence in Education* 52, no. 4 (October 2, 2019): 370–72.

5. Brockenbrough, "Queer of Color Agency in Educational Contexts"; Cris Mayo, "Intersections, Ambivalence, and Racial Justice in Schools: Black Queer Students Remap Complexity," *Teachers College Record* 120, no. 14 (2018): 1–22; Lance T. McCready, *Making Space for Diverse Masculinities: Difference, Intersectionality, and Engagement in an Urban High School* (New York: Peter Lang, 2010).

6. Tyrone C. Howard, "Culture," chap. 3 in *Why Race and Culture Matter in Schools: Closing the Achievement Gap in America's Classrooms,* 2nd ed. (New York: Teachers College Press, 2020).

7. Sonia Nieto, *The Light in Their Eyes: Creating Multicultural Learning Communities,* 10th anniversary ed. (New York: Teachers College Press, 2015).

8. Nieto, *The Light in Their Eyes*, 78.
9. I use *responsive* in my work because of the relationality it entails. To be responsive, practitioners must pay attention and respond to the cultural sensibilities—which, as in the definition of culture I quoted from Nieto, are ever-evolving—of the learners they serve. Yet as others have noted, *culturally relevant* and *culturally responsive* index a shared set of pedagogical concerns and actions. See Brittany Aronson and Judson Laughter, "The Theory and Practice of Culturally Relevant Education: A Synthesis of Research Across Content Areas," *Review of Educational Research* 86, no. 1 (March 1, 2016): 163–206; Felicia Moore Mensah, "Culturally Relevant and Culturally Responsive: Two Theories of Practice for Science Teaching," *Science and Children* 58, no. 4 (March–April 2021): 10–13.
10. See Gloria Ladson-Billings, *Culturally Relevant Pedagogy: Asking a Different Question* (New York: Teachers College Press, 2021); Geneva Gay, *Culturally Responsive Teaching: Theory, Research, and Practice*, 3rd ed. (New York: Teachers College Press, 2018); H. Richard Milner, "Culturally Relevant Pedagogy in a Diverse Urban Classroom," *Urban Review* 43, no. 1 (2011): 66–89; Howard, *Why Race and Culture Matter in Schools;* Ana María Villegas and Tamara Lucas, "Preparing Culturally Responsive Teachers: Rethinking the Curriculum," *Journal of Teacher Education* 53, no. 1 (2002): 20–32.
11. Ladson-Billings, *Culturally Relevant Pedagogy;* Gay, *Culturally Responsive Teaching;* Tamara Beauboeuf-Lafontant, "A Womanist Experience of Caring: Understanding the Pedagogy of Exemplary Black Women Teachers," *Urban Review* 34, no. 1 (2002): 71–86; Adrienne D. Dixson, "Let's Do This!: Black Women Teachers' Politics and Pedagogy," *Urban Education* 38, no. 2 (2003): 217–35; Carla R. Monroe, "Teachers Closing the Discipline Gap in an Urban Middle School," *Urban Education* 44, no. 3 (2009): 322–47; Marvin Lynn, "Education for the Community: Exploring the Culturally Relevant Practices of Black Male Teachers," *Teachers College Record* 108, no. 12 (2006): 2497–522.
12. H. Samy Alim and Django Paris, "What Is Culturally Sustaining Pedagogy and Why Does It Matter?," in *Culturally Sustaining Pedagogies: Teaching and Learning for Justice in a Changing World,* ed. Django Paris and H. Samy Alim (New York: Teachers College Press, 2017), 4.
13. Alim and Paris, "What Is Culturally Sustaining Pedagogy and Why Does It Matter?," 5.
14. Wargo, "Queer, Quare, and [Q]ulturally Sustaining"; Wargo, "Lights! Cameras! Genders?"; Wargo, "'I Don't Write So Other People Notice Me, I Write So I Can Notice Myself.'"
15. Wargo, "'I Don't Write So Other People Notice Me, I Write So I Can Notice Myself'"; Wargo, "Lights! Cameras! Genders?"
16. Although I focus on US-based scholarship, some of McCready's work on BQY reaches into Canada as well. See Lance T. McCready, "Conclusion to the

Special Issue: Queer of Color Analysis: Interruptions and Pedagogic Possibilities," *Curriculum Inquiry* 43, no. 4 (September 1, 2013): 512–22; Lance McCready, "A Double Life: Black Queer Youth Coming of Age in Divided Cities," *Educational Forum* 79, no. 4 (2015): 353–58.
17. Zaretta Hammond, "5 Common Myths About Culturally Responsive Pedagogy," *Culturally Responsive Teaching and the Brain* (blog), July 18, 2012, https://crtandthebrain.com/5-common-myths-about-culturally-responsive-pedagogy/; Howard, *Why Race and Culture Matter in Schools*.
18. Howard, *Why Race and Culture Matter in Schools*.
19. For explanations of being a "warm demander," see Franita Ware, "Warm Demander Pedagogy: Culturally Responsive Teaching That Supports a Culture of Achievement for African American Students," *Urban Education* 41, no. 4 (2006): 427–56; Amy Carpenter Ford and Kelly Sassi, "Authority in Cross-Racial Teaching and Learning: (Re)Considering the Transferability of Warm Demander Approaches," *Urban Education* 49, no. 1 (2014): 39–74.
20. In addition to using Howard's work, I encourage pre-service teachers to consider the guiding principles for culturally responsive pedagogy in the following texts: Ladson-Billings, *Culturally Relevant Pedagogy;* Gay, *Culturally Responsive Teaching;* Aronson and Laughter, "The Theory and Practice of Culturally Relevant Education."
21. Howard, *Why Race and Culture Matter in Schools;* Aronson and Laughter, "The Theory and Practice of Culturally Relevant Education."
22. Beauboeuf-Lafontant, "A Womanist Experience of Caring"; Rosalie Rolón-Dow, "Critical Care: A Color(full) Analysis of Care Narratives in the Schooling Experiences of Puerto Rican Girls," *American Educational Research Journal* 42, no. 1 (2005): 77–111; Mia Angélica Sosa-Provencio, "A 'Revolucionista' Ethic of Care: Four Mexicana Educators' Subterraneous Social Justice Revolution of Fighting and Feeding," *American Educational Research Journal* 56, no. 4 (2019): 1113–47; Angela Valenzuela, *Subtractive Schooling: U.S.-Mexican Youth and the Politics of Caring* (New York: SUNY Press, 1999).
23. Andrea del Carmen Vázquez, "Joaquin's Refusal: An Embodied and Geographic Active Subjectivity," *Journal of the Association of Mexican American Educators* 14, no. 2 (2020): 87–104; Johnson, "Writing the Self"; Therese M. Quinn, "'You Make Me Erect!': Queer Girls of Color Negotiating Heteronormative Leadership at an Urban All-Girls' Public School," *Journal of Gay & Lesbian Issues in Education* 4, no. 3 (2007): 31–47; Savannah Shange, "Play Aunties and Dyke Bitches: Gender, Generation, and the Ethics of Black Queer Kinship," *Black Scholar* 49, no. 1 (2019): 40–54; Wargo, "'I Don't Write So Other People Notice Me, I Write So I Can Notice Myself.'"
24. Cindy Cruz, "LGBTQ Youth of Color Video Making as Radical Curriculum: A Brother Mourning His Brother and a Theory in the Flesh," *Curriculum Inquiry* 43, no. 4 (2013): 441–60; Shange, "Play Aunties and Dyke Bitches."

25. del Carmen Vázquez, "Joaquin's Refusal," 9.
26. Tomás Boatwright, "Flux Zine: Black Queer Storytelling," *Equity & Excellence in Education* 52, no. 4 (2019): 383–95; Mollie V. Blackburn, "Disrupting the (Hetero)Normative: Exploring Literacy Performances and Identity Work with Queer Youth," *Journal of Adolescent & Adult Literacy* 46, no. 4 (December 2002–January 2003): 312–24; Mollie Blackburn, "Exploring Literacy Performances and Power Dynamics at the Loft: 'Queer Youth Reading the World and the Word,'" *Research in the Teaching of English* 37, no. 4 (2003): 467–90; Mollie V. Blackburn, "Agency in Borderland Discourses: Examining Language Use in a Community Center with Black Queer Youth," *Teachers College Record* 107, no. 1 (2005): 89–113; Ed Brockenbrough, "Further Mothering: Reconceptualizing White Women Educators' Work with Black Youth," *Equity & Excellence* 47, no. 3 (July 3, 2014): 253–72; Brockenbrough, "Becoming Queerly Responsive"; Ed Brockenbrough and Tomás Boatwright, "In the MAC: Creating Safe Spaces for Transgender Youth of Color," in *Cultural Transformations: Youth and Pedagogies of Possibility,* ed. Korina Jocson (Cambridge, MA: Harvard Education Press, 2013), 165–82.
27. Shamari Reid, "Exploring the Agency of Black LGBTQ+ Youth in Schools and in NYC's Ballroom Culture," *Teachers College Record* 124, no. 6 (2022): 92–117; Shamari Reid, "Using a Queer of Color Critique to Work Toward a Black LGBTQ+ Inclusive K–12 Curriculum," *Curriculum Inquiry* 53, no. 2 (March 15, 2023): 105–25; Brockenbrough, "Becoming Queerly Responsive." See also Marlon M. Bailey, *Butch Queens Up in Pumps: Gender, Performance, and Ballroom Culture in Detroit* (Ann Arbor: University of Michigan Press, 2013); Philadelphia Inquirer, "LEGENDARY: 30 Years of Philly Ballroom," YouTube video, 18:42, December 10, 2019, https://www.youtube.com/watch?v=t6EaBvrV6QI; Ricky Tucker, *And the Category Is . . . : Inside New York's Vogue, House, and Ballroom Community* (Boston: Beacon Press, 2022). *Houses* are kinship groups that emerged in urban Black and Latinx LGBTQ+ communities over the last third of the twentieth century. Usually headed by house *mothers* or *fathers*—surrogate parental figures who mentor and care for younger community members—houses compete against one another in performative, pageant-like *balls,* hence the name *House Ball* community.
28. Brockenbrough, "Further Mothering"; Brockenbrough, "Becoming Queerly Responsive"; Michael D. Bartone, "'Nothing Has Stopped Me. I Keep Going:' Black Gay Narratives," *Journal of LGBT Youth* 14, no. 3 (2017): 317–29; Blackburn, "Agency in Borderland Discourses"; Quinn, "'You Make Me Erect!'"
29. Bailey, *Butch Queens Up in Pumps;* Brockenbrough, "Becoming Queerly Responsive"; Ed Brockenbrough, "'We Don't See a Lot of People Like You': Black Queer Men Mentoring Black Queer Male Youth," in *Youth Sexualities: Public Feelings and Contemporary Cultural Politics,* vol. 1, ed. Susan Talburt

(Santa Barbara, CA: Praeger, 2018), 229–54; Cindy Cruz, "Notes on Immigration, Youth, and Ethnographic Silence," *Theory Into Practice* 47, no. 1 (2008): 67–73; del Carmen Vázquez, "Joaquin's Refusal"; Johnson, "Writing the Self"; Shange, "Play Aunties and Dyke Bitches"; Boni Wozolek, "'It's Not Fiction, It's My Life': LGBTQ Youth of Color and Kinships in an Urban School," *Theory Into Practice* 60, no. 1 (2021): 94–102.
30. Brockenbrough and Boatwright, "In the MAC," 177.
31. Boatwright, "Flux Zine"; del Carmen Vázquez, "Joaquin's Refusal"; Reid, "Exploring the Agency of Black LGBTQ+ Youth in Schools and in NYC's Ballroom Culture"; Wozolek, "'It's Not Fiction, It's My Life'"; Bailey, *Butch Queens Up in Pumps;* Brockenbrough, "Further Mothering"; Tucker, *And the Category Is. . . .*
32. Brockenbrough, "Further Mothering"; Brockenbrough, "Becoming Queerly Responsive."
33. Wozolek, "'It's Not Fiction, It's My Life.'"
34. Brockenbrough, "Queer of Color Agency in Educational Contexts"; Mayo, "Intersections, Ambivalence, and Racial Justice in Schools"; McCready, *Making Space for Diverse Masculinities.*
35. Blackburn, "Agency in Borderland Discourses"; Boatwright, "Flux Zine"; Reid, "Exploring the Agency of Black LGBTQ+ Youth in Schools and in NYC's Ballroom Culture"; Susan Talburt, Eric Rofes, and Mary Louise Rasmussen, "Introduction: Transforming Discourses of Queer Youth and Educational Practices Surrounding Gender, Sexuality, and Youth," in *Youth and Sexualities: Pleasure, Subversion, and Insubordination In and Out of Schools,* ed. Mary Louise Rasmussen, Eric Rofes, and Susan Talburt (New York: Palgrave Macmillan, 2004), 1–13.
36. This applies to practically all of the scholarship on QYC cited throughout this chapter.
37. For analyses of hegemonic constructions of masculinity and femininity, see Callier, "Gendered Violences and Queer of Color Critiques in Educational Spaces"; McCready, *Making Space for Diverse Masculinities;* Quinn, "'You Make Me Erect!'"; Joan Ariki Varney, "Undressing the Normal: Community Efforts for Queer Asian and Asian American Youth," in *Troubling Intersections of Race and Sexuality: Queer Students of Color and Anti-Oppressive Education,* ed. Kevin K. Kumashiro (Lanham, MD: Rowman and Littlefield, 2001), 87–103; Sabina Vaught, "The Talented Tenth: Gay Black Boys and the Racial Politics of Southern Schooling," *Journal of Gay & Lesbian Issues in Education* 2, no. 2 (2004): 5–26. Examples of the increased attention to transphobia include Blackburn, "Exploring Literacy Performances and Power Dynamics at the Loft"; Brockenbrough and Boatwright, "In the MAC"; Louis F. Graham, "Navigating Community Institutions: Black Transgender Women's Experiences in Schools, the Criminal Justice System, and Churches," *Sexuality Research &*

*Social Policy* 11, no. 4 (2014): 274–87; Reid, "Using a Queer of Color Critique to Work Toward a Black LGBTQ+ Inclusive K–12 Curriculum."
38. Blackburn and McCready, "Voices of Queer Youth in Urban Schools"; Sam Stiegler, "Under the Trees in Lincoln Center: Queer and Trans Homeless Youth Coming Together in the City," *Equity & Excellence in Education* 52, no. 4 (2019): 373–82; Veronica Terriquez, "Intersectional Mobilization, Social Movement Spillover, and Queer Youth Leadership in the Immigrant Rights Movement," *Social Problems* 62, no. 3 (2015): 343–62.
39. Blackburn, "Exploring Literacy Performances and Power Dynamics at the Loft"; Blackburn and McCready, "Voices of Queer Youth in Urban Schools"; Cindy Cruz, "LGBTQ Street Youth Talk Back: A Meditation on Resistance and Witnessing," *International Journal of Qualitative Studies in Education* 24, no. 5 (2011): 547–58; Cruz, "LGBTQ Youth of Color Video Making as Radical Curriculum"; Graham, "Navigating Community Institutions"; Stiegler, "Under the Trees in Lincoln Center"; Sam Stiegler, "Walking to the Pier and Back," *Qualitative Inquiry* 28, no. 2 (February 1, 2022): 200–208; Kai Wright, *Drifting Toward Love: Black, Brown, Gay, and Coming of Age on the Streets of New York* (Boston: Beacon Press, 2008).
40. Bailey, *Butch Queens Up in Pumps;* Brockenbrough and Boatwright, "In the MAC"; Cruz, "LGBTQ Youth of Color Video Making as Radical Curriculum"; Graham, "Navigating Community Institutions"; Stiegler, "Under the Trees in Lincoln Center"; Wright, *Drifting Toward Love.*
41. Johnson, "Writing the Self"; Wargo, "'I Don't Write So Other People Notice Me, I Write So I Can Notice Myself.'"
42. Quinn, "'You Make Me Erect!'"
43. Cruz, "LGBTQ Youth of Color Video Making as Radical Curriculum"; Blackburn, "Disrupting the (Hetero)Normative"; Blackburn, "Agency in Borderland Discourses"; Boatwright, "Flux Zine."
44. Blackburn, "Disrupting the (Hetero)Normative," 317.
45. Johnson, "Writing the Self"; Wargo, "'I Don't Write So Other People Notice Me, I Write So I Can Notice Myself.'"
46. Shange, "Play Aunties and Dyke Bitches."
47. Reid, "Using a Queer of Color Critique to Work Toward a Black LGBTQ+ Inclusive K–12 Curriculum."
48. As a reminder, I defined agency in chapter 1 as the degree to which BQY can determine their actions and shape their sense of self at the intersections of white supremacy, cisheteronormativity, adultism, and other hierarchies that produce their alterity. This builds on Wozolek's work with BQY, in which agency is defined as a contingent phenomenon negotiated with other actors amidst the power dynamics of a given time and place, ultimately producing shifting degrees of determination over one's actions and being. See Wozolek, "'It's Not Fiction, It's My Life.'"

49. Dominique Johnson, "'This Is Political!' Negotiating the Legacies of the First School-Based Gay Youth Group," *Children, Youth and Environments* 17, no. 2 (2007): 380–87.
50. Johnson, "'This Is Political!'"; Stephan Cohen, "Liberationists, Clients, Activists: Queer Youth Organizing, 1966–2003," *Journal of Gay & Lesbian Issues in Education* 2, no. 3 (2005): 67–86.
51. del Carmen Vázquez, "Joaquin's Refusal"; Quinn, "'You Make Me Erect!'"
52. Quinn, "'You Make Me Erect!'"
53. McCready, *Making Space for Diverse Masculinities*.
54. Blackburn, "Exploring Literacy Performances and Power Dynamics at the Loft"; Blackburn and McCready, "Voices of Queer Youth in Urban Schools"; McCready, *Making Space for Diverse Masculinities*.
55. Susan Driver, *Queer Youth Cultures* (Albany, NY: SUNY Press, 2008); Terriquez, "Intersectional Mobilization, Social Movement Spillover, and Queer Youth Leadership in the Immigrant Rights Movement."
56. Examples include the following: GSA Network (https://gsanetwork.org/); "Texas GSA Network," Out Youth, accessed July 11, 2023, https://www.outyouth.org/txgsa; GLYS WNY [Growing LGBTQ+ Youth Support, Western New York] (https://www.glyswny.org/); "Massachusetts Gender and Sexuality Alliance (GSA) Leadership Council: What Is the GSA Leadership Council?," Massachusetts Department of Elementary and Secondary Education, May 3, 2023, https://www.doe.mass.edu/sfs/lgbtq/gsalcouncil.html.
57. Johnson, "Writing the Self."
58. Blackburn, "Exploring Literacy Performances and Power Dynamics at the Loft"; Brockenbrough and Boatwright, "In the MAC."
59. Blackburn, "Agency in Borderland Discourses."
60. Shange, "Play Aunties and Dyke Bitches"; Wargo, "'I Don't Write So Other People Notice Me, I Write So I Can Notice Myself.'" For discussions of femiphobia and hegemonic masculinity politics in queer cultures, see Jay Clarkson, "Contesting Masculinity's Makeover: Queer Eye, Consumer Masculinity, and 'Straight-Acting' Gays," *Journal of Communication Inquiry* 29, no. 3 (2005): 235–55; Brooke E. Love, "Lesbians, Masculinities, and Privilege: The Privileging of Gender and the Gendering of Sexuality," *Dissenting Voices* 5 (Spring 2016): 1–24.
61. Shange, "Play Aunties and Dyke Bitches," 40.
62. Cindy Cruz, "Toward an Epistemology of a Brown Body," *International Journal of Qualitative Studies in Education* 14, no. 5 (2001): 665.
63. Cindy Cruz, "LGBTQ Street Youth Doing Resistance in Infrapolitical Worlds," in *Youth Resistance Research and Theories of Change*, ed. Eve Tuck and K. Wayne Yang (New York: Routledge, 2013), 209–17.
64. Varney, "Undressing the Normal"; Brockenbrough and Boatwright, "In the MAC."

65. Blackburn, "Exploring Literacy Performances and Power Dynamics at the Loft"; del Carmen Vázquez, "Joaquin's Refusal"; Shange, "Play Aunties and Dyke Bitches."
66. See Kimberly Cosier, "Creating Safe Schools for Queer Youth," in *Handbook of Social Justice in Education*, ed. William Ayers, Therese Quinn, and David Stovall (New York: Routledge, 2009), 285–303; Emily S. Fisher and Karen Komosa-Hawkins, eds., *Creating Safe and Supportive Learning Environments: A Guide for Working with Lesbian, Gay, Bisexual, Transgender, and Questioning Youth and Families* (New York: Routledge, 2013); GLSEN, *Safe Space Kit: A Guide to Supporting Lesbian, Gay, Bisexual, Transgender, and Queer Students in Your School*, 2019, https://www.glsen.org/sites/default/files/2019-11/GLSEN%20English%20SafeSpace%20Book%20Text%20Updated%202019.pdf.
67. See Brian Arao and Kristi Clemens, "From Safe Spaces to Brave Spaces: A New Way to Frame Dialogue Around Diversity and Social Justice," in *The Art of Effective Facilitation: Reflections from Social Justice Educators*, ed. Lisa M. Landreman (Sterling, VA: Stylus, 2013), 135–50; "Safer Space Policy/Community Agreements," The Anti-Oppression Network, accessed September 5, 2023, https://theantioppressionnetwork.com/resources/saferspacepolicy/; SACE: Sexual Assault Centre of Edmonton, "Creating a Safer Space Program," July 2020, https://www.sace.ca/wp-content/uploads/2020/07/Safer-Spaces.pdf; Timothy J. San Pedro, "'This Stuff Interests Me': Re-Centering Indigenous Paradigms in Colonizing Schooling Spaces," in Paris and Alim, *Culturally Sustaining Pedagogies*, 99–116.
68. See GLSEN, "Building an Inclusive GSA," February 2023, https://www.glsen.org/sites/default/files/2023-02/GLSEN_GSA_Resources_2023_Building_Inclusive_GSA.pdf; ImFromDriftwood, "Woman Stands Up Against Biphobia in the LGBTQ Community: 'I Have to Be Who I Am,'" YouTube video, 7:05, February 26, 2020, https://www.youtube.com/watch?v=UzZYgIzK1O8; Cut, "Do Lesbians & Gay Men Think the Same Way?," YouTube video, 5:57, December 7, 2022, https://www.youtube.com/watch?v=iVr9fGZHGF4.
69. Blackburn, "Exploring Literacy Performances and Power Dynamics at the Loft"; McCready, *Making Space for Diverse Masculinities;* Quinn, "'You Make Me Erect!'"
70. Bailey, *Butch Queens Up in Pumps;* Brockenbrough, "Becoming Queerly Responsive."
71. Terriquez, "Intersectional Mobilization, Social Movement Spillover, and Queer Youth Leadership in the Immigrant Rights Movement"; Driver, *Queer Youth Cultures.*
72. Eric Blanc, "The Chicago Teachers' Strike Ten Years On: Organizing for the Common Good, Then and Now," *New Labor Forum,* August 2022, https://

newlaborforum.cuny.edu/2022/08/15/the-chicago-teachers-strike-ten-years-on-organizing-for-the-common-good-then-and-now/.
73. Blanc, "The Chicago Teachers' Strike Ten Years On."
74. Rhiannon Maton, "WE Learn Together: Philadelphia Educators Putting Social Justice Unionism Principles into Practice," *Workplace: A Journal for Academic Labor* 26 (2016): 5–19; Farima Pour-Khorshid, "Cultivating Sacred Spaces: A Racial Affinity Group Approach to Support Critical Educators of Color," *Teaching Education* 29, no. 4 (2018): 318–29. See also the Teacher Activists Groups website: https://teacheractivists.org/.
75. Deborah P. Britzman, "Is There a Queer Pedagogy? Or, Stop Reading Straight," *Educational Theory* 45, no. 2 (June 1995): 151–65; Deborah P. Britzman, "Queer Pedagogy and Its Strange Techniques," *Counterpoints* 367 (2012): 292–308; Susanne Luhmann, "Queering/Querying Pedagogy? Or, Pedagogy Is a Pretty Queer Thing," in *Queer Theory in Education,* ed. W. Pinar (Mahwah, NJ: Lawrence Erlbaum Associates, 1998), 141–55; Cris Mayo and Nelson M. Rodriguez, eds., *Queer Pedagogies: Theory, Praxis, Politics* (Cham, Switzerland: Springer Nature, 2019).
76. Britzman, "Is There a Queer Pedagogy?"; Mayo and Rodriguez, *Queer Pedagogies.*

## Chapter 3

1. See Jeremy Hubbard, "Fifth Gay Teen Suicide in Three Weeks Sparks Debate," *ABC News,* October 3, 2010, https://abcnews.go.com/US/gay-teen-suicide-sparks-debate/story?id=11788128; Jesse McKinley, "Suicides Put Light on Pressures of Gay Teenagers," *New York Times,* October 4, 2010, https://www.nytimes.com/2010/10/04/us/04suicide.html.
2. See Mary Louise Kelly, Melissa Block, and Dan Savage, "Dan Savage's Message to Gay Youth: 'It Gets Better,'" *NPR,* October 12, 2010, https://www.npr.org/templates/story/story.php?storyId=130519806.
3. Elizabethe Payne and Melissa Smith, "LGBTQ Kids, School Safety, and Missing the Big Picture: How the Dominant Bullying Discourse Prevents School Professionals from Thinking about Systemic Marginalization or . . . Why We Need to Rethink LGBTQ Bullying," *QED: A Journal in GLBTQ Worldmaking* (Fall 2013): 1–36; Elizabethe C. Payne and Melissa J. Smith, "Safety, Celebration, and Risk: Educator Responses to LGBTQ Professional Development," *Teaching Education* 23, no. 3 (2012): 265–85.
4. Payne and Smith, "LGBTQ Kids, School Safety, and Missing the Big Picture"; Sandra J. Schmidt, "Un/Scripting Queer Subjectivity: Queer Futures Envisioned in 'It Gets Better,'" *High School Journal* 105, no. 1 (2021): 43–59; Jacqueline Ullman, "Breaking Out of the (Anti)Bullying 'Box': NYC Educators Discuss Trans/Gender Diversity-Inclusive Policies and Curriculum," *Sex Education* 18, no. 5 (2018): 495–510.

5. Josephine Lee, "A 'Dark Vision' of Discipline: Zero Tolerance Makes a Comeback," *Texas Observer,* March 10, 2023, https://www.texasobserver.org/zero-tolerance-makes-a-comeback/; Patrick Wall, "Lawmakers Across U.S. Push for Harsher School Discipline as Safety Fears Rise," Chalkbeat, March 30, 2023, https://www.chalkbeat.org/2023/3/28/23658974/school-discipline-violence-safety-state-law-suspensions-restorative-justice.
6. Kimberlé Crenshaw, Priscilla Ocen, and Jyoti Nanda, *Black Girls Matter: Pushed Out, Overpoliced and Underprotected,* African American Policy Forum, 2015, https://www.aapf.org/_files/ugd/b77e03_e92d6e80f7034f30bf843ea7068f52d6.pdf; Erica R. Meiners, "The Problem Child: Provocations Toward Dismantling the Carceral State," *Harvard Educational Review* 87, no. 1 (2017): 122–46.
7. Tara J. Yosso, "Whose Culture Has Capital? A Critical Race Theory Discussion of Community Cultural Wealth," *Race Ethnicity and Education* 8, no. 1 (2005): 69–91.
8. Stellan Vinthagen, "Editorial: An Invitation to Develop 'Resistance Studies,'" *Journal of Resistance Studies* 1, no. 1 (2015): 5–17; Sarah Murru and Abel Polese, *Resistances: Between Theories and the Field* (London: Rowman and Littlefield, 2020); Terence Renaud, "Seminar Syllabus: HUMS 287/HIST 455J/WGSS 347/GMAN 373: Resistance in Theory & Practice," Yale University, 2020, https://humanities.yale.edu/sites/default/files/files/Syllabus%20-%20Resistance%20SP20.pdf.
9. Eve Tuck and K. Wayne Yang, eds., *Youth Resistance Research and Theories of Change* (New York: Routledge, 2013); Ken McGrew, "A Review of Class-Based Theories of Student Resistance in Education: Mapping the Origins and Influence of Learning to Labor by Paul Willis," *Review of Educational Research* 81, no. 2 (2011): 234–66; Boni Wozolek, *Black Lives Matter in US Schools: Race, Education, and Resistance* (Albany, NY: SUNY Press, 2022); Brandon Andrew Robinson and Rachel M. Schmitz, "Beyond Resilience: Resistance in the Lives of LGBTQ Youth," *Sociology Compass* 15, no. 12 (2021): Article e12947.
10. Yosso, "Whose Culture Has Capital?"
11. Yosso, "Whose Culture Has Capital?," 77.
12. See Rebeca Burciaga and Rita Kohli, "Disrupting Whitestream Measures of Quality Teaching: The Community Cultural Wealth of Teachers of Color," *Multicultural Perspectives* 20, no. 1 (2018): 5–12; Jihea Maddamsetti, "Navigating Emotion Work by Using Community Cultural Wealth: Student Teaching Experiences of Teacher Candidates of Color," *Equity & Excellence in Education* 54, no. 3 (2021): 252–70; Stacy D. Saathoff, "Funds of Knowledge and Community Cultural Wealth: Exploring How Pre-Service Teachers Can Work Effectively with Mexican and Mexican American Students," *Critical Questions in Education* 6, no. 1 (2015): 30–40; Erin Crosby, "Leveraging Students'

Community Cultural Wealth," *At The Center* (blog), March 14, 2017, https://blog.smu.edu/atthecenter/2017/03/14/leveraging-students-community-cultural-wealth/; WeTeachNYC, "Recognizing and Honoring Community Cultural Wealth," accessed July 21, 2023, https://www.weteachnyc.org/resources/resource/recognizing-and-honoring-community-cultural-wealth-during-remote-learning/.

13. Yosso, "Whose Culture Has Capital?," 80.
14. Yosso, "Whose Culture Has Capital?"
15. For undergraduate contexts, see Renata A. Revelo and Lorenzo D. Baber, "Engineering Resistors: Engineering Latina/o Students and Emerging Resistant Capital," *Journal of Hispanic Higher Education* 17, no. 3 (2018): 249–69; Erica Morales, "'Beasting' at the Battleground: Black Students Responding to Racial Microaggressions in Higher Education," *Journal of Diversity in Higher Education* 14, no. 1 (2021): 72–83. For graduate contexts, see Michelle M. Espino, "Exploring the Role of Community Cultural Wealth in Graduate School Access and Persistence for Mexican American PhDs," *American Journal of Education* 120, no. 4 (2014): 545–74; Tatiana Pumaccahua and Margaret R. Rogers, "Academic Warriors: Community Cultural Wealth Among Latinx and Black STEM Doctoral Students at Predominately White Institutions," *Journal of Latinos and Education* 22, no. 5 (2023), 1870–84. For teacher preparation contexts, see Gisela Ernst-Slavit et al., "Latina Paraeducators' Stories of Resistance, Resilience, and Adaptation in an Alternative Route to Teaching Program," *Journal of Career Development* 49, no. 5 (2022): 1021–38; Angelica Monarrez, Amy Wagler, and Ron Wagler, "Latinx STEM Teacher Formation Through a Cultural Wealth Lens," *Journal of Hispanic Higher Education* 20, no. 2 (2021): 164–78. For K–12 student contexts, see Erin L. Papa, "Using Photovoice as a Tool for Advocacy and Policy Change," *Journal of Southeast Asian American Educational Advancement* 14, no. 1 (2019): 1–23; Jason Salisbury, "'It'll Make My Brother's Education Better Than Mine. We Need That.': Youth of Color Activating Their Community Cultural Wealth for Transformative Change," *Leadership and Policy in Schools* 21, no. 3 (2022): 522–42.
16. For the college selection process, see Marcela G. Cuellar, "Creating Hispanic-Serving Institutions (HSIs) and Emerging HSIs: Latina/o College Choice at 4-Year Institutions," *American Journal of Education* 125, no. 2 (2019): 231–58. For out-of-school and informal learning contexts, see Amy Wilson-Lopez and Jorge Acosta-Feliz, "Transnational Latinx Youths' Workplace Funds of Knowledge and Implications for Assets-Based, Equity-Oriented Engineering Education," *Journal of Pre-College Engineering Education Research* 11, no. 1 (2021): Article 7; Bobby Habig, Preeti Gupta, and Jennifer D. Adams, "Disrupting Deficit Narratives in Informal Science Education: Applying Community

Cultural Wealth Theory to Youth Learning and Engagement," *Cultural Studies of Science Education* 16, no. 2 (2021): 509–48.

17. Summer Melody Pennell, "Queer Cultural Capital: Implications for Education," *Race Ethnicity and Education* 19, no. 2 (2016): 324–38; Summer Melody Pennell, "Transitional Memoirs: Reading Using a Queer Cultural Capital Model," in *Teaching, Affirming, and Recognizing Trans and Gender Creative Youth: A Queer Literacy Framework,* ed. S. J. Miller (New York: Palgrave Macmillan, 2016), 199–230; Summer M. Pennell, "Queer Transgressive Cultural Capital," in *Critical Concepts in Queer Studies and Education: An International Guide for the Twenty-First Century,* ed. Nelson M. Rodriguez et al. (New York: Palgrave Macmillan, 2016), 319–28; Antonio Duran and David Pérez II, "The Multiple Roles of Chosen Familia: Exploring the Interconnections of Queer Latino Men's Community Cultural Wealth," *International Journal of Qualitative Studies in Education* 32, no. 1 (2019): 67–84.

18. See Jennifer DeClue, "Theorize for What? Reading Black Queer Film and Popular Culture," *Palimpsest* 9, no. 2 (2020): 43–54, 61–62; Tadashi Dozono, "Queer of Color Literacies as Subversive Reading Practice: How Queer Students of Color Subvert Power in the Classroom," *Equity & Excellence in Education* 56, nos. 1–2 (2023): 28–41; Jafari S. Allen, *There's a Disco Ball Between Us: A Theory of Black Gay Life* (Durham, NC: Duke University Press, 2022).

19. My emphasis is on reading that pushes back against anti-queerness, but the practice can be deployed against other forms of oppression as well.

20. E. Patrick Johnson, "Snap! Culture: A Different Kind of 'Reading,'" *Text and Performance Quarterly* 15, no. 2 (1995): 125.

21. Henry Louis Gates Jr., *The Signifying Monkey: A Theory of African American Literary Criticism* (New York: Oxford University Press, 2014); Claudia Mitchell-Kernan, "Signifying, Loud-Talking and Marking," in *Signifyin(g), Sanctifyin', & Slam Dunking: A Reader in African American Expressive Culture,* ed. Gena Dagel Caponi (Amherst: University of Massachusetts Press, 1999), 309–30; Joseph A. Guzman, "Talking Shit, Egos, and Tough Skin: Humor Among Elite Black Men," *Journal of Contemporary Ethnography* 49, no. 5 (2020): 613–37. *Dozens* and *signifying* are playful yet competitive forms of teasing in Black culture that, like reading, demonstrate the speakers' quick wit and performativity. Though they have the potential to become antagonistic, they are not used to challenge anti-queerness in the way that reading is deployed by Black queer speakers.

22. *Pose,* series 2, episode 9, "Life's a Beach," directed by Gwyneth Horder-Payton, aired August 13, 2019, FX Productions.

23. Jeremy Helligar, "'Pose' Highlights the Beauty of Being Queer, Gifted, and Black," *LEVEL,* June 8, 2021, https://level.medium.com/pose-made-history-by-giving-queer-talents-of-color-the-spotlight-656025f27f93.

24. Horder-Payton, "Life's a Beach."
25. "Elektra Reading a Transphobe for Filth—Full Scene | Pose," episode 2, "Life's a Beach," directed by Gwyneth Horder-Payton, written by Janet Mock and Our Lady J, August 12, 2019, FX Network, YouTube video, 1:57, October 6, 2020, https://www.youtube.com/watch?v=O_17-LX36Io.
26. For more examples of reading, see Kid Fury and Crissle, "Hit the Road, Jack," April 13, 2023, in *The Read,* produced by Avalon Television, podcast, MP3 audio, 1:56:07, https://www.podparadise.com/Podcast/619369512/Listen/1681410111/0; *Paris Is Burning,* directed by Jennie Livingston (United States: Academy Entertainment / Off White Productions, 1990); "Ima Read," Tidal, track 1 on Zebra Katz and Njena Reddd Foxxx, *Ima Read,* Mad Decent, 2012, https://tidal.com/browse/track/241880531; *Tongues Untied,* directed by Marlon Riggs (United States: Frameline, California Newsreel, 1989). For discussions and examples of shade, see Seth E. Davis, "Shade: Literacy Narratives at Black Gay Pride," *Literacy in Composition Studies* 7, no. 2 (2019): 56–89; Livingston, *Paris Is Burning;* E. Patrick Johnson, ed., *No Tea, No Shade: New Writings in Black Queer Studies* (Durham, NC: Duke University Press, 2016).
27. Mollie V. Blackburn, "Agency in Borderland Discourses: Examining Language Use in a Community Center with Black Queer Youth," *Teachers College Record* 107, no. 1 (2005): 106.
28. See Durell Callier, "Gendered Violences and Queer of Color Critiques in Educational Spaces: Remembering Sakia, Carl, and Jaheem," in *Encyclopedia of Educational Philosophy and Theory,* ed. Michael A. Peters (Singapore: Springer, 2017), 914–19; Lala B. Holston-Zannell, "Black Trans Women Are Being Murdered in the Streets. Now the Trump Administration Wants to Turn Us Away from Shelters and Health Care," American Civil Liberties Union, May 24, 2019, https://www.aclu.org/news/lgbtq-rights/black-trans-women-are-being-murdered-streets-now-trump; National Black Justice Coalition, "LGBTQ Violence," accessed July 21, 2023, https://nbjc.org/category/nbjc-issues-lgbtq-violence/; Gabrielle Orum Hernández and Chris Barcelos, "Queer Punishments: School Safety and Youth of Color in the United States," *Equity & Excellence in Education* 56, nos. 1–2 (2023): 87–99; Orion Rummler, "LGBTQ+ People of Color Face Greatest Risk from Spike in Hate Crimes. Why Doesn't FBI Data Include Them?," *Nextgov/FCW,* September 3, 2021, https://www.nextgov.com/digital-government/2021/09/lgbtq-people-color-face-greatest-risk-spike-hate-crimes-why-doesnt-fbi-data-include-them/185074/; Vanessa Taylor, "'Safety Isn't Just Physical': How Martial Arts Can Help Black Queer People Build Every Kind of Strength," *Mic,* June 30, 2021, https://www.mic.com/impact/safety-isnt-just-physical-how-martial-arts-can-help-black-queer-people-build-every-kind-of-strength-81524487.
29. *Check It,* directed by Dana Flor and Toby Oppenheimer (United States: Olive Productions / RadicalMedia, 2016).

30. Flor and Oppenheimer, *Check It.*
31. See Taylor, "'Safety Isn't Just Physical'"; *Noah's Arc,* series 2, episode 7, "Baby, Can I Hold You," directed by Mina Shum, aired September 27, 2006, on Logo; Eva Reign, "Meet the Organizers Offering Self-Defense Tools and Training to the Trans Community," *Them,* January 11, 2021, https://www.them.us/story/in-bloom-thorn-molasses-offering-self-defense-tools-training-trans-community.
32. For a discussion of chosen family, see Boni Wozolek, "'It's Not Fiction, It's My Life': LGBTQ Youth of Color and Kinships in an Urban School," *Theory Into Practice* 60, no. 1 (2021): 94–102.
33. Nhan L. Truong, Adrian D. Zongrone, and Joseph G. Kosciw, *Erasure and Resilience: The Experiences of LGBTQ Students of Color—Black LGBTQ Youth in U.S. Schools* (New York: GLSEN, 2020).
34. GSA Network and Crossroads Collaborative at the University of Arizona, *LGBTQ+ Youth of Color: Discipline Disparities, School Push-Out, and the School-to-Prison Pipeline,* n.d., https://gsanetwork.org/wp-content/uploads/2018/08/LGBTQ_brief_FINAL.pdf.
35. NBJConTheMove, "Black LGBTQ+/SGL Thriving in Schools, Part I," YouTube video, 106:59, March 19, 2021, https://www.youtube.com/watch?v=UKSi3gIXG2E.
36. NBJConTheMove, "Black LGBTQ+/SGL Thriving in Schools, Part I."
37. See Duran and Pérez, "The Multiple Roles of Chosen Familia"; Salisbury, "'It'll Make My Brother's Education Better Than Mine'"; Blanca E. Rincón and Sarah Rodriguez, "Latinx Students Charting Their Own STEM Pathways: How Community Cultural Wealth Informs Their STEM Identities," *Journal of Hispanic Higher Education* 20, no. 2 (2021): 149–63.
38. See Papa, "Using Photovoice as a Tool for Advocacy and Policy Change"; Morales, "'Beasting' at the Battleground."
39. See nn. 8 and 9 above.
40. To protect the anonymity of study participants, I do not cite any data sources on Midtown, as those sources would reveal Midtown's actual name.
41. Therese M. Quinn, "'You Make Me Erect!': Queer Girls of Color Negotiating Heteronormative Leadership at an Urban All-Girls' Public School," *Journal of Gay & Lesbian Issues in Education* 4, no. 3 (2007): 31–47; Mollie V. Blackburn and Lance T. McCready, "Voices of Queer Youth in Urban Schools: Possibilities and Limitations," *Theory Into Practice* 48, no. 3 (2009): 222–30; GSA Network and Crossroads Collaborative at the University of Arizona, *LGBTQ+ Youth of Color;* Rigoberto Marquez and Ed Brockenbrough, "Queer Youth v. the State of California: Interrogating Legal Discourses on the Rights of Queer Students of Color," *Curriculum Inquiry* 43, no. 4 (2013): 461–82; Fox 11 Los Angeles, "Protest Planned in Support of Black Transgender Student Attacked in Lancaster," YouTube video, 3:04, November 19, 2021, https://www.youtube.com/watch?v=vi0d-z3xoM0.

42. Yosso, "Whose Culture Has Capital?"
43. Yosso, "Whose Culture Has Capital?"
44. For examples, see Russell J. Skiba, Kavitha Mediratta, and M. Karega Rausch, eds., *Inequality in School Discipline: Research and Practice to Reduce Disparities* (New York: Palgrave Macmillan, 2016); Dorothy Hines-Datiri and Dorinda J. Carter Andrews, "The Effects of Zero Tolerance Policies on Black Girls: Using Critical Race Feminism and Figured Worlds to Examine School Discipline," *Urban Education* 55, no. 10 (2020): 1419–40; Vincent Basile, Adam York, and Ray Black, "Who Is the One Being Disrespectful? Understanding and Deconstructing the Criminalization of Elementary School Boys of Color," *Urban Education* 57, no. 9 (2022): 1592–1620.
45. See Joseph Kosciw, Caitlin Clark, and Leesh Menard, *The 2021 National School Climate Survey: The Experiences of LGBTQ+ Youth in Our Nation's Schools* (New York: GLSEN, 2022).

## Chapter 4

1. See chapter 1 for a detailed description of the MAC study.
2. Ed Brockenbrough and Tomás Boatwright, "In the MAC: Creating Safe Spaces for Transgender Youth of Color," in *Cultural Transformations: Youth and Pedagogies of Possibility*, ed. Korina Jocson (Cambridge, MA: Harvard Education Press, 2013), 165–82.
3. Brian Arao and Kristi Clemens, "From Safe Spaces to Brave Spaces: A New Way to Frame Dialogue Around Diversity and Social Justice," in *The Art of Effective Facilitation: Reflections from Social Justice Educators,* ed. Lisa M. Landreman (Sterling, VA: Stylus, 2013), 135–50; Zeus Leonardo and Ronald K. Porter, "Pedagogy of Fear: Toward a Fanonian Theory of 'Safety' in Race Dialogue," *Race, Ethnicity and Education* 13, no. 2 (2010): 139–57; "Safer Space Policy/Community Agreements," The Anti-Oppression Network, March 21, 2017, https://theantioppressionnetwork.com/resources/saferspacepolicy/; Timothy J. San Pedro, "'This Stuff Interests Me': Re-Centering Indigenous Paradigms in Colonizing Schooling Spaces," in *Culturally Sustaining Pedagogies: Teaching and Learning for Justice in a Changing World,* ed. Django Paris and H. Samy Alim (New York: Teachers College Press, 2017), 99–116.
4. Mollie Blackburn, "Exploring Literacy Performances and Power Dynamics at the Loft: 'Queer Youth Reading the World and the Word,'" *Research in the Teaching of English* 37, no. 4 (2003): 467–90; Cris Mayo, *Gay-Straight Alliances and Associations Among Youth in Schools* (New York: Palgrave Macmillan, 2017); Lance T. McCready, *Making Space for Diverse Masculinities: Difference, Intersectionality, and Engagement in an Urban High School* (New York: Peter Lang, 2010); Jon Wargo, "'I Don't Write So Other People Notice Me, I Write So I Can Notice Myself': Locating Queer at the Intersection of Rhetoric, Resistance, and Resource-Based Pedagogy," in *Queer, Trans,*

*and Intersectional Theory in Educational Practice Student, Teacher, and Community Experiences,* ed. Cris Mayo and Mollie V. Blackburn (New York: Routledge, 2021), 50–63.

5. Since my analysis is set in a predominantly Black queer space, I use transmisogyny instead of transmisogynoir—the contempt and suspicion toward, and the pathologization and marginalization of, Black trans girls and women—because the role of anti-blackness in the study data is unclear. For a discussion of transmisogyny, see Julia M. Serano, "Transmisogyny," in *The SAGE Encyclopedia of Trans Studies,* ed. Abbie E. Goldberg and Genny Beemyn (Thousand Oaks, CA: SAGE, 2021). For a discussion of transmisogynoir, see Kelsey N. Whipple, "Transmisogynoir," in Goldberg et al., *The SAGE Encyclopedia of Trans Studies.*

6. See Joseph Kosciw, Caitlin Clark, and Leesh Menard, *The 2021 National School Climate Survey: The Experiences of LGBTQ+ Youth in Our Nation's Schools* (New York: GLSEN, 2022); Louis F. Graham, "Navigating Community Institutions: Black Transgender Women's Experiences in Schools, the Criminal Justice System, and Churches," *Sexuality Research & Social Policy* 11, no. 4 (2014): 274–87; "Attacks on Gender Affirming Care by State Map," Human Rights Campaign, last modified November 13, 2023, https://www.hrc.org/resources/attacks-on-gender-affirming-care-by-state-map; Jo Yurcaba, "Over 30 New LGBTQ Education Laws Are in Effect as Students Go Back to School," *NBC News,* August 30, 2023, https://www.nbcnews.com/nbc-out/out-politics-and-policy/30-new-lgbtq-education-laws-are-effect-students-go-back-school-rcna101897.

7. Kosciw et al., *The 2021 National School Climate Survey;* N. Eugene Walls, Sarah B. Kane, and Hope Wisneski, "Gay–Straight Alliances and School Experiences of Sexual Minority Youth," *Youth & Society* 41, no. 3 (2010): 307–32; V. Paul Poteat et al., "GSA Advocacy Predicts Reduced Depression Disparities Between LGBQ+ and Heterosexual Youth in Schools," *Journal of Clinical Child and Adolescent Psychology* (2023): 1–13, https://doi.org/10.1080/15374416.2023.2169924; Carolyn M. Porta et al., "LGBTQ Youth's Views on Gay-Straight Alliances: Building Community, Providing Gateways, and Representing Safety and Support," *Journal of School Health* 87, no. 7 (2017): 489–97; V. Paul Poteat, Jerel P. Calzo, and Hirokazu Yoshikawa, "Promoting Youth Agency Through Dimensions of Gay-Straight Alliance Involvement and Conditions That Maximize Associations," *Journal of Youth and Adolescence* 45, no. 7 (2016): 1438–51.

8. GLSEN, *Safe Space Kit: A Guide to Supporting Lesbian, Gay, Bisexual, Transgender, and Queer Students in Your School,* 2019, https://www.glsen.org/sites/default/files/2019-11/GLSEN%20English%20SafeSpace%20Book%20Text%20Updated%202019.pdf; Lambda Legal, "Gay-Straight Alliances," accessed September 3, 2023, https://legacy.lambdalegal.org/know-your-rights/article/youth-gay-straight-alliances.

9. Cindy Cruz, "LGBTQ Youth of Color Video Making as Radical Curriculum: A Brother Mourning His Brother and a Theory in the Flesh," *Curriculum Inquiry* 43, no. 4 (2013): 441–60; Lori Chung, "NYC School Gives LGBTQ Students a Safe Place to Learn," *Spectrum News NY1,* June 27, 2022, https://ny1.com/nyc/all-boroughs/news/2022/06/26/nyc-school-gives-lgbtq-students-a-safe-place-to-learn.
10. Marlon M. Bailey, *Butch Queens Up in Pumps: Gender, Performance, and Ballroom Culture in Detroit* (Ann Arbor: University of Michigan Press, 2013); Shamari Reid, "Exploring the Agency of Black LGBTQ+ Youth in Schools and in NYC's Ballroom Culture," *Teachers College Record* 124, no. 6 (2022): 92–117.
11. German Lopez, "What the Conservative Caricature of 'Safe Spaces' Gets Wrong," *Vox,* August 29, 2016, https://www.vox.com/2016/8/29/12684042/safe-spaces-college-university; Greg Lukianoff and Jonathan Haidt, "The Coddling of the American Mind," *The Atlantic,* August 11, 2015, https://www.theatlantic.com/magazine/archive/2015/09/the-coddling-of-the-american-mind/399356/.
12. San Pedro, "'This Stuff Interests Me,'" 102.
13. Leonardo and Porter, "Pedagogy of Fear"; Cheryl E. Matias and Robin DiAngelo, "Beyond the Face of Race: Emo-Cognitive Explorations of White Neurosis and Racial Cray-Cray," *Educational Foundations* 27 (2013): 3–20.
14. Blackburn, "Exploring Literacy Performances and Power Dynamics at the Loft"; Mayo, *Gay-Straight Alliances and Associations Among Youth in Schools;* McCready, *Making Space for Diverse Masculinities;* Wargo, "'I Don't Write So Other People Notice Me, I Write So I Can Notice Myself.'"
15. Blackburn, "Exploring Literacy Performances and Power Dynamics at the Loft."
16. Arao and Clemens, "From Safe Spaces to Brave Spaces."
17. Stephen Best and Saidiya Hartman, "Fugitive Justice," *Representations* 92, no. 1 (2005): 1–15; Tina Campt, "Black Feminist Futures and the Practice of Fugitivity," video, 1:15:46, October 7, 2014, Barnard Center for Research on Women, https://bcrw.barnard.edu/videos/tina-campt-black-feminist-futures-and-the-practice-of-fugitivity/; Stefano Harney and Fred Moten, *The Undercommons: Fugitive Planning & Black Study* (New York: Autonomedia, 2013); Fred Moten, *Stolen Life* (Durham, NC: Duke University Press, 2018); C. Riley Snorton, *Black on Both Sides: A Racial History of Trans Identity* (Minneapolis: University of Minnesota Press, 2017).
18. Saidiya Hartman, *Lose Your Mother: A Journal Along the Atlantic Slave Route* (New York: Farrar, Straus, and Giroux, 2007), 6.
19. For a primer on Cedric Robinson's formulation of racial capitalism, see Robin D. G. Kelley, "What Did Cedric Robinson Mean by Racial Capitalism?," *Boston Review,* January 12, 2017, https://www.bostonreview.net/articles/robin-d-g-kelley-introduction-race-capitalism-justice/.

20. Damien M. Sojoyner, "Another Life Is Possible: Black Fugitivity and Enclosed Places," *Cultural Anthropology* 32, no. 4 (2017): 516. For Campt's work, see Campt, "Black Feminist Futures and the Practice of Fugitivity."
21. In his explanation of anti-blackness, Dumas states: "Antiblackness marks an irreconcilability between the Black and any sense of social or cultural regard. The aim of theorizing antiblackness is not to offer solutions to racial inequality, but to come to a deeper understanding of the Black condition within a context of utter contempt for, and acceptance of violence against the Black." Michael J. Dumas, "Against the Dark: Antiblackness in Education Policy and Discourse," *Theory Into Practice* 55, no. 1 (2016): 11–19.
22. See Carl A. Grant, Ashley N. Woodson, and Michael J. Dumas, eds., *The Future Is Black: Afropessimism, Fugitivity, and Radical Hope in Education* (New York: Routledge, 2021).
23. Jarvis R. Givens, "Literate Slave, Fugitive Slave: A Note on the Ethical Dilemma of Black Education," in Grant et al., *The Future Is Black,* 23.
24. Dumas, "Against the Dark"; Givens, "Literate Slave, Fugitive Slave"; kihana miraya ross, "Black Space in Education: Fugitive Resistance in the Afterlife of School Segregation," in Grant et al., *The Future Is Black,* 47–54.
25. Michael J. Dumas, "'Losing an Arm': Schooling as a Site of Black Suffering," *Race Ethnicity and Education* 17, no. 1 (January 1, 2014): 1–29.
26. Jamila Lyscott, "Fugitive Literacies as Inscriptions of Freedom," *English Education* 52, no. 3 (2020): 256–63; kihana miraya ross, "On Black Education: Anti-Blackness, Refusal, and Resistance, in Grant et al., *The Future Is Black,* 7–15; Ashley N. Woodson, "Afropessimism for Us in Education: In Fugitivity, Through Fuckery and with Funk," in Grant et al, *The Future Is Black,* 8–21; Esther O. Ohito, "'The Creative Aspect Woke Me Up': Awakening to Multimodal Essay Composition as a Fugitive Literacy Practice," *English Education* 52, no. 3 (April 2020); Ross, "Black Space in Education."
27. Lyscott, "Fugitive Literacies as Inscriptions of Freedom."
28. Ross, "Black Space in Education," 47.
29. Grace D. Player et al., "Enacting Educational Fugitivity with Youth of Color: A Statement/Love Letter from the Fugitive Literacies Collective," *High School Journal* 103, no. 3 (2020): 140–56.
30. Karen Zaino, "Teaching in the Service of Fugitive Learning," *#CritEdPol: Journal of Critical Education Policy Studies at Swarthmore College* 3, no. 1 (2021): 64–80.
31. Ohito, "'The Creative Aspect Woke Me Up,'" 188.
32. To protect the anonymity of study participants, I do not cite any data sources on Midtown, as those sources would reveal Midtown's actual name.
33. Graham, "Navigating Community Institutions"; Sa Whitley, "We Call Them Bandos: Black Trans Fugitivity in Baltimore's Geographies of Foreclosure," *TSQ: Transgender Studies Quarterly* 9, no. 2 (2022): 266–88; Lala B. Holston-

Zannell, "Black Trans Women Are Being Murdered in the Streets. Now the Trump Administration Wants to Turn Us Away from Shelters and Health Care," American Civil Liberties Union, May 24, 2019, https://www.aclu.org/news/lgbtq-rights/black-trans-women-are-being-murdered-streets-now-trump.
34. Graham, "Navigating Community Institutions"; Whitley, "We Call Them Bandos"; Holston-Zannell, "Black Trans Women Are Being Murdered in the Streets."
35. "MSM" is the nomenclature used in the field of public health. I include it when citing discourses that used it.
36. As explained in Table 1.1, MAC study participants who identified as male were not asked about the "cis" identity label. Hence, "cis-presenting" is used to describe those in this chapter.
37. At the time, "trannies" was still an accepted term within the MAC community, which is why I included it here.
38. Ohito, "'The Creative Aspect Woke Me Up'"; Woodson, "Afropessimism for Us in Education"; ross, "On Black Education."
39. I should note that Peggy Lee followed young people's lead on pronoun usage; that both of the youth referenced in this interview were still wrestling with their gender identity may account for the use of *he* as a pronoun.
40. Elizabethe Payne and Melissa Smith, "LGBTQ Kids, School Safety, and Missing the Big Picture: How the Dominant Bullying Discourse Prevents School Professionals from Thinking About Systemic Marginalization or . . . Why We Need to Rethink LGBTQ Bullying," *QED: A Journal in GLBTQ Worldmaking* no. 1 (2013): 1–36; Sandra J. Schmidt, "Un/Scripting Queer Subjectivity: Queer Futures Envisioned in 'It Gets Better,'" *High School Journal* 105, no. 1 (2021): 43–59; Jacqueline Ullman, "Breaking Out of the (Anti) Bullying 'Box': NYC Educators Discuss Trans/Gender Diversity-Inclusive Policies and Curriculum," *Sex Education* 18, no. 5 (2018): 495–510.
41. Susan Talburt, "Introduction: Public Feelings and Youth Sexualities," in *Youth Sexualities: Public Feelings and Contemporary Cultural Politics,* vol. 1, ed. Susan Talburt (Santa Barbara, CA: Praeger, 2018), xi–xxxiv.
42. Max Osborn, "U.S. News Coverage of Transgender Victims of Fatal Violence: An Exploratory Content Analysis," *Violence Against Women* 28, no. 9 (2022): 2033–56.
43. Osborn, "U.S. News Coverage of Transgender Victims of Fatal Violence," 2046.
44. Epigraph: Julian Glover, "Representation, Respectability, and Transgender Women of Color in Media," *AAIHS—African American Intellectual History Society* (blog), April 27, 2017, https://www.aaihs.org/representation-respectability-and-transgender-women-of-color-in-media/.https://www.aaihs.org/representation-respectability-and-transgender-women-of-color-in-media/, para 7. See Anushka Patil, "How a March for Black Trans Lives Became a Huge

Event," *New York Times,* June 16, 2020, https://www.nytimes.com/2020/06/15/nyregion/brooklyn-black-trans-parade.html; Mia Fischer, "Making Black Trans Lives Matter," *QED: A Journal in GLBTQ Worldmaking* 8, no. 1 (2021): 111–18.

45. Cindy Cruz, "LGBTQ Street Youth Talk Back: A Meditation on Resistance and Witnessing," *International Journal of Qualitative Studies in Education* 24, no. 5 (2011): 547–58; Sam Stiegler, "Under the Trees in Lincoln Center: Queer and Trans Homeless Youth Coming Together in the City," *Equity & Excellence in Education* 52, no. 4 (2019): 373–82.

46. For an example of this type of racial consciousness space for white people, see Ali Michael and Eleonora Bartoli, *Our Problem, Our Path: Collective Antiracism for White People* (Thousand Oaks, CA: Corwin Press, 2022).

47. Brockenbrough and Boatwright, "In the MAC."

## Chapter 5

1. *The Skinny,* directed by Patrik-Ian Polk (United States: Tall Skinny Black Boy Productions / Logo, 2012).
2. Polk, *The Skinny.*
3. I use "cishetero-presenting" because none of my colleagues publicly articulated noncisheteronormative identities.
4. As explained in chapter 1, MAC study participants who identified as male also presented as such, but they were not specifically asked about their identification with the "cis" label. In this chapter, I use YBQM to refer to both the cis-presenting, male-identified MAC study participants and the SENT study participants, all of whom identified as cis males.
5. See the following regarding LGBTQ+ youth's reliance on out-of-school resources to learn about and explore queer sexual identities, desires, and practices: Brittnie E. Bloom et al., "Responsiveness of Sex Education to the Needs of LGBTQ+ Undergraduate Students and Its Influence on Sexual Violence and Harassment Experiences," *American Journal of Sexuality Education* 17, no. 3 (2022): 368–99; Joseph M. Currin et al., "How Gay and Bisexual Men Compensate for the Lack of Meaningful Sex Education in a Socially Conservative State," *Sex Education* 17, no. 6 (2017): 667–81; Steven Hobaica and Paul Kwon, "'This Is How You Hetero': Sexual Minorities in Heteronormative Sex Education," *American Journal of Sexuality Education* 12, no. 4 (2017): 423–50; Emily Sweetnam Pingel et al., "Creating Comprehensive, Youth Centered, Culturally Appropriate Sex Education: What Do Young Gay, Bisexual and Questioning Men Want?," *Sexuality Research & Social Policy* 10, no. 4 (2013), http://dx.doi.org/10.1007/s13178-013-0134-5.
6. Future of Sex Education Initiative, *National Sex Education Standards: Core Content and Skills, K-12,* 2nd ed. (Washington, DC: American School Health Association, 2020), 6.

7. Future of Sex Education Initiative, *National Sex Education Standards*.
8. Eva S. Goldfarb and Lisa D. Lieberman, "Three Decades of Research: The Case for Comprehensive Sex Education," *Journal of Adolescent Health* 68, no. 1 (2021): 13–27; Kelli Stidham Hall et al., "The State of Sex Education in the United States," *Journal of Adolescent Health* 58, no. 6 (2016): 595–97; Caitlin Howlett, *Against Sex Education: Pedagogy, Sex Work, and State Violence* (London: Bloomsbury Academic, 2021); Emily Meadows, "Sexual Health Equity in Schools: Inclusive Sexuality and Relationship Education for Gender and Sexual Minority Students," *American Journal of Sexuality Education* 13, no. 3 (2018): 297–309.
9. Guttmacher Institute, "Sex and HIV Education," September 1, 2023, https://www.guttmacher.org/state-policy/explore/sex-and-hiv-education.
10. Joseph M. Currin, Randolph D. Hubach, and Julie M. Croff, "Sex-Ed Without the Stigma: What Gay and Bisexual Men Would Like Offered in School Based Sex Education," *Journal of Homosexuality* 67, no. 13 (2020): 1779–97; Hall et al., "The State of Sex Education in the United States"; Meadows, "Sexual Health Equity in Schools."
11. Guttmacher Institute, "Sex and HIV Education."
12. Joseph Kosciw, Caitlin Clark, and Leesh Menard, *The 2021 National School Climate Survey: The Experiences of LGBTQ+ Youth in Our Nation's Schools* (New York: GLSEN, 2022).
13. Goldfarb and Lieberman, "Three Decades of Research."
14. Bloom et al., "Responsiveness of Sex Education to the Needs of LGBTQ+ Undergraduate Students and Its Influence on Sexual Violence and Harassment Experiences"; Nova J. Bradford et al., "Sex Education and Transgender Youth: 'Trust Means Material by and for Queer and Trans People,'" *Sex Education* 19, no. 1 (2019): 84–98; Currin et al., "How Gay and Bisexual Men Compensate for the Lack of Meaningful Sex Education in a Socially Conservative State"; Currin et al., "Sex-Ed Without the Stigma"; Christopher Micheal Fisher, "Queer Youth Experiences with Abstinence-Only-Until-Marriage Sexuality Education: 'I Can't Get Married so Where Does That Leave Me?,'" *Journal of LGBT Youth* 6, no. 1 (2009): 61–79; Hobaica and Kwon, "'This Is How You Hetero'"; Steven Hobaica, Kyle Schofield, and Paul Kwon, "'Here's Your Anatomy . . . Good Luck': Transgender Individuals in Cisnormative Sex Education," *American Journal of Sexuality Education* 14, no. 3 (2019): 358–87; Elizabeth Jarpe-Ratner, "How Can We Make LGBTQ+-Inclusive Sex Education Programmes Truly Inclusive? A Case Study of Chicago Public Schools' Policy and Curriculum," *Sex Education* 20, no. 3 (2020): 283–99; Sanjana Pampati et al., "Sexual and Gender Minority Youth and Sexual Health Education: A Systematic Mapping Review of the Literature," *Journal of Adolescent Health* 68, no. 6 (2021): 1040–52; Pingel et al., "Creating Comprehensive, Youth Centered, Culturally Appropriate Sex Education."

15. Currin et al., "How Gay and Bisexual Men Compensate for the Lack of Meaningful Sex Education in a Socially Conservative State"; Currin et al., "Sex-Ed Without the Stigma"; Hobaica and Kwon, "'This Is How You Hetero'"; Pingel et al., "Creating Comprehensive, Youth Centered, Culturally Appropriate Sex Education."
16. Hobaica et al., "'Here's Your Anatomy . . . Good Luck'"; Katrina Kubicek et al., "In the Dark: Young Men's Stories of Sexual Initiation in the Absence of Relevant Sexual Health Information," *Health Education & Behavior* 37, no. 2 (2010): 243–63.
17. Fisher, "Queer Youth Experiences with Abstinence-Only-Until-Marriage Sexuality Education"; Hobaica and Kwon, "'This Is How You Hetero'"; Hobaica et al., "'Here's Your Anatomy . . . Good Luck'"; Kubicek et al., "In the Dark."
18. Bloom et al., "Responsiveness of Sex Education to the Needs of LGBTQ+ Undergraduate Students and Its Influence on Sexual Violence and Harassment Experiences"; Currin et al., "How Gay and Bisexual Men Compensate for the Lack of Meaningful Sex Education in a Socially Conservative State"; Currin et al., "Sex-Ed Without the Stigma"; Hobaica and Kwon, "'This Is How You Hetero'"; Katrina Kubicek et al., "Use and Perceptions of the Internet for Sexual Information and Partners: A Study of Young Men Who Have Sex with Men," *Archives of Sexual Behavior* 40, no. 4 (2011): 803–16; Kimberly M. Nelson, David W. Pantalone, and Michael P. Carey, "Sexual Health Education for Adolescent Males Who Are Interested in Sex with Males: An Investigation of Experiences, Preferences, and Needs," *Journal of Adolescent Health* 64, no. 1 (2019): 36–42.
19. Currin et al., "How Gay and Bisexual Men Compensate for the Lack of Meaningful Sex Education in a Socially Conservative State"; Hobaica and Kwon, "'This Is How You Hetero'"; Kubicek et al., "Use and Perceptions of the Internet for Sexual Information and Partners."
20. Hobaica and Kwon, "'This Is How You Hetero'"; Kubicek et al., "In the Dark."
21. Nelson et al., "Sexual Health Education for Adolescent Males Who Are Interested in Sex with Males"; Pingel et al., "Creating Comprehensive, Youth Centered, Culturally Appropriate Sex Education."
22. For examples, see Bloom et al., "Responsiveness of Sex Education to the Needs of LGBTQ+ Undergraduate Students and Its Influence on Sexual Violence and Harassment Experiences"; Bradford et al., "Sex Education and Transgender Youth"; Currin et al., "How Gay and Bisexual Men Compensate for the Lack of Meaningful Sex Education in a Socially Conservative State"; Currin et al., "Sex-Ed Without the Stigma"; Fisher, "Queer Youth Experiences with Abstinence-Only-Until-Marriage Sexuality Education"; Goldfarb and Lieberman, "Three Decades of Research"; Hobaica and Kwon, "'This Is How You Hetero'"; Hobaica et al., "'Here's Your Anatomy . . . Good Luck'"; Kubicek

et al., "Use and Perceptions of the Internet for Sexual Information and Partners"; Nelson et al., "Sexual Health Education for Adolescent Males Who Are Interested in Sex with Males."
23. For examples of scholarly work on the gender and sexual politics of blackness, see Patricia Hill Collins, *Black Sexual Politics: African Americans, Gender, and the New Racism* (New York: Routledge, 2004); Adrienne D. Davis and BSE Collective, eds., *Black Sexual Economies: Race and Sex in a Culture of Capital* (Champaign: University of Illinois Press, 2019); E. Patrick Johnson, ed., *No Tea, No Shade: New Writings in Black Queer Studies* (Durham, NC: Duke University Press, 2016).
24. Michelle L. Estes, "'If There's One Benefit, You're Not Going to Get Pregnant': The Sexual Miseducation of Gay, Lesbian, and Bisexual Individuals," *Sex Roles* 77, no. 9 (2017): 615–27; Goldfarb and Lieberman, "Three Decades of Research"; Hobaica and Kwon, "'This Is How You Hetero'"; Jarpe-Ratner, "How Can We Make LGBTQ+-Inclusive Sex Education Programmes Truly Inclusive?"; Ester McGeeney, "A Focus on Pleasure? Desire and Disgust in Group Work with Young Men," *Culture, Health & Sexuality* 17, suppl. 2 (2015): 223–37.
25. Goldfarb and Lieberman, "Three Decades of Research," 23.
26. Centers for Disease Control and Prevention, "New Multi-Year Data Show Annual HIV Infections in U.S. Relatively Stable," August 3, 2011, http://www.cdc.gov/nchhstp/newsroom/2011/HIVIncidencePressRelease.html.
27. For an analysis of how public health discourses pathologize Black queer males, see Derrick D. Matthews et al., "Reconciling Epidemiology and Social Justice in the Public Health Discourse Around the Sexual Networks of Black Men Who Have Sex with Men," *American Journal of Public Health* 106, no. 5 (2016): 808–14.
28. For visuals from the "I Love My Boo" campaign, see Jaya Saxena, "'I Love My Boo' Campaign Hits Subways," *Gothamist,* October 5, 2010, https://gothamist.com/news/i-love-my-boo-campaign-hits-subways.
29. Paul Butler, *Chokehold: Policing Black Men* (New York: New Press, 2018); Michael P. Jeffries, *Thug Life: Race, Gender, and the Meaning of Hip-Hop* (Chicago: University of Chicago Press, 2011).
30. "DL," or "down low," describes men who have sex with other men while not identifying as queer and/or remaining in the closet. In Black queer male circles, DL is also associated with a masculine gender presentation that helps to conceal one's sex life with other men.
31. Here, Kris is using "trade" (or in his words, "trady") to describe Black men with a thuggish, hypermasculine gender presentation.
32. "Bareback" here refers to condomless penile-anal intercourse.
33. Examples of websites include Scarleteen (https://www.scarleteen.com/); Sex, Etc. (https://sexetc.org/); Q Chat Space (https://www.qchatspace.org/). See also

Genderqueer Australia, "Trans Youth Sexual Health Booklet," May 24, 2012, https://www.genderqueer.org.au/trans-youth-sexual-health-booklet/; It Gets Better Project, "Queer Sex Ed," accessed October 17, 2022, https://itgetsbetter.org/queer-sex-ed/; Pam Segall, "Queer Creators Are Using TikTok to Provide the Sex Education They Wish They'd Received," *Insider,* November 14, 2022, https://www.insider.com/queer-educators-are-providing-sex-education-on-tiktok-2022-11.

34. Monique Y. Perry, "Supporting Sexuality Education Pedagogy: A Cross-Curricular Analysis of Middle School Classrooms (PhD diss. proposal, University of Pennsylvania, 2022).
35. GLSEN, *2021 High School Booklist,* July 2021, https://www.glsen.org/sites/default/files/2021-07/GLSEN_NSC_Booklist_High_School_2021.pdf; History UnErased (https://unerased.org/).
36. Paul Byron et al., "Reading for Realness: Porn Literacies, Digital Media, and Young People," *Sexuality & Culture* 25, no. 3 (2021): 786–805.
37. Byron et al., "Reading for Realness"; Paul Byron, "Porn Literacy and Young People's Digital Cultures," *Porn Studies* (March 2023): 1–8; Alanna Goldstein, "Beyond Porn Literacy: Drawing on Young People's Pornography Narratives to Expand Sex Education Pedagogies," *Sex Education* 20, no. 1 (2020): 59–74.
38. See n. 33 above.
39. See n. 33 above.
40. For relatively accessible examples, see Wesley Morris, "Why Pop Culture Just Can't Deal with Black Male Sexuality," *New York Times,* October 27, 2016, https://www.nytimes.com/interactive/2016/10/30/magazine/black-male-sexuality-last-taboo.html; "Sex Stereotypes of African Americans Have Long History," *NPR,* May 7, 2007, https://www.npr.org/templates/story/story.php?storyId=10057104.

## Chapter 6

1. For the documentary, see *Out of the Past: The Struggle for Gay and Lesbian Rights in America,* directed by Jeff Dupre (United States: Allumination, 1998), DVD; Michael Wigglesworth, *The Day of Doom: or, A Poetical Description of the Great and Last Judgment,* 6th ed. (New York: American News Company, 1867).
2. Jonathan Edwards, *Sinners in the Hands of an Angry God: Sermon* (Louisville, KY: Pentecostal Publishing, n.d.).
3. Andrew O'Hehir, "The Sexual Life of Abraham Lincoln," *Salon.com,* January 12, 2005, https://www.salon.com/2005/01/12/lincoln_7/.
4. For examples, see Dupre, *Out of the Past;* Kevin Jennings, ed., *One Teacher in Ten in the New Millennium: LGBT Educators Speak Out About What's Gotten Better . . . and What Hasn't* (Boston: Beacon Press, 2015); Lillian Faderman, *The Gay Revolution: The Story of the Struggle* (New York: Simon and Schuster, 2015).

5. For examples, see Sarah Baughey-Gill, "When Gay Was Not Okay with the APA: A Historical Overview of Homosexuality and Its Status as Mental Disorder," *Occam's Razor* 1, no. 2 (2011), https://cedar.wwu.edu/cgi/viewcontent.cgi?article=1001&context=orwwu; *Boys Beware*, directed by Sid Davis (United States: Sid Davis Productions, 1961); Gillian Frank, "'The Civil Rights of Parents': Race and Conservative Politics in Anita Bryant's Campaign Against Gay Rights in 1970s Florida," *Journal of the History of Sexuality* 22, no. 1 (2013): 126–60; Karen Graves, *And They Were Wonderful Teachers: Florida's Purge of Gay and Lesbian Teachers* (Urbana: University of Illinois Press, 2009); Keith Boykin, *Beyond the Down Low: Sex, Lies, and Denial in Black America* (New York: Carroll and Graf, 2006).
6. For an example, see the critique of this blame rhetoric targeted at Black men on the down low in Boykin, *Beyond the Down Low*.
7. Christian George Gregory, "The Closet," in *Encyclopedia of Queer Studies*, ed. Kamden K. Strunk and Stephanie Anne Shelton (Boston: Brill, 2022), 93–102.
8. Diana Fuss, *Inside/Out: Lesbian Theories, Gay Theories* (New York: Routledge, 1991).
9. Edward Brockenbrough, *Black Men Teaching in Urban Schools: Reassessing Black Masculinity* (New York: Routledge, 2018), 26.
10. Aaron Betsky, *Queer Space: Architecture and Same-Sex Desire* (New York: William Morrow, 1997); Shawn A. Trivette, "Secret Handshakes and Decoder Rings: The Queer Space of Don't Ask/Don't Tell," *Sexuality Research & Social Policy* 7, no. 3 (2010): 214–28; James Kirchick, *Secret City: The Hidden History of Gay Washington* (New York: Henry Holt, 2022); Matthew B. Cox, "Working Closets: Mapping Queer Professional Discourses and Why Professional Communication Studies Need Queer Rhetorics," *Journal of Business and Technical Communication* 33, no. 1 (January 1, 2019): 1–25.
11. Beatrice Fanucci, "Exploring the Secret History of Queer Coded Language," *GCN*, June 2, 2023, https://gcn.ie/exploring-queer-coded-language/; Trivette, "Secret Handshakes and Decoder Rings"; Kirchick, *Secret City*.
12. Eve Kosofsky Sedgwick, *Epistemology of the Closet* (Berkeley: University of California Press, 1990).
13. Rogério Diniz Junqueira, "Pedagogy of the Closet: Heterosexism and Gender Surveillance on Brazilian Everyday School Life," *Annual Review of Critical Psychology* 11 (2014): 173–88.
14. Stephen Best and Saidiya Hartman, "Fugitive Justice," *Representations* 92, no. 1 (2005): 1–15; Tina Campt, "Black Feminist Futures and the Practice of Fugitivity," video, 1:15:46, October 7, 2014, Barnard Center for Research on Women, https://bcrw.barnard.edu/videos/tina-campt-black-feminist-futures-and-the-practice-of-fugitivity/; Stefano Harney and Fred Moten, *The Undercommons: Fugitive Planning & Black Study* (New York: Autonomedia, 2013);

C. Riley Snorton, *Black on Both Sides: A Racial History of Trans Identity* (Minneapolis: University of Minnesota Press, 2017).

15. To be clear, I am not critiquing other frameworks for understanding teacher resistance. What I am suggesting here is that a pedagogy of the closet provides a distinct context for naming and nurturing teachers' resistance against antiqueerness. To compare this chapter to other insightful analyses of teacher resistance, see Bree Picower, "Resisting Compliance: Learning to Teach for Social Justice in a Neoliberal Context," *Teachers College Record* 113, no. 5 (2011): 1105–34; Jordan Levy, "Reforming Schools, Disciplining Teachers: Decentralization and Privatization of Education in Honduras," *Anthropology & Education Quarterly* 50, no. 2 (2019): 170–88; David Bruce Tyack and Larry Cuban, *Tinkering Toward Utopia: A Century of Public School Reform* (Cambridge, MA: Harvard University Press, 1995); Sarah Jewett and Katherine Schultz, "Toward an Anthropology of Teachers and Teaching," in *A Companion to the Anthropology of Education,* ed. Mica Pollock and Bradley A. U. Levinson (Oxford: Blackwell Publishing, 2011), 425–44; Jesse Hagopian, ed., *More Than a Score: The New Uprising Against High-Stakes Testing* (Chicago, IL: Haymarket Books, 2014).

16. Amity Buxton, *The Other Side of the Closet: The Coming-Out Crisis for Straight Spouses and Families,* revised and expanded ed. (New York: Wiley, 1994); Juliet E. Hart, Jon E. Mourot, and Megan Aros, "Children of Same-Sex Parents: In and Out of the Closet," *Educational Studies* 38, no. 3 (July 1, 2012): 277–81; Kimberly Walpot, "Coming Out as a Straight Ally in the Workplace," LinkedIn, October 31, 2016, https://www.linkedin.com/pulse/coming-out-straight-ally-workplace-kimberly-walpot.

17. See Janet Penner-Williams, "Formal Curriculum," in *Encyclopedia of Curriculum Studies,* ed. Craig Kridel (Los Angeles: SAGE, 2010), 376–77; William H. Schubert, "Curriculum Venues," in Kridel, *Encyclopedia of Curriculum Studies,* 272–74.

18. Katie Burkholder, "Teacher Officially Fired for Reading Gender Identity Book to Students," *Georgia Voice,* August 21, 2023, https://thegavoice.com/today-in-gay-atlanta/teacher-officially-fired-for-reading-gender-identity-book-to-students/; Lexi McMenamin, "Florida Teacher Fired over LGBTQ+ Pride Flag Lesson," *Teen Vogue,* May 6, 2022, https://www.teenvogue.com/story/dont-say-gay-firing-pansexual.

19. John D'Emilio, *Lost Prophet: The Life and Times of Bayard Rustin,* 2nd ed. (Chicago: University of Chicago Press, 2004); Henry Louis Gates Jr., "Who Designed the March on Washington?," The African Americans: Many Rivers to Cross, January 20, 2013, https://www.pbs.org/wnet/african-americans-many-rivers-to-cross/history/100-amazing-facts/who-designed-the-march-on-washington/.

20. Pennsylvania State Department of Education, "View Standards," *Standards Aligned System,* accessed November 25, 2022, https://pdesas.org/Standard/View.
21. See James A. Banks, "Approaches to Multicultural Curriculum Reform," in *Multicultural Education: Issues and Perspectives,* 10th ed., ed. James A. Banks and Cherry A. McGee Banks (Indianapolis: John Wiley, 2019), 137–57.
22. Eric Marcus, "Bayard Rustin," January 10, 2019, in *Making Gay History,* produced by Pineapple Street Media, podcast, MP3 audio, 34:09, https://makinggayhistory.com/podcast/bayard-rustin/.
23. *Brother Outsider: The Life of Bayard Rustin,* directed by Bennet Singer and Nancy Kates (United States: Question Why Films, 2003); D'Emilio, *Lost Prophet.*
24. Pat Parker, "Where Will You Be?," *The Slant,* January 1996.
25. Martin Niemöller, "First They Came," Holocaust Memorial Day Trust, accessed September 19, 2023, https://www.hmd.org.uk/resource/first-they-came-by-pastor-martin-niemoller/.
26. Audre Lorde, "Who Said It Was Simple," Poetry Foundation, accessed September 19, 2023, https://www.poetryfoundation.org/poems/42587/who-said-it-was-simple.
27. Nella Larsen, *Quicksand* and *Passing,* ed. Deborah McDowell (New Brunswick, NJ: Rutgers University Press, 1986).
28. Deborah E. McDowell, introduction to Larsen, *Quicksand* and *Passing,* ix–xxxv; Elizabeth Dean, "The Gaze, the Glance, the Mirror: Queer Desire and Panoptic Discipline in Nella Larsen's *Passing,*" *Women's Studies* 48, no. 2 (2019): 97–103.
29. Mara D. Johnson and monét cooper, "Toward Loving and Legibility: Understanding Black LGBTQ Girls' School Experiences and Navigational Strategies in Educational Research" (paper presented at the American Educational Research Association Annual Meeting, Chicago, IL, April 16, 2023); Torie Wheatley, "Hidden in Plain Sight: The Mental Health Epidemic for Black Queer Womxn in Educational Spaces" (paper presented at the American Educational Research Association Annual Meeting, Chicago, IL, April 16, 2023); Savannah Shange, "Play Aunties and Dyke Bitches: Gender, Generation, and the Ethics of Black Queer Kinship," *Black Scholar* 49, no. 1 (2019): 40–54; Latrise P. Johnson, "Writing the Self: Black Queer Youth Challenge Heteronormative Ways of Being in an After-School Writing Club," *Research in the Teaching of English* 52, no. 1 (2017): 13–33; Sam Stiegler, "Under the Trees in Lincoln Center: Queer and Trans Homeless Youth Coming Together in the City," *Equity & Excellence in Education* 52, no. 4 (2019): 373–82; Lance T. McCready, *Making Space for Diverse Masculinities: Difference, Intersectionality, and Engagement in an Urban High School* (New York: Peter Lang, 2010); Tomás

Boatwright, "Flux Zine: Black Queer Storytelling," *Equity & Excellence in Education* 52, no. 4 (2019): 383–95; Jon Wargo, "'I Don't Write So Other People Notice Me, I Write So I Can Notice Myself': Locating Queer at the Intersection of Rhetoric, Resistance, and Resource-Based Pedagogy," in *Queer, Trans, and Intersectional Theory in Educational Practice Student, Teacher, and Community Experiences,* ed. Cris Mayo and Mollie V. Blackburn (New York: Routledge, 2021), 50–63.

# Acknowledgments

My father's sudden passing, my own health issues, the chaos of the COVID-19 pandemic, and seemingly endless bouts with racial and queer battle fatigues repeatedly forced this project onto the backburner. I owe a huge debt of gratitude to Lance McCready and Roland Sintos Coloma for helping me to rediscover my writing voice, offering me feedback on early chapter drafts, and being a constant source of joy and affirmation. Our fellowship gives me life. #TodayIsAReadingDay (smile).

The work featured in chapter 5 was supported by the University of Rochester's Center for AIDS Research (grant #T30AI078498), as well as by the Calvin Bland Faculty Fellowship at the University of Pennsylvania, funded by the Robert Wood Johnson Foundation. I am grateful to both initiatives for making such a critical portion of my scholarship possible.

Thank you to my former research assistants—Tomás Boatwright, Monique Perry, Luis Ramirez, and Luciano Zuniga—who provided invaluable support with data collection and analysis for my research projects. And to Mitchell Wharton, my SENT study research partner: This work could not have happened without you. And I wouldn't have wanted it to.

I want to send an exuberant shout-out to the fabulous circle of scholars and scholar-friends who have advanced educational studies on queer youth and students of color. Those folks include Mollie Blackburn, Reginald Blockett, Tomás Boatwright, Durell Callier, Cindy Cruz, Kia Darling-Hammond, Tadashi Dozono, Antonio Duran, Dominique Hill, Latrise Johnson, Kevin Kumashiro, Luis Leyva, Lisa Loutzenheiser, Bettina Love, Rigoberto Marquez, Cris Mayo, Erica Meiners, Liz Meyer, Steve Mobley, Z Nicolazzo, Steven Thurston Oliver, Therese Quinn, Shamari Reid, Christopher Sewell, Savannah Shange, Sam Stiegler, Mario Suarez, Lisa Weems, and Jon Wargo, among others. It is a pleasure and an honor to take up space with you.

To the "up-and-coming children" who are pushing queer of color educational scholarship in new and exciting directions: I see you, and I got your back. And to my parents: the more I do this work, the more I appreciate the journey you had to take to understand it.

Last, but certainly not least, I want to thank the young people who graciously and courageously shared the stories and insights that are presented throughout this book. Your Black queer brilliance and resilience inspire me, and I hope the impact of this book is (further) evidence that your struggles and successes have not been in vain.

# About the Author

**Ed Brockenbrough** is an associate professor at the University of Pennsylvania's Graduate School of Education in Philadelphia, where he teaches courses on diversity and social justice in education, trains prospective urban secondary teachers, and offers professional development sessions to K–12 educators on culturally responsive pedagogy and LGBTQ+ issues in schools. His research focuses on the educational experiences of LGBTQ+ youth, and he is the author of *Black Men Teaching in Urban Schools: Reassessing Masculinity* (Routledge, 2018).

# Index

abstinence education, 95, 99
abstinence only until marriage (AOUM), 95
adults, critical ethic of care and, 27–29, 81–83, 89
advocacy, 37–40
advocacy groups, support for, 40
advocacy incubators, 39
agency, 6–8, 30–35, 114–115, 123–124
Alim, H. Samy, 23
alternative educational programs, 26, 68
anti-queer harassment. *See* Black queer resistant capital
asset-based pedagogies, 21–24, 33

Bailey, Marlon M., 27, 38
bargaining for the common good, 39–40
"Becoming Queerly Responsive: Culturally Responsive Pedagogy for Black and Latino Urban Queer Youth" (Brockenbrough), 19, 40–41
Black, use of term, 4
Blackburn, Mollie V., 31, 33, 35–36, 38, 50, 70
Black Queens Collective, 83–84
Black queer resistant capital
 overview, 16–17, 45–46
 accounts of, 53–60
 critical ethic of care and, 46, 60–63
 cultural context of, 48–53
 preliminary boundaries for, 62–63
 recommendations about, 63–64
 transformative resistant capital, 48, 60, 62
 what constitutes, 46–48
Black queer youth (BQY), 43–44, 71–73. *See also* Black queer resistant capital; intersectionality; queerly responsive pedagogy (QRP); queer youth of color (QYC); sexual education; trans fugitivity; young Black queer males (YBQM)
Black thuggery, 106–110, 115
Black trans female youth (BTFY), 65. *See also* trans fugitivity
Boatwright, Tomás, 28, 31, 35, 36, 135
boyd, danah, 11–12
brave spaces, 70
Brockenbrough, Ed, 19, 35, 36, 38, 40–41
bullying, 54–55. *See also* Black queer resistant capital
Byron, Paul, 115

Campt, Tina, 71
care, ethic of. *See* critical ethic of care
caring spaces, 30
*Check It*, 51
chosen families, 28–30, 51
cisgender (cis), use of term, 5, 6
cisheteronormativity, 5, 94–95

173

closet. *See* pedagogy of the closet
collective teacher organization, 39–40
community-based organizations, 29, 97–102, 111–114. *See also* Midtown AIDS Center (MAC) study
community cultural wealth, 47, 52
community networks, 26–27
condom use, 98
critical ethic of care
  overview, 25–30
  Black queer resistant capital and, 46, 60–63
  trans fugitivity and, 81–83, 89
Crossroads Collaborative, 51–52
Cruz, Cindy, 31, 36, 88–89
culturally responsive pedagogy, 19, 21–25. *See also* queerly responsive pedagogy (QRP)
culturally sustaining pedagogy, 22–23
culture, defined, 21
curriculum
  formal versus taught, 126
  guiding questions for, 35, 129–131
  pedagogy of the closet and, 126–133
  professional development on, 34–35
  queerly responsive pedagogy and, 32
  sexual education across, 114

data analysis, 9–11, 14
data collection, 9, 12–14
data sources for book, 8–15
"Day of Doom, The" (Wigglesworth), 119
del Carmen Vásquez, Andrea, 26–27, 28, 32, 36
dental dams, 99
DiAngelo, Robin, 70
disconnected youth, use of term, 5

Driver, Susan, 38
Dumas, Michael, 72
Duran, Antonio, 48

educational and social justice, 37–40, 133–135
education as anti-Black, 71–73
educators/school personnel. *See also* pedagogy of the closet
  anti-queer harassment by, 54–55, 58–60
  collective teacher organization, 39–40
  intervention training for, 64
  professional development for, 33–35, 63–64, 90
  sexual education, risks of providing, 1–2, 94, 101, 113–114
*Epistemology of the Closet* (Sedgwick), 124
ethic of care. *See* critical ethic of care

family engagement, 29–30
Ferguson, Roderick, 6
fighting back. *See* Black queer resistant capital
"First They Came" (Niemöller), 132
fugitive spaces, 37, 89
funding, research participants limited due to source of, 15, 36, 67, 76, 93
Fuss, Diana, 122–123

"gay club" as critical ethic of care, 26–27
gay-straight alliances (GSAs), 51–52, 68, 70
George Washington High School, 32
Givens, Jarvis, 72
Glover, Julian, 87
GLSEN, 29, 40, 51, 95, 114
Goldfarb, Eva, 97

GSA Network, 51–52
Guttmacher Institute, 94–95

harassment. *See* Black queer resistant capital
Hartman, Saidiya, 71
history instruction standards, 127–128
HIV infections, 2, 97. *See also* sexual education
House Ball community, 27, 32, 49
Howard, Tyrone, 24–25
Human Rights Campaign, 29, 40

incident logs, 64
Internet Usage Scale for Sexual Purposes—Modified, 12
intersectionality
  culture and, 21–22
  marginality increased due to, 2, 3–4
  missing in traditional scholarship, 20–21
  pairing intersectional analysis with opportunities for agency, 30–35, 114–115
  professional development on, 33–34
  [q]ulturally sustaining pedagogy and, 23
  spaces and peer interactions and, 37
  types of, 30–31

Johnson, E. Patrick, 49
Johnson, Latrise P., 31, 32, 34, 135
Johnson, Mara, 134
journal writing, 31, 34
Junqueira, Rogério Diniz, 124
Justine, author of "Pride," 31–32

kinship formation, 27–28. *See also* chosen families

Larsen, Nella, 132–133
leadership training for queer youth of color, 34
legislation, anti-queer and anti-trans, 61–62, 112, 126
Leonardo, Zeus, 69–70
LGBTQ+, use of term, 6. *See also* headings beginning with queer
Lieberman, Lisa, 97
literacy practices, 31–32, 34
Lorde, Audre, 131, 132
Lyscott, Jamila, 73

MAC (Midtown AIDS Center) study, 8–11, 14–15. *See also* sexual education; trans fugitivity
*Making Gay History* podcast, 130–131
marginalization. *See also* queerly responsive pedagogy (QRP); systemic subjugations
  intersectionality and, 2, 3–4
  queer of color critique and, 6–7
  in sexual education, 94–96
  of trans youth by cis peers, 70, 75
Matias, Cheryl, 70
Mayo, Cris, 70
McCready, Lance, 33, 38, 70, 135
men who have sex with men (MSM), 2, 76
Midtown AIDS Center (MAC) study, 8–11, 14–15. *See also* sexual education; trans fugitivity

name change, 86
National Black Justice Coalition, 29, 40
National LGBTQ Task Force, 29, 40
National Sex Education Standards (NSES), 17–18, 92–93
Niemöller, Martin, 132
Nieto, Sonia, 21–22

Ohito, Esther, 73–74, 80
opportunity youth, use of term, 5
oral sex, 98

Paris, Django, 23
Parker, Pat, 131–132
partnerships, 113
*Passing* (Larsen), 132–133
Patel, Leigh, 69
pedagogy of the closet
　overview, 18, 121–122
　application of, 125–133
　defined, 122–125
　educational and social justice and, 133–135
　need for, 119–121
peer connections, 26–27
Pennell, Summer, 48
Pérez, David, II, 48
Perry, Monique, 114
Player, Grace, 73
political organization training, 39
porn
　Black thuggery and, 106–110
　curation issues, 107–108
　literacy training about, 116
　as source of sexual education, 96, 102–106, 114–116
Porter, Ronald, 70
*Pose*, 49–50
"Pride" (Justine), 31–32
professional development, 33–35, 63–64, 90
professional risks. *See* risks to educators
publication lead time, 40–41
punishment in schools, as one-sided, 52, 57

[q]ulturally sustaining pedagogy, 23–24
queer, use of term, 5

queerly responsive pedagogy (QRP).
　*See also* pedagogy of the closet
　overview, 16, 19–21, 24
　addressing tensions among variously identified queer youth of color, 35–37, 66–67, 70
　critical ethic of care and, 25–30, 46, 60–63, 81–83, 89
　culturally responsive and sustaining pedagogies and, 21–25
　defined, 3
　educational and social justice and, 37–40, 133–135
　growing of, 40–44
　lack of in secondary schools, 14
　Midtown AIDS Center (MAC) as, 8–9
　pairing intersectional analysis with opportunities for agency, 30–35, 114–115
　queer pedagogy missing from, 41–42
　sexual education and, 110–117
　white queer youth and, 20–21, 42–43
queer of color critique, 6–8
queer pedagogy, 41–42
queer sexual health, 1–2, 7, 97.
　*See also* sexual education
queer victimhood trope, 45, 85. *See also* Black queer resistant capital
queer youth of color (QYC). *See also* Black queer youth (BQY)
　culturally responsive pedagogy lacking for, 19–20
　as having a culture, 22
　intersectionality and, 3–4
　leadership training for, 34
　scholarship about increasing, 35
　subgroup identities and tensions among, 35–37
　use of term, 20
Quinn, Therese M., 27, 31, 32–33, 38

racially minoritized youth, use of term, 4–5
reading, 49–50. *See also* Black queer resistant capital
recommendations
   addressing tensions among variously identified queer youth of color, 37
   Black queer resistant capital and, 63–64
   critical ethic of care and, 28–30
   educational and social justice and, 39–40
   fugitivity and, 89–90
   pairing intersectional analysis with opportunities for agency, 33–34
   sexual education and, 113–116
recruitment of adults, 28–29
Reid, Shamari, 28, 32
repercussions for practitioners. *See* risks to educators
"Representation, Respectability, and Transgender Women of Color in Media" (Glover), 87
resistance, 46–47. *See also* Black queer resistant capital
retaliation. *See* Black queer resistant capital
risks to educators. *See also* pedagogy of the closet
   collective teacher organization and, 39–40
   providing sexual education and, 1–2, 94, 101, 113–114
ross, kihana miraya, 73
Rustin, Bayard, curriculum about, 126–129

safe spaces. *See also* trans fugitivity
   overview, 17, 68–70
   alternatives to, 30, 37, 69, 70, 89
   issues with, 65–66, 67
   sex workers excluded from, 84–87
Sage, 52
San Pedro, Timothy, 69
scholarship, lead time for, 40–41
school discipline, 52, 57, 63
school personnel. *See* educators/school personnel
Sedgwick, Eve Kosofsky, 124
self-defense. *See* Black queer resistant capital
sexual education
   Black thuggery and, 106–110, 115
   current landscape for, 94–97
   lack of in secondary schools, 2, 7, 91–92
   MAC provision of, 97–102, 111–114
   pleasure, inclusion in, 96–97, 99–100, 106
   queerly responsive pedagogy and, 110–117
   recommendations about, 113–116
   risks to educators teaching about, 1–2, 94, 101, 113–114
   self-discovery and mechanics by youth, 103–106
   SENT study findings on, 102–110, 114–116
   Standards for, 17–18, 92–93
   vulnerability about, 117
Sexual Engagements with Networked Technologies (SENT) study, 11–15. *See also* sexual education
sexual innocence, 85
sex work
   professional development on, 90
   stigma of, 77–80, 84–89
   as survival sex, 31, 75
Shange, Savannah, 32, 36, 135
*Skinny, The*, 91
slavery, impacts of, 70–71

social justice, 37–40, 133–135
Sojoyner, Damien, 71
standards, educational, 17–18, 92–93, 127–128
Stiegler, Sam, 88–89, 135
survival sex, 31, 75. *See also* sex work
suspensions, 52, 57, 63
systemic subjugations. *See also* pedagogy of the closet
  critical ethic of care and, 26
  educational and social justice and, 37–40
  intersectionality and, 2, 3–4, 20–21, 30–35, 114–115
  safe spaces in response to, 68–70
  slavery, impacts of, 71
  transformative resistant capital and, 48, 60, 62

Talburt, Susan, 85
terminology, use of, 4–6
Terriquez, Veronica, 38
training, 34, 39, 64. *See also* professional development
transformative resistant capital, 48, 60, 62
trans fugitivity
  overview, 65–67, 70–74
  closet compared with, 124–125
  defined, 17
  "good" versus "bad" trans kids and, 84–87
  implications about, 87–89
  paradigm shift from safe spaces to, 67–74
  recommendations about, 89–90
  social and institutional contexts for, 74–77
  supports and, 81–84
  transmisogyny and sex work stigma, 77–80, 88–89
transgendered persons (trans). *See also* trans fugitivity
  anti-trans legislation, 61–62, 112, 126
  caring adults and, 27–28
  marginalization by cis peers, 70, 75
  safe spaces dialogue and, 17, 84–87
  use of term, 6
transmisogyny, defined, 66. *See also* trans fugitivity
truth spaces, 69

Varney, Joan Ariki, 36
victimhood trope, 45, 85. *See also* Black queer resistant capital
violence, zero tolerance policies, 62, 63. *See also* Black queer resistant capital

Wargo, Jon, 23–24, 31, 32, 36, 70, 135
Wharton, Mitchell, 11
Wheatley, Torie, 134–135
"Where Will You Be?" (Parker), 131–132
white queer youth, queerly responsive pedagogy and, 20–21, 42–43
white supremacy, 30–31
"Who Said It Was Simple" (Lorde), 132
Wigglesworth, Michael, 119
Woodson, Ashley, 80
Wozolek, Boni, 8, 28, 29–30
writing, 31–32, 34

Yosso, Tara, 47–48, 52, 53, 55, 60
young Black queer males (YBQM), 11–15, 36. *See also* Black queer youth (BQY)
youth of color, use of term, 4–5
youth/young people, use of term, 5

Zaino, Karen, 73, 74
zero tolerance policies, 62, 63